MOBILIZE

MOBILIZE

How to Reboot
THE AMERICAN
INDUSTRIAL BASE
and Stop
WORLD WAR III

SHYAM SANKAR

and Madeline Hart

BOMBARDIER
BOOKS

Published by Bombardier Books
An Imprint of Post Hill Press
ISBN: 979-8-89565-516-0
ISBN (eBook): 979-8-89565-517-7

Mobilize:
How to Reboot the American Industrial Base and Stop World War III

Cover Design by Chris Allen

Post Hill Press
New York • Nashville
posthillpress.com

Published in the United States of America
2 3 4 5 6 7 8 9 10

To the Americans who support and defend our nation, from the factory floor to the frontlines.

And to the heretics, unappreciated in their time but without whom we'd be lost.

From Shyam: To Pooja, my pyaari the patini

From Madeline: To Gordon, my husband and forever editor

TABLE OF CONTENTS

FIGURES AND ILLUSTRATIONS

Figures

Illustrations

FOREWORD

My father raised me with a deep appreciation for our adoptive country. He would remind me: but for the grace of God and America, I'd be dead in a ditch in Lagos.

My father was born in rural India in a single-room mud hut, the youngest of nine children. He could never drink Dr. Pepper—the smell reminded him of the blood-sucking red insects that lived in the mud walls. He escaped poverty through education financed by the Jesuit order and the shared sacrifices of his eight older siblings.

He moved to Nigeria to build and run the first pharmaceutical factory in Africa. Ultimately, this opportunity did not bring him prosperity, only peril. When I was two years old, five armed robbers broke into our house, pistol whipped my father, killed our dog, threatened my mother with unspeakable things, and took our valuables.

We immigrated to America after the robbery. My father started over by selling T-shirts and gift store items in Orlando's growing theme parks. It was not the storybook immigrant success story. His business ventures failed and ended in bankruptcy. Life repeatedly kicked him in the teeth, but he never became cynical.

He felt blessed to be in America and to provide unimaginable opportunities for his children. He reminded us that here, we would only be limited by our ability and ambition. Every day after that dreadful night in Lagos was a gift.

About the same age my father was when he set off to Nigeria, I joined Palantir Technologies as the thirteenth employee in 2006. I had heard about a small group of technologists from the PayPal Mafia who wanted to build a company focused on national security. I had found my calling.

I built Palantir's Forward Deployed Engineering team and our unique way of building products, which sends engineers as close to the problem as possible—from remote firebases in Afghanistan to factory floors in America—so they learn firsthand what's broken and how to fix it. This approach was initially reviled by investors but has now been adopted by many technology companies.

This is not a book about Palantir. This book is, however, informed by my perspective building the only defense tech company to go public in the twenty-first century so far.

When Palantir started there was essentially one way for commercial technology companies to work with the US Intelligence Community (through its venture capital arm, In-Q-Tel) and none for the Department of Defense. (It has now been renamed the Department of War. In general, this book uses "Department of War" in the present tense, and "Department of Defense" when discussing the institution before the name change.) This book couldn't have been written in 2006 because there was nothing to mobilize. Now there is. Venture capitalists have invested $130 billion in defense tech since 2021. A host of founders have rallied to the mission, following in the footsteps of the greatest of the greats of the past century of American power: Kaiser, Ford, Northrop, Hughes, Higgins, Rickover, Schriever, and many, many more. The time is ripe for reform.

In October 2024, I authored *The Defense Reformation,* a treatise that explained what's broken with the Pentagon and how to bring innovation back to our military (you can read the full thing at 18theses.com). I didn't actually nail my theses to the Pentagon door, but they caused quite a stir. The response was incredible—I was flooded with messages from uniformed servicemembers, industry insiders, and other patriots who had seen the same problems up close and who wanted to get in the fight to fix them. That was the point. The house was (and is) on fire, and I wanted to shake people awake before it's too late. I still do.

Mobilize is a book-length treatment of that short document. It tells the stories of how our nation successfully mobilized during the twentieth century, through the eyes of heroes from industry and government. It examines the bad if often well-intentioned policies that created our broken military-industrial complex, a system that's endlessly criticized yet remarkably resistant to change. And it offers a fundamentally optimistic vision of the future—if we're brave enough to build it. This vision will require the right people to change the culture, inside government and industry, and implement the right policies: fierce internal competition within the Department of War for the best technology, enforcement of current laws to buy commercial solutions, and fast and flexible government contracting that values time saved above all else. Because time is the scarcest resource we Americans have.

The broader goal of this book is to remind Americans that mobilization isn't a narrow issue best left to the Washington think-tank crowd. If we're going to be successful, it *can't* be. Rebooting the American industrial base affects our national security, yes, but also our economy and even our democracy. As in World War II and the Cold War, the ability to produce is core to our conception of what it means to be an American. Production is the foundation of mobilization—production of AI models and drones, of munitions and autonomous vehicles. The notion that only a few defense companies can provide for America's defense has been definitively proven wrong. We need founders and workers from Silicon Valley, the Heartland, and every corner of the country. We need heretics, whether they have two bars or four stars on their shoulder. Above all, we need patriots.

The pieces for the Defense Reformation are in place: the capital class has shown up, the founders are busy building, and the Department of War is ready to innovate. And not a moment too soon as we face the worst threat since the Cold War. Will we look back at this moment and realize that World War III had already started, and we just didn't know it?

Now more than ever, the mission feels personal. In June 2025, I became a reservist in the US Army, direct commissioning as a lieutenant colonel alongside executives of other premier American technology companies. We're following in the footsteps of many patriots from the business world who rallied during crises, like Bill Knudsen, the General Motors president commissioned as a three-star general during World War II. Our country's best and brightest have an obligation to give back to our country, and increasingly they are answering the call. When I put my children to bed at night, I want to know I've done everything in my power to build them a secure future in an uncertain world.

It's up to all of us to mobilize and rebuild the Arsenal of Democracy. It'll take grit, hard work, and ingenuity—all the things my father taught me to love about America—to prevent World War III and win the battle for the twenty-first century. But we can do it. This book shows how.

—*Shyam Sankar,*
Chief Technology Officer, Palantir

CHAPTER 1

The Precipice

In May 2023, Russian conscript Ruslan Anitin surrendered to an armed robot. Miles away, Ukraine's 92nd Mechanized Brigade controlled this cheap but effective grenade-equipped drone. It spent the previous hours hunting the man's comrades. The two Russian soldiers with Anitin were dead. After sustaining serious injuries, one detonated a grenade near his head; the other shot himself. Anitin chose differently, pleading with his unseen enemy for mercy. After some deliberation, the Ukrainians decided Anitin's intentions were genuine. They spared his life, directing him by drone across no man's land and into captivity as a prisoner of war.

The Ukraine War has been called the "first AI war" and the "first large-scale drone war." There have been many firsts in this war, which has employed AI models and autonomous systems to hound the enemy on land, by sea, and most of all from the air. On June 1, 2025, Ukraine smuggled dozens and perhaps hundreds of small kamikaze drones in cargo containers to locations near Russian airfields. The drones then self-deployed from the containers and destroyed potentially one-third of Russia's strategic bombers, some as far away as Murmansk above the Arctic Circle. Command and control for the operation rode on the back of Russia's local cell network. Billions of dollars of hardware were eliminated for an estimated cost of $1 million. Russia's centuries-old advantage of size, which has thwarted would-be conquerors from Charles XII to Napoleon to Hitler, was overcome by a tenacious adversary weaponizing Russia's own logistics and telecommunications networks against it. Ukraine is redefining the David and Goliath fight and forcing introspection about how to adapt to this brave new world.

For all the innovation and novelty, though, one thing has remained constant: war is hell. Humans will not be outsourcing the suffering of combat to robots any time soon. Russia's invasion of Ukraine on February 24, 2022, started the bloodiest European war since World War II. Drones darken the skies. Exposing yourself for more than a few minutes means death. Medics can't treat the injured. Dead bodies pile up because there's no way to evacuate them without incurring further losses. There have been nearly one million casualties.

Russia's invasion of Ukraine is an existential threat to Europe and an omen of what could lie in its future if it doesn't rearm. But most of the countries involved, for all their alarmist and moralizing rhetoric, haven't acted like it. Ukraine has been called a "dumping ground" for Cold War–era weapons and other obsolete equipment. France has provided lightly armored fighting vehicles from the 1980s that are "too flimsy for frontal assaults." After much prodding, Germany provided eighteen of its prized Leopard 2 tanks. Most were lost within months. The United States shipped thirty-one Abrams tanks to much fanfare, but the Ukrainians found them ill-suited for modern warfare, too. The Russians offered a blunter assessment, equating the Abrams with "empty tin cans."

Perhaps, as some say, the West would be in a better negotiating position to end the war—and Ukrainian lives might've been saved—if Western countries had sold more (and more modern) arms to Ukraine sooner. But that possibility depends not only on political leadership and democratic support but sheer industrial capacity. It's far from clear whether Western defense production could have risen to the occasion on a relevant timeline.

While Ukraine has ramped its production of drones to well above 100,000 per month, the United States is currently capable of making fewer than 5,000 per month. Russian tank production exceeds ours by an order of magnitude. The problem is perhaps most dire when it comes to munitions. General Christopher Cavoli, then commander of US European Command, testified in early 2025 that Russia is producing almost 250,000 artillery shells per month, putting it "on track to build a stockpile three times greater than the United States and Europe combined." One of the most useful weapons we've provided to Ukraine has been the Patriot air defense system, which shoots down Russian missiles. But we can't give Ukraine enough Patriot interceptors because we don't make enough of them to go around.

Military industrial production cannot be switched on and off at will. It is a capability, like strength or endurance, that must be maintained through practice and repetition. Today, our ability to make the things we need to defend ourselves and our allies has atrophied. The grim implications of this fact extend far beyond Ukraine.

The hidden hand behind this conflict, keeping Russia in the fight, is China. In 2021, the two countries pledged their "unbreakable" friendship. China's foreign ministry said "Russia and China are united like a mountain." And China has acted on that pledge, lending its world-leading industrial base to Russia to ramp up its war production. It is sending a steady supply of machine tools, microelectronics (used in everything from missiles to tanks), and drones. In return, China is buying huge quantities of sanctioned Russian oil at a discount.

This is a strategic partnership, part of both countries' efforts to humble the United States and its allies and put themselves on top. As Xi Jinping told Vladimir Putin at a Moscow summit in 2023, "[t]here are changes—the likes of which we haven't seen for 100 years—and we are the ones driving these changes together."

China wasn't always so bold about its intentions. For many years, the Chinese Communist Party (CCP) flew under the radar, following Deng Xiaoping's maxim to "hide your strength, bide your time." Now, China has been strengthened by years of trade and investment into a manufacturing—and military—powerhouse. Under Xi, China has decided to flex its muscles.

In 2014, China began the militarization of the Spratly Islands in the South China Sea, where it built thousands of acres of artificial islands using massive dredgers. China transformed what was previously rocks and coral into full-fledged military outposts, complete with airstrips, anti-aircraft guns, and other weapons. These actions marked a step-change in China's maritime insurgency to enforce its claims in the Pacific.

China is also in the middle of a massive military buildup. It has doubled the size of its nuclear arsenal, and may triple or quadruple it in the years ahead. Its navy already has more ships than ours. And it's going all-in on advanced technology, from hypersonic missiles to AI to satellites with grappling arms that could wrestle ours out of orbit.

This military buildup isn't just for parades in Tiananmen Square. China is preparing for war. Xi's goal, as he has expressed time and again, is to recover from the so-called century of humiliation by bringing about "the great rejuvenation of the Chinese nation." The deadline for accomplishing this dream is 2049, the centennial year of the People's Republic of China. A few things need to happen by that time. First and foremost, China needs to "reunite" with Taiwan—by force, if necessary. Xi has instructed the People's Liberation Army (PLA) to be ready to invade Taiwan by 2027. Second, and more ambitiously, China seeks to replace the United States as the world's dominant power.

China is a long way from achieving that dream—but it isn't fantasy, the way many assumed a decade ago. China's rocket stockpiles and ability to shuttle troops and equipment across the Taiwan Strait grow by the day. Its military is practicing missile strikes on outlines of US aircraft carriers in the desert. And as China's "no limits" partnership with Russia shows, increasingly it is enlisting other countries to its team with offers of trade, infrastructure, and technology to spy on their political opponents.

American tech companies and the CCP have at least one thing in common: both possess a deep-seated belief in the ability of technology to solve societal problems. But the communist vision of technology is drastically different from our own. The CCP is methodically building and exporting the operating system for techno-authoritarianism. Its vertically integrated stack of software and hardware is used for state surveillance and the "re-education" and repression of disfavored groups, such as the Uyghurs. As China grows more powerful, its model is spreading. China is shipping its operating system for the unfree world as you read these words.

And the unfree world is increasingly aligned. Iran and North Korea, like China, are supplying the Russians. The Ukraine war has only accelerated an existing pattern of arms sales and cooperation between the four nations. In 2024, Putin and Kim Jong Un signed a "comprehensive strategic partnership" that has sent North Korean troops halfway around the world to die on European battlefields.

Iran, for its part, continues to serve as a chaos agent in the Middle East, funding and equipping Islamic terror groups and firing barrages of drones, cruise missiles, and ballistic missiles at Israel. During the Twelve-Day War in June 2025, Israel fired back. Using a novel combination of pre-positioned, small explosive drones and high-end military aircraft, Israel took out key figures in Iran's military and scientific leadership. The United States provided missile interceptors and then intervened directly, bombing three underground Iranian nuclear sites. Stealthy B-2s dropped 30,000-pound bunker buster bombs, the first known operational usage of the Massive Ordnance Penetrators. It was a stunning display of American and allied air superiority and flawless military execution—in marked contrast to many US military operations in the past twenty-plus years.

Yet there were red flags. The United States reached deep into its stockpiles over those twelve days, expending some 15 to 20 percent of its total supply of interceptors for the Terminal High Altitude Air Defense (THAAD) system. Admiral James Kilby remarked that the US Navy had blown through Standard Missile-3 ship-based interceptors at an "alarming rate." Both interceptors cost tens of millions of dollars per shot. In a protracted conflict—one that lasts years or months, not days—the United States would be bled dry of its best weapons within weeks. Our enemies are counting on it.

They are already using battlefields across the globe to test their weapons against ours. In May 2025, intense but brief fighting broke out along the border of India and Pakistan. China armed Pakistan. The West armed India. Chinese-made fighters shot down at least one French-made Rafale, marking the fighter's first combat loss—and one of the first modern demonstrations of Chinese offensive power. Painful lessons are being learned on the battlefield.

The most painful lesson is that the West has lost technological overmatch, initiative, and deterrence. This is an emergency, and it demands an urgent response if we in the West are to avoid a much darker future.

The ratcheting intensity of conflict recalls the run-up to World War II. Americans are taught that Germany's invasion of Poland in 1939 was the clear and obvious beginning of the bloodiest war in history. The reality was not so neat. Different conflicts all over the globe foreshadowed what was to come.

Japan invaded Manchuria in 1931, seizing it from China and exposing the League of Nations as useless. Fascist Italy invaded Ethiopia in 1935, again proving the ineffectiveness of the League of Nations. The 1936–1939 Spanish Civil War was the so-called dress rehearsal for World War II. In this proxy war, the Nationalists were backed by Germany and Italy, while the Republicans were backed by the Soviet Union. The Nationalists won, providing momentum to the war's fascist backers, who went on to form the Axis alliance. In 1937, Japan plunged deeper into China during the Second Sino-Japanese War, which included such horrors as the Rape of Nanjing. And in 1939, Germany invaded Czechoslovakia and, later that year, invaded Poland in partnership with the Soviet Union. World War II had officially begun.

There is a common thread to these events. In each case, an authoritarian power—often supported by other, like-minded powers—saw a window of opportunity to strike, and so it did. Authoritarian powers took the chance because they thought no one would stop them. The democracies didn't have their act together. The bad guys took full advantage.

Will we look back on the Ukraine–Russia war as the dress rehearsal for World War III? If we want to avoid such a fate, we need to ask these kinds of troubling questions.

The morbid truth is that war provides a unique opportunity to learn. No amount of testing or training exercises will ever simulate operational conditions. During the Spanish Civil War, the German Luftwaffe refined a doctrine of close-air support to ground forces on the move. This revolution in military affairs came to full flower during World War II; we know it as *Blitzkrieg*, or lightning war. Defense analyst Andrew Krepinevich notes, "By the time Germany invaded Poland, more than 19,000 Luftwaffe airmen had rotated through Europe's best training center, gaining deadly experience in modern air warfare." What is most notable about Germany's tactical innovations is that they occurred despite considerable handicaps. Part of Germany's punishment after World War I was its disarmament under the Treaty of Versailles. Germany's economy was a basket case, its level of development lower than all its eventual enemies on the Western Front. The German military was learning even while in the process of rebuilding and rearming.

Germany in the interwar years is a reminder that an intelligent and determined enemy can impose asymmetric costs, despite serious disadvantages. The Ukraine war is a drain on Russian resources, but Russia is also learning and adapting to a changing battlefield. Russia's electronic warfare capabilities improved so much that the accuracy of Ukraine's precision-guided artillery rounds dropped from 70 percent to 6 percent within six weeks of the invasion. The lifespan of a radio in Ukraine is about three months before it needs to be reprogrammed or swapped out. For a drone, it's weeks.

The best way for the United States to avoid calamity is to learn from today's wars, as well as the past, and ruthlessly change what no longer works. Failure to adapt comes at great human cost on modern battlefields.

The Arsenal of Democracy Is Empty

America forged the arsenal of democracy to deliver victory in World War II. By now, we all know the incredible true story. This period of unprecedented industrial mobilization has obtained mythical status, and rightfully so.

In 1939, when President Roosevelt announced that the United States would make 50,000 planes a year to supply the Allies via Lend-Lease, it seemed like a pipe dream. The inventory of fighters and bombers across the US Army Air Corps and Navy totaled fewer than 2,000. But the United States would go on to produce 324,750 planes over the course of the war; during peak production, more than 250 planes were produced per day. America's production engine was so effective it outproduced the combined Axis powers across all major categories of weapons, including planes, tanks, ships, and munitions.

The American industrial base's mobilization for World War II remains a singularly impressive feat. Given the parallels to today, it is often referenced as something the United States did before and, therefore, could easily do again. It's a comforting thought, but as we've seen, wartime mobilization isn't a switch that can be flipped on and off at will. It wasn't back then, either. We primed the pump for defense production via Lend-Lease while building new factories and retooling existing ones. Yes, Ford built B-24s at Willow Run, but it required two painful years before production was in full swing. The United States didn't hit peak production until 1944. Now, with 2027 fast approaching, Taiwan is waiting on a massive backlog of defense articles, including 66 F-16 fighters from the United States. The delivery is years behind schedule and is now slated for the end of 2026. If that date slips any further, it might be too late.

Worse, by not aggressively ramping up production to support Ukraine, the United States missed the equivalent of Lend-Lease. Instead of priming the pump with new production, the United States mostly drew down stockpiles of weapons and equipment made decades ago. This is painful because, as historian Arthur Herman said, "it's through making things that we learn what can be made better." The alternative to learning in peacetime is learning in wartime, precisely when stakes are highest and the margin for error is smallest.

There is, of course, one other crucial difference between now and 1939. The United States was the world leader in manufacturing going into World War II. Although it took time to mobilize, America started the competition far ahead of any country. Two of the three major Axis powers never completed an aircraft carrier. The US Navy built 151, in large part because it had such a deep bench of construction, shipbuilding, and manufacturing power to draw on.

The world looks different today.

The United States now has a peer adversary: China. (Washington prefers the term "near-peer," which is a euphemism to avoid the embarrassment of acknowledging a peer when the country was once peerless.) Today, China is the world leader in manufacturing, with a nearly one-third share of global production. It's not just cheap toys and lawn furniture, either. China has the capacity to make nearly half the world's ships—and it has more than *230 times* the shipbuilding capacity of the United States. In 2024, a single Chinese shipbuilder produced more ships than the United States has built since World War II ended. Meanwhile, the global market for small drones is dominated by Chinese companies—precisely the technology proving so vital on the battlefields of Ukraine. China is the world's largest producer and exporter of cars, gas-powered and electric. China also makes a greater share of the world's semiconductors than the United States. Even in the technology that the United States invented, and that has revolutionized the world in the span of a lifetime, the United States has ceded the manufacturing lead to its greatest adversary.

Worse, the US defense industry is deeply dependent on China. Nine percent of the major subcontractors to the big defense companies on Department of War contracts are Chinese. Those contracts support everything from missile defense to munitions and nuclear deterrence.

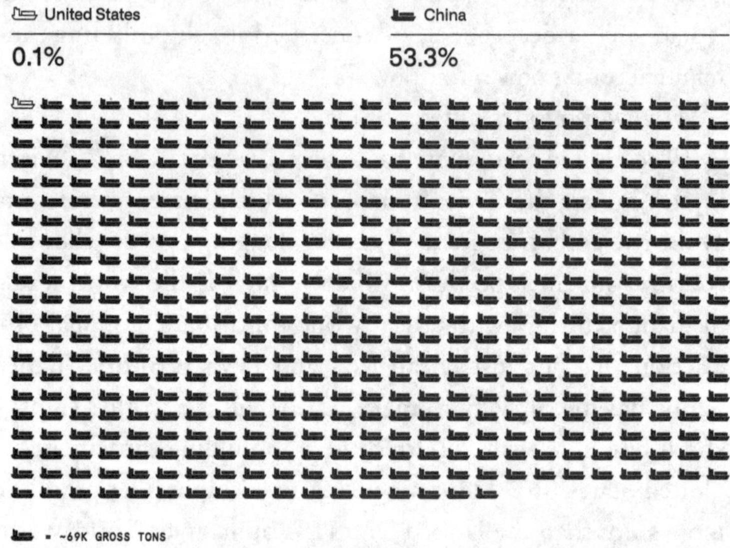

Figure 1

America's production problems will have consequences if they aren't fixed—and soon. Most Americans aren't old enough to remember World War II as anything but a story. But many Americans *are* old enough to remember the televised "Highway of Death" from the Persian Gulf War, where America's military hammered Saddam Hussein's army with seemingly limitless precision-guided munitions. We may not have that luxury in the next fight. Simulations of war with China over Taiwan usually find that the United States runs out of its most advanced missiles within days. Far from a cakewalk, we're now staring at the very real possibility of a humiliating and bloody defeat.

Preventing such a war should be our number one priority. But if we're going to do that on our terms, we'll need to produce.

What Money Can't Buy

It's not just that we can't build the way we used to. We've also forgotten how to buy.

The Department of War's acquisition process looks remarkably like Soviet central planning. Faceless bureaucrats with no ability to deviate from the five-year plan repeatedly try and fail to predict the future. The warfighter pays the price. It takes an average of seventeen years to field a new capability. Across domains, from deep sea to space, the one thing that's remarkably consistent is our inability to field the right weapons on relevant timelines.

The F-35 fifth-generation fighter was more than ten years late and $183 billion over budget. The program to modernize intercontinental ballistic missiles (ICBMs)—the land-based leg of the US nuclear triad—is 81 percent over budget and years behind schedule. The new ground stations for our GPS satellites were supposed to go online in 2016; they still aren't finished and their cost has increased by more than $3 billion. These are eye-watering figures, yet we've come to accept them as business as usual.

The most damning aspect of these procurement failures isn't even the billions in cost overruns and waste. The Apollo program, the Manhattan Project, and the Pentagon were all over budget. Nobody remembers that. We remember that the United States deployed critical capabilities at blazing speed; we spent money to buy time. Today, defense programs are supposedly optimized for the trifecta of cost, schedule, and performance. Yet they routinely fail to deliver all three.

It would be *easier* if funding was the blocker. Then the solution to our problems would be simple: just add dollars. But as the RAND Corporation's Mike Mazarr argues,

> Our problems are a function of the deeply ingrained inefficiencies, bureaucratic and political egotism, vague conceptual foundations, self-defeating policies, and often pointless rules, regulations, and restrictions that keep the Defense Department from gaining the full value of the money it already spends. To be prepared for a more dangerous era, the United States should overhaul its defense institutions before it pours more resources into them.

Given today's threat environment, the United States probably does need to increase the amount of money it spends on defense. Today's $850 billion budget is only 2.7 percent of gross domestic product (GDP). During the Cold War military buildup of the 1950s and '60s, the Department of Defense's budget was between six percent and eight percent of GDP. But money isn't magic, and Americans shouldn't expect to fix our problems simply by sluicing more defense-contractor dollars through the same leaky pipes. When we think about how to reform the Pentagon, we should heed the warning of Chuck Spinney, a Pentagon analyst and voice for reform in the twentieth century: "We need more money to strengthen our military.… [But] unless we change the way we do business, more money could actually make our problems worse." Indeed, when bad outcomes are rewarded with billions of dollars, we shouldn't be surprised when more bad outcomes follow.

This book is about how to restore deterrence—fast. The stakes are high. If we do it right, we'll make every American safer and richer. If we fail, we could live to see the United States dethroned as the world's most powerful country—if we live to see it at all. Thankfully, mobilization is still possible. But it will require massive changes in how the government and the military do business. And it will require an unrelenting and intense focus on winning above all else—above box-checking, bureaucracy, and everything standing in the way of speed and action.

In the first half of the book, we explain the problems that have contributed to the present crisis. Chief among these problems is the disconnection between America's vast, innovative private sector and its walled-off, small defense sector. Relying on a handful of defense contractors has failed the country. Mobilization demands a whole-of-nation effort, and that requires the participation of the full *American* industrial base—not a narrow *defense* industrial base.

The country ended up with a defense industrial base divorced from the broader economy because, to put it simply, the Department of War is a difficult customer. In fact, it's the *only* customer for the entire defense market, a situation referred to in economics as a "monopsony" (the mirror image of a monopoly). The Pentagon has used its leverage over defense contractors to dictate what gets built, when, and for how much. It has created an arcane system of rules and regulations that privilege well-connected and slippery Washington insiders over innovative startups. In short, the Pentagon has tried to centrally plan its way to success. To no one's surprise, it has found that Americans are bad commies.

The second half of this book discusses the road back to mobilization, renewal, and strength. Policy changes must play a role, and this book recommends some. But mobilization also requires bold leaders, risk-taking entrepreneurs, and organizational cultures biased toward action to start winning again. It takes visionaries, rebels, and even heretics to overcome the bureaucratic inertia that has always stood in the way of tectonic shifts. We'll meet a few of these heretical heroes from American history, including Louisiana shipbuilder Andrew Higgins, whose World War II landing craft were so effective that Ike proclaimed him "the man who won the war for us," and Admiral Hyman Rickover, the father of the nuclear Navy. We'll share the untold stories of modern-day heroes, like Colonel Drew Cukor, who brought AI to the Department of Defense with Project Maven, as well as the business titans who are on a mission to reindustrialize America.

Silicon Valley is fond of the 80–20 rule, which says that 80 percent of the outcomes result from 20 percent of the inputs. A few key levers have a disproportionate impact on our ability to mobilize. We need to identify and pull those levers. Everything else is noise.

It's reassuring to think that when things go south, we'll abandon harmful policies, swap out our peacetime generals for wartime generals, and unshackle our iconoclastic entrepreneurs who will step in to save the day. We hope that's the case, but hope is not a strategy or a substitute for preparation. It's time to stop banking on hope and commit to doing the hard things now.

Mobilization day was yesterday.

CHAPTER 2

Colonel Cukor's Odyssey

Khalid lay in a ditch, closed his eyes, and prepared to die alongside his family and friends. Shouts of *Allahu Akbar!* mixed with rapid gunfire. Bullets pierced his hand and foot, and he felt the blood of his neighbors soak his clothes. The firing stopped. Eventually, the ISIS (Islamic State of Iraq and Syria) terrorists moved on. Khalid was still breathing. He should be dead, but he wasn't. After lying still for some five hours, he chanced a look around. Somehow his childhood friend Idrees was still alive, but both of his feet had been shot. Khalid desperately tried to pull Idrees out of the mass grave, but they both lacked the strength. Distraught, Khalid promised Idrees he would come back for him. Idrees later discovered the strength to climb out of the death pit and survive. He left behind a dead son and brother.

Meanwhile, Khalid stumbled for miles, aware that if blood loss didn't kill him, thirst would. He came across a home with the door propped open—a door he could only hope would lead to help. It did. The owner took Khalid in, dressed his swollen wounds, and gave him food and water. Eventually, Khalid made it to a hospital, and then a refugee camp.

Many of Khalid's family were murdered or died of exhaustion trying to escape ISIS, but his daughter, Nazik, survived. Just nine years old, she escaped after watching captors sell her mother and two siblings into slavery. Khalid's sister, Nadia, also survived a brutal ordeal. She was separated from her husband and sold to an ISIS terrorist. Her captor and his friends raped her in front of her three children. Then he made Nadia watch while he beat her children. The family was forced to make rockets twelve hours a day for three months. They escaped after Nadia called her cousin while her captor was away. He sent a smuggler to extract the family.

These are only a few of the stories of the Yazidi genocide, carried out by ISIS in August 2014 during its conquest of northern Iraq. The Yazidis are a Kurdish-speaking minority who primarily live in Iraq's Sinjar region. They practice an ancient monotheistic religion and, before the genocide, had managed to coexist alongside their Sunni neighbors. As ISIS surged to power, however, it moved to systematically purge the Yazidi "infidels." ISIS acted with devastating effectiveness. More than 400,000 Yazidis were displaced in a matter of days. Thousands of men and older women were killed. The young women became sex slaves. The boys were indoctrinated and forced to fight for the terrorist group.

The United States was aware of the impending massacre. It had been made possible, in part, by US withdrawal from the country in 2011. As the Yazidis fled ISIS, thousands ended up on Mount Sinjar, trapped in the punishing heat with no food or water and surrounded by a monstrous enemy who wished them dead or enslaved. This humanitarian crisis unfolded publicly, in the new age of social media. President Barack Obama authorized air strikes and food drops, while an even bigger operation was considered. A small number of US Marines flew V-22 Ospreys to Mount Sinjar to assess the situation and determine if it would be possible to safely deploy a larger force to evacuate the Yazidis. General James Amos, the Marine Corps commandant, later revealed that "the plan was to pick everyone off the mountain. It was going to be a 'round the clock operation."

But it never happened. The direct intervention was called off, allegedly because intelligence from video feeds suggested the ISIS presence was too dangerous for Ospreys to land and carry out the evacuation. Versions of Khalid, Nazik, and Nadia's stories would play out thousands of times over the subsequent days.

These stories are documented in *The Beekeeper: Rescuing the Stolen Women of Iraq*, a moving but disturbing book about how a local Yazidi beekeeper, Abdullah Shrem, rescued hundreds of his people with the help of a smuggler network. Marine Corps Colonel Drew Cukor gifted this book to every Silicon Valley company he visited in 2017 as he doggedly pursued the companies to work with the Department of Defense on a nascent AI effort called Project Maven. *The Beekeeper* may seem an odd gift to bring to tech engineers accustomed to high salaries, free food, and nap pods, but Cukor wanted to appeal to their hearts.

You see, Cukor believed the Yazidi genocide could have been prevented. The ISIS forces that appeared around Mount Sinjar sufficiently spooked top brass and political leaders into suspending the operation. Cukor believed that if better intelligence had existed—intelligence integrated with real-time operations and leveraging the best software, processing capabilities, algorithms, and computing power—then better planning and a less risky evacuation could have taken place. Instead, the Yazidis were condemned to death.

Cukor started Project Maven as a one-man show in a dusty cubicle in the literal Pentagon basement. Project Maven was the first operationally deployed instantiation of AI at the Department of Defense. It would go on to become a billion-dollar program, but more important, it revolutionized how the Intelligence Community analyzed intelligence, how the Combatant Commands fought, and how the Department of Defense worked with Silicon Valley in the twenty-first century. When Russia invaded Ukraine, the US Army set up shop in Germany and put Maven on its command screens. When the United States evacuated from Kabul in 2021, Maven kept track of the people, logistics, and threats involved in the massive airlift. When Iranian proxies in Iraq and Syria mobilized for battle following Hamas's massacre in Israel on October 7, 2023, US Central Command used Maven to strike more than eighty-five targets.

The technical challenges of Project Maven were matched only by the political challenges. Over five years, Cukor had to battle anonymous enemies from inside the house who accused him of everything from embezzlement and bribery to undermining the national security of the United States. He faced multiple, serious Inspector General (IG) investigations. He survived them all and managed to build something great.

Legendary fighter pilot and military strategist John Boyd coined a timeless maxim: "to be or to do." It challenges individuals to consider whether they are more focused on achieving status and titles ("being") or on making a real impact ("doing"). Cukor chose to do. As a result, his story is largely unknown. Yet he is as responsible for Project Maven's existence and success as Hyman Rickover was for nuclear submarines or Bernard Schriever was for ICBMs.

This book relates the story of Cukor's odyssey into the inner workings of the Pentagon for the first time. Colonel Cukor's story shows that exceptional people can still accomplish great things in government, but only if they are willing to endure the slings and arrows of an outrageous bureaucracy—and push forward relentlessly to victory, at great personal cost.

We include Cukor's story at the outset of this book because—in addition to being a page-turner—it's a microcosm of the book's themes: the primacy of people, the interconnection of a thriving private sector and our nation's security, and the importance of competition, both *within* government and *among* defense companies. Cukor's story is a primer on how the Pentagon machinery works (or, more often, doesn't work) to deliver a weapon. Like many a heretic before him, Cukor had to break the machine to deliver the goods.

A Marine on a Mission

Cukor grew up poor, raised by a single mom in Los Angeles in the 1980s. There was no money for college, which left two options: the trades or the military. Cukor chose the latter, attending the University of Southern California on a Reserve Officers' Training Corps (ROTC) scholarship. Cukor was also a member of the Church of Jesus Christ of Latter-day Saints (LDS)—commonly known as a Mormon. Famously, every LDS young adult is encouraged to go on a mission. Cukor switched his major to linguistics after his mission in Panama and Costa Rica. He would eventually return to Panama wearing an entirely different uniform than he had before.

In appearance, Cukor is closer to a California rebel than a clean-cut missionary. He later picked up the nickname "Shaggy" for the old, disheveled uniforms he wore. Cukor had a tough commission. He entered as a Marine ground intelligence officer. This marked him as either a black sheep or a unicorn, depending on your perspective. Just as the Air Force has a culture of promoting pilots, the Marine Corps is run by infantryman and aviators. Even though Cukor was a ground intel officer who served in infantry units, the intel role was still viewed as a supporting element. Cukor would need to be truly exceptional to survive and advance, and very few young intelligence officers survived the defense drawdown of the early 1990s.

Cukor started in the 2nd Battalion 7th Marine Regiment based at Twentynine Palms, California, in the Mojave Desert, a "hot, miserable, and not a very interesting place to live." Still, he loved every minute. The remote desert environment meant the Marines could have some fun shooting and blowing things up.

But what Cukor really loved was being deployed, doing intel in the field, and looking for ways he could burn down the old way of doing things and build something better. He deployed to Somalia, Okinawa, and Panama. In Central America, the missions included humanitarian relief, border operations, and the war on drugs. There were plenty of opportunities for an intel officer to learn his trade.

While Cukor relished the physical side of being a Marine, he had an intellectual side. A fellow Marine who later worked with him on Maven described him as the "smartest Marine I ever met." Intelligence collection is about data and how to make sense of data. Cukor thought nonstop about how to better integrate intelligence and operations. His technical background in information and linguistics lent itself to this challenge. Cukor's early deployments convinced him that technology would make or break his vision. Many people complain about how bad the military's technology is; Cukor was one of the few people to do something about it.

Part of his job as an intel officer was typing up daily field reports. In Somalia in 1993, Lieutenant Cukor and his fellow Marines had access to a single computer. The machine cost $200,000 and was coated in fifty pounds of metal to prevent adversaries from intercepting any signals coming off of it. The computer ran just one software program, "Enable," written by Marines in St. Louis. "Enable" was so broken that Cukor and others called it "Disable"—after typing more than three pages, it would often fail and lose everything.

While the Information Revolution had arrived, it clearly hadn't arrived at the Department of Defense. The military used practically no commercial software. It was even an ordeal to deploy Microsoft products like Word and PowerPoint, as the services preferred building their own office productivity software to avoid the license costs of commercial software. Not only that, but little had changed about intelligence analysis and collection since World War II. Cukor would receive reams of notes and field reports and try to make sense of them, connecting dots without technology. That was the state-of-the-art methodology. Further, threat assessments by Marine intelligence were stuck in the Cold War. The focus was on nuclear weapons. Ground forces were, in Cukor's words, "for general deterrence and small dust-ups." Tanks against tanks, infantry against infantry—this remained the type of battle the Marine Corps wanted to fight. While manhunts for high-value targets would gain elevated importance with the War on Terror, that evolution would take time, and Cukor would help to advocate for the type of intelligence processes and technology needed for human targeting.

After a few years of deployments, Cukor set off to the Naval Postgraduate School. Cukor's 1997 thesis, *Marine Ground Intelligence Reform: How to Redesign Ground Intelligence for the Threats of the 21st Century*, was ahead of its time. Cukor pulled no punches. He argued that Marine intelligence "faces a serious dilemma: it can either reform or face ever-decreasing relevance and effectiveness." The reform Cukor suggested was moving away from a "rote information processing machine bureaucracy" and toward an "intellect-centric network organization." But encoding human intelligence into a digital network required the best technology—technology that wouldn't come from the government. "Therefore a significant challenge for Marine Corps ground intelligence will be to harness the revolution in information technology occurring in private industry." He suggested the Marine Corps look to innovative enterprises like "Intel, GE and Silicon Graphics." And he railed against "the 10–15 year acquisition cycle," arguing that it "cannot continue to be the way things are done."

Presciently, Cukor used a potential invasion of Taiwan by China as a primary case study in his thesis. Despite the Tiananmen Square Massacre and a flare-up in the Taiwan Strait, in 1997 it was rare to be as clear-eyed as Cukor on the nature of the China threat:

> With a focus on power projection and survivability, China is transforming its army from large Soviet style formations to smaller airborne and marine forces. Second, recognizing its inability to outperform Western air power, China has invested in a low tech, inexpensive asymmetric response.

The US military was not designed to respond to such a threat.

Cukor began to put theory into practice at Marine Corps Systems Command, the Quantico-based command that buys weapons and technology for the Marines. For three years, Cukor assessed software acquisitions that were, except for Microsoft Office, always late, overpriced, and underpowered. As he learned about software development and how the government bought technology, he also learned what made such acquisitions problematic. Part of the problem was that the only companies selling software to the government were traditional defense contractors, not software companies. He also observed that the Marines tended to buy custom hardware that happened to have software, almost as an afterthought. Cukor thought the emphasis should be reversed: the software should follow human workflows, and the hardware should be interchangeable commodity components. But back then—as now, with few exceptions—acquisition remained hardware-centric.

After the desk job, Cukor experienced two of the most significant world events of the 2000s while deployed as an intelligence officer with the 26th Marine Expeditionary Unit (MEU). These elite Marines deploy on ships in the middle of the ocean so that they are prepared to respond to a crisis at a moment's notice. Cukor's first deployment was just days after 9/11, so he soon found himself on the frontlines of Operation Enduring Freedom: the invasion of Afghanistan. Two years later, he participated in the 2003 invasion and stabilization of northern Iraq during Operation Iraqi Freedom. Then, as the 26th MEU was on its way back to the United States, the Marines were diverted to war-torn Liberia for a bonus deployment.

During these combat tours, the themes from his previous deployments were the same: functional software was non-existent. At this point, the Microsoft Office suite was widely available, and while it was gratifying to go from paper products to digital ones, this was also when Cukor decided that PowerPoint and Word were "where data goes to die, buried within impossible-to-find file folders." Outgoing units would literally do hard-drive transfers with incoming units in the middle of the ocean. They'd wish them luck, and the incoming unit would ask what data was in the giant hard drive. Nobody had the tools to answer that question.

Drew "Shaggy" Cukor, all cleaned up, as a US Marine Corps colonel.

In 2008, Cukor was promoted to lieutenant colonel and assumed command of a 400-Marine reserve intelligence battalion. While never one to play politics for the next promotion, as subsequent events will make clear, his contributions to the philosophy and execution of integrating intelligence with operations were impossible to ignore. In his first command, Cukor would also face his first, but certainly not last, IG investigation.

As part of his new, larger responsibilities, Cukor was asked to scale the counterinsurgency intelligence project he had designed and fielded in his previous billet as the Middle East Branch Chief for Marine Corps Intelligence Activity. Called Project Legacy, the initiative remains almost entirely classified, but even the unclassified details read like a Tom Clancy novel. Legacy was an initiative to teach the Iraqis and Afghans how to do intelligence. Cukor was inspired by the special branch organization of the Northern Ireland police, which was able to penetrate the Irish Republican Army like Swiss cheese during the Troubles. The UK intelligence agency MI5 then operated on top of the special branch force. Cukor concluded that the best opportunity to build an intelligence organization was with the police, reasoning that it would be better for the Iraqis and Afghans to become competent at intelligence rather than relying wholly on the Americans. After all, the Iraqis and Afghans natively knew the language, culture, and terrain, and they lived there permanently, whereas the Americans cycled in and out every six months.

In the mid-2000s, the United States was already building up the Iraqi police as part of reconstruction, but nobody had thought to use it for intelligence. Cukor started by hiring former special branch officers from Northern Ireland to train the Iraqis at a few police stations in Anbar Province. It was quite the cultural fusion, but it was so successful in improving targeting that Cukor was authorized to scale Legacy all over Iraq and then Afghanistan. Cukor was able to quickly secure hundreds of millions of dollars for this task because he knew the ins and outs of contracting from his acquisition days. The program later grew to more than a billion dollars. Eventually, Cukor was asked to run the same program in Mexico during an upsurge in cartel violence.

It was an entirely unorthodox operation. Even worse, from the establishment's point of view, it was effective. Legacy and Cukor took serious heat. Critics charged that teaching foreign countries how to do human intelligence was illegal. Cukor insists that the program had the proper agreements and that everything was approved, but people didn't like the optics. In 2017, years after Cukor had left Legacy for a different assignment, the Special Inspector General for Afghanistan Reconstruction accused the program of lacking sufficient performance metrics to assess its impact. Per Cukor, these accusations "rained down on an amazing team of hardworking professionals, but the metrics part was entirely wrong. Host nation intelligence reports from Iraqi and Afghan police were some of the best intel out there and saved a lot of lives."

Cukor emerged on the other side of Legacy only to find himself embroiled in yet another military intelligence controversy. Here's where his story intersects with Palantir—and more specifically, with the Army's disastrous military intelligence system, the Distributed Common Ground System (DCGS), which you will hear about again in Chapter 9. In 2010, Cukor became the analysis and futures chief at the Marine Corp's Intelligence Department. His boss was Brigadier General Vincent Stewart, the director of intelligence. They had a professional relationship stretching back almost fifteen years, and Stewart trusted Cukor. Together, they advanced the concept of fully integrating intelligence and operations using new analytic systems and processes.

Palantir, then the spunky underdog of defense contractors, had the best technology in the market to meet their goals. Cukor, who had spent every waking hour since his first deployments using broken software and thinking about how to fix the problem, knew a winner when he saw one. And when Cukor saw Palantir, he saw software that worked. It was a stark contrast with DCGS, the Army's gigantic and broken program of record.

It's worth pausing to explain some of the jargon the Pentagon uses when it buys things. It will come in handy throughout the book. A "program of record" is a funded acquisition program that has the blessing of the establishment. It's a desired, protected status gained after years spent jumping through hoops in the government's requirements and funding processes. Once established, a program of record has the momentum to keep going indefinitely until stopped. A "requirement," for that matter, is a formal, specific criterion that a weapon must satisfy to be considered effective and useful for military operations. A rifle, for instance, might have requirements for weight, effective range, and other desired characteristics. While requirements for most systems should be simple, short documents, the process of creating requirements is lengthy and political. In an effort to satisfy all stakeholders, requirements frequently number in the hundreds or thousands and often have little bearing on the operational needs of troops on the ground. Once formalized, programs of record and their mountains of requirements are virtually untouchable. Challenging them is ill advised.

That didn't stop Cukor. In his words, DCGS was a "melting pot of everyone's problems, and it could never deliver on so many impossible requirements." The Marines were also procuring their own system, the Intelligence Analysis System (IAS), which "consistently and dramatically fell short of user requirements." He wanted the Marines to have something better. So, working with partners, he procured Palantir, packed Palantir servers into a C-17 transport aircraft headed to Afghanistan, delivered it to users, and plugged it in. The whole process happened at blazing speed, thanks in part to anonymous users and their bosses who helped Cukor to speedrun the myriad network and cyber requirements. Word spread, and soon everyone wanted what the Marines had in Helmand Province.

There were just a few small problems. Palantir software wasn't a program of record, and it wasn't what the Department of Defense had rallied behind. DCGS, IAS, and other service-built systems were the chosen ones. Making matters worse, from the establishment's point of view, Cukor was a Pentagon insider ignoring the chosen systems in favor of procuring commercial software—it was a betrayal by one of their own!

When General Stewart found out about the unexpected software deployment, he was angry. Fortunately for Cukor, his boss trusted him, and when Cukor told him that Palantir was making a difference, Stewart let the mayhem continue. But Cukor had once again been marked as a target and a rebel. "Everyone was mad at us," he recalls, "but no one could fight the fact that it was working."

The Marine Corps got a brief reprieve from Cukor's creative destruction when he went to graduate school again, this time to write his magnum opus, *Operate to Know.* The thesis would provide the intellectual foundations for Project Maven (emphasis ours):

> After immense investment fighting in Iraq and Afghanistan, joint expeditionary forces operate without the ability to continuously process sensor information in near-real time. Even with the ability to process it, the joint force still does not have a C2 [command and control] system to supply a *near real-time enemy situation picture to immerse planners in the details of the problem and for fires and maneuver to fight with.*

There was no such system because intelligence continued to be treated as a subordinate and supporting function. The focus on extensive, detailed, commander-level planning made it harder to adjust plans in response to new information and a rapidly changing adversary. Also, intelligence had a perception problem. Per Cukor, "in the minds of operational leadership, it [the force] cannot win battles with nonphysical means, only fires and maneuver can do this." But deadlier munitions and longer-range mobility would be wasted in a future fight if they were not connected to a continuously updating intelligence-operations system.

In 2014, Cukor was assigned as the commanding officer of the Marine Corps Information Operations Center, where he was responsible for information and deception operations. It was a secondary command position for officers not on the golden path for further promotion, but Cukor loved the mission, the work, and the Marines. There were still big things he could accomplish, but he'd already picked up too many investigations and gone against the establishment too many times to ever be one of the elect. In his own words, he was "relentless and unapologetic." What's more, the United States was (relatively) at peace; Cukor was not a peacetime leader.

After that assignment, Cukor descended from command to, in his words, "the dark bowels of oblivion inside the Pentagon, a place no one wanted to land," supporting the under secretary of defense for intelligence (USD(I))—renamed under secretary of defense for intelligence and security (USD(I&S)) in 2019. His final military assignment was in the Pentagon, in office 1B 855. The Pentagon is arranged in concentric rings, A to E, with offices in every ring. The E Ring is the most desirable (it has outward-facing windows). The further away from E Ring, the further from the center of power—and from the sun. Cukor's B Ring office, buried deep in a secure facility, was therefore about as low-status as it could get. Given Cukor's previous work on deception operations, it was only too fitting that Project Maven would emerge from such an unassuming location, literally from the shadows of the Pentagon's back office.

CHAPTER 3

Project Maven

For more than two decades, Drew Cukor fought his way across continents trying to bring good software to American and allied troops. With Project Maven, it was time to bring that fight to the Pentagon. Cukor learned many lessons over the years about procurement and technology, but also about hierarchy and human nature. He'd need every one of them for the fight ahead. As we're about to see, the culmination of Cukor's military career would require him to cross the Rubicon and take on the bureaucracy in its own backyard.

But first, it'll be helpful to briefly review the history of AI to that point. Little about Cukor's odyssey can be attributed to luck, but 2016 was, at the very least, a good year to bring AI to the Department of Defense. The mid-2010s were a breakthrough period, when the promise and hype of the technology could finally be translated into powerful applications for end users.

The theoretical groundwork for AI was laid in the mid-twentieth century by pioneers like Alan Turing, who asked the iconic question "Can machines think?" Turing's work on computation and his famous "Turing Test" provided a philosophical basis for what would become AI research. In 1956, Dartmouth hosted a workshop, the Dartmouth Summer Research Project, which marked the formal inauguration of AI as a field. Researchers were optimistic about rapid progress and believed that machines capable of human-like reasoning were just around the corner.

The 1960s and early 1970s saw significant developments in symbolic AI and rule-based systems. Researchers developed programs that could solve problems, manipulate symbols, and even play games. A classic example of a rule-based system was MYCIN, developed in the 1970s to diagnose bacterial infections and recommend antibiotics. MYCIN used rules like: "*If* the patient has a high fever and a sore throat, *then* consider the possibility of a bacterial infection." In this example, MYCIN applied a series of rules to analyze patient symptoms and lab results to make medical recommendations. This period was characterized by ambitious goals and predictions that general intelligence was not far off.

Expectations soon outpaced reality. Limited processing power and data storage hindered the training of more complex algorithms, and rule-based systems that relied on humans encoding different "if, then" statements were not broadly generalizable. Throughout the 1980s, the field encountered substantial setbacks. Technical limitations, overhyped promises, and funding cuts led to a period known as the AI winter. Progress in AI research slowed dramatically as both government and private agencies reduced their investments, hesitant to fund a technology that repeatedly failed to deliver on its grandiose promises.

The latter part of the twentieth century saw renewed interest in AI, thanks to improvements in computational power, the advent of more sophisticated algorithms, and increased availability of data. Techniques such as machine learning started to gain traction as alternatives to purely rule-based approaches. In machine learning, algorithms make predictions based on data, similar to how humans learn from experience. For example, you don't need to have seen every cat in the world to be able to identify a cat you've never seen before. Then, another milestone. In 1997, IBM's Deep Blue defeated Gary Kasparov in chess. Such a public and relatable event helped to catalyze broader interest in the field of AI.

But it would be almost another twenty years before the research breakthroughs Cukor needed for Project Maven would finally occur. Deep learning, an advanced subset of machine learning, uses neural networks to mimic the neurons and synapses of the human brain. Specifically, convolutional neural networks (CNNs) became the standard for computer vision tasks, such as image classification and object detection. Landmark successes like the ImageNet competitions underscored the power of deep CNNs, fueling innovations in facial recognition, self-driving car technology, and medical-image analysis. Meanwhile, recurrent neural networks showed great promise in processing sequential data. They were widely adopted for applications like speech recognition, natural language processing, and time series forecasting. In 2016, deep learning received a public spotlight when Google DeepMind's AlphaGo defeated world champion Lee Sedol in Go, a game many times more complex than chess.

Although the technical breakthroughs had finally occurred as Colonel Cukor arrived in the back office of the Pentagon, belief in the transformative power of AI was still eccentric and contrarian, especially in the government. There was no 2022 "ChatGPT moment" where individual consumers felt the power of AI at their fingertips. The research advances described were primarily appreciated by those already working at technology companies and in certain parts of academia, all far from Washington.

That history brings us to the final and most important chapter of Cukor's odyssey: Maven. When Cukor started his new job, the deputy secretary of defense was Robert Work, who had recently rolled out the Third Offset Strategy. As the name implies, this type of strategy seeks to *offset* an enemy advantage, often by using new technology or changing the composition of one's forces. During the Cold War, the First Offset leveraged nuclear weapons to make up for the Soviet Union's numerical superiority. In the 1970s, the Second Offset used advances in digital computing to go from "dumb" bombs to precision-guided munitions, something we'll learn more about in Chapter 6. Work's Third Offset sought to use AI, autonomous systems, and human-machine collaboration to deliver an asymmetric advantage over China and Russia. This roughly mapped with Cukor's vision of developing an AI brain to accelerate intelligence and operations. The stars were aligned.

Much to Work's surprise, Cukor started showing up to Third Offset meetings. He wormed his way in when he learned there weren't any senior intelligence officers representing the intelligence function or USD(I). Cukor had zero money and zero staff, but these indignities didn't bother him. In fact, he saw the job as an opportunity, a challenge. The aperture was wide open.

It quickly became apparent to Cukor that while the working group knew AI was a critical technology for the future, no one was doing much to advance it within the department. And this was where Cukor saw his opportunity. To an intel guy like Cukor, AI had blindingly obvious use cases. Intelligence was an information-intensive specialty that required many, many people to do the required data wrangling. AI was now perfectly suited to automate such labor-intensive jobs as image classification, speech recognition, and document extraction.

Cukor's idea was to start the Algorithmic Warfare Cross Functional Team (AWCFT), which would house the program known as Project Maven (later known simply as "Maven"). Cukor pitched Work, explaining that he would need around $500 million over five years to realize his vision, at which point the program would permanently transition to an intelligence agency. Work thought it was a great idea, as did Jack Shanahan, the three-star general who sat above Cukor as the director for defense intelligence (Warfighter Support) in USD(I). Shanahan and Cukor had a great relationship in part because they'd held similar jobs in the past as overseers of information and deception programs. With Work and Shanahan on board, Cukor had top cover. He also gained the support of his agency head, Under Secretary of Defense for Intelligence Joseph Kernan, a former Navy SEAL and retired vice admiral whose attitude toward the matter, Cukor recalls, was essentially "Good luck. You know how the building works." Cukor knew only too well.

On April 26, 2017, Bob Work published a memo, just over one page in length, titled "Establishment of an Algorithmic Warfare Cross-Functional Team (Project Maven)." The contents, heavily influenced by Cukor's steady hand, are remarkable for their specificity, concision, and focus on outcomes. While not technically a requirements document, this one-page memo served as the guiding requirements for Project Maven, putting 500-page requests for proposals to shame: "The AWCFT's first task is to field technology to augment or automate Processing, Exploitation, and Dissemination (PED) for tactical Unmanned Aerial System (UAS) and Mid-Altitude Full-Motion Video (FMV) in support of the Defeat-ISIS campaign." In other words, automate the detection of bad guys on drone feeds.

Then the memo clearly laid out how AWCFT would go about augmenting or automating human analysis:

1. Organize a data-labeling effort, and develop, acquire, and/or modify algorithms to accomplish key tasks;
2. Identify required computational resources and identify a path to fielding that infrastructure;
3. Integrate algorithmic-based technology with Programs of Record in 90-day sprints.

That was it. This brief memo contained the seeds of one of the most consequential programs in Pentagon history. Acquisition officers should take note before killing a forest for their next project.

Cukor was already moving with impressive speed in his new role. Because Work was a political appointee, he would soon be out of a job due to the change in administration. It was therefore of the utmost importance to capitalize on the momentum of Work's enthusiasm for the Third Offset Strategy to get the AWCFT formed and funded before the window closed and a new deputy secretary of defense arrived who may or may not share that enthusiasm.

Money stymies many a program manager. Without funds, you can't do anything. Work was able to give Cukor $65 million right away, sourced mostly from underperforming programs and the fuels fund, which had spare money because of the low price of fuel. Cukor then put in the leg work on Capitol Hill to secure the consistent, future funding for a five-year program. Cukor's background in acquisitions was a boon, but going to bat for Maven on the Hill required salesmanship of a higher order. He would have to match Maven against existing priorities, communicate the value of the technology, and transparently map how the money would be spent and what it would buy. Then he would have to deliver results. This was no small feat for a one-man show operating out of the Pentagon basement. Cukor recalls, "I spent all night, all day, all weekend building all the necessary expositions that are required, and spent lots of time on the Hill working to convince everybody."

Money in hand, the first thing Cukor did was hire an all-star team. Like any good founder, Cukor was a talent magnet. One of his greatest strengths was the team he assembled, and he did it with one hand tied behind his back. Reallocating permanent, active-duty service members for a temporary program takes a lot of time and effort. Cukor didn't have the luxury of hand-picking who he wanted. So he got creative. Since he had money, he could activate reservists on active-duty orders. The Maven team ended up consisting primarily of Marine reservists, because Cukor had identified likeminded people over the years and knew who was crazy enough to fit into the new mission.

The primary drawback of having reservists on Project Maven was that they had to take orders on one-year cycles, with a renewal required every year. Many wanted to stay longer but couldn't. This put even more pressure on Cukor, who was effectively the program's sole source of continuity. Project Maven was sometimes criticized for its transient staffing model, a critique that fails to acknowledge the broken Department of Defense personnel system at the root of the program. For a program on a tight timeline, it was reservists and contractors or nothing. Cukor took what he could get.

As the AWCFT memo explained, the initial Project Maven objective was to assist operators in analyzing the huge amounts of drone footage from Iraq and Syria in the fight against ISIS. Hundreds of General Atomics MQ-1 Predator drones and MQ-9 Reaper drones—not to mention smaller drones, like Boeing MQ-27 ScanEagles—were collecting hundreds of thousands of hours of footage for human analysis. Analysts used this footage to create "pattern of life" analysis to figure out what the bad guys were doing and predict what they might do next. This analysis was used to protect our troops, prepare the battlefield, and kill terrorists.

Before Maven, several people would stand around a video feed studying everything that was going on. There would be a digital map next to them and they'd manually annotate the map with relevant activity. The formal name for this process was "Extract, Transform, and Load," or ETL. Humans would manually extract relevant information, transform it by digitally placing it on a map using a mouse, and then load it into a system to be tracked and used by others. The product produced was static, useful for a particular moment and then lost to history. As bad, the process was inefficient and didn't scale. An estimated 85 percent of video was never viewed—there just weren't enough people. It was also expensive. Every 1,000 analysts burned a billion dollars. Finally, it was a disturbing job with high rates of post-traumatic stress disorder. Watching endless hours of terrorist atrocities isn't easy on anyone.

Cukor's early goal was for Project Maven to be the ETL killer, replacing labor-intensive analysis with speedy computers, but he also hoped to make ETL an all-around more effective process. Cukor saw real value in creating a central data platform that could remember every activity and then start to reason about events. Algorithms would assist humans in identifying trends and predicting future actions, not just identifying immediate targets.

With a clear vision and a government team, Cukor had to figure out who was going to bring the vision to life. That meant Silicon Valley companies, which would soon pose a problem for Cukor in more ways than one. He would have to go West.

After twenty-five years of trying to make government software work for warfighters, it was obvious to Cukor that he needed the support of technology companies. But putting tech companies on contract was not the easy path. The Cold War was long over, as were the days when Southern California was a magnet of defense dollars. Most tech companies had little work with the government, much less the Department of Defense. Cukor would need to embark on a mission. Which brings us back to *The Beekeeper.*

Cukor literally went door to door, pitching tech companies and PhD students on why working for the government to stop the Yazidi genocide and other atrocities was a more noble calling than anything else they were doing. In other words, Cukor ran the missionary playbook, going door to door with a book and a message. And he won converts. Some were true believers, while others (some of the PhD students) were enticed by the prospect of a bigger check than they could get in academia.

Cukor built a team with tech companies, big and small, including Google, Amazon, Microsoft, Maxar, and Palantir, as well as Clarifai and CrowdAI. Perhaps anticipating blowback from the bureaucracy, Cukor first completed a much-beloved artifact of the Pentagon to justify his actions: a study. Cukor surveyed Silicon Valley companies as well as government agencies and labs to document anywhere cutting-edge AI could plausibly exist. Silicon Valley software companies came out ahead, which of course was his hunch all along—but it had the added virtue of being true.

In the early days of the program, Cukor also had traditional defense companies on contract, like Raytheon and Lockheed Martin. Even still, the antibodies to Cukor's approach were strong. First, some agencies were mad that Cukor was leading Project Maven, period. The Defense Advanced Research Projects Agency (DARPA) thought it should own AI and that, consequently, Cukor was guilty of the rankest insubordination. Further, it argued that AI was not ready for prime time and that Cukor was going to get people killed by pushing AI products into the field. In a similar vein, the Army, the Air Force, and the National Geospatial-Intelligence Agency (NGA) felt that Cukor was encroaching on their turf.

But of course, it would be absurd for any single agency to have a monopoly on something as broad and amorphous as "AI." Furthermore, nobody was stopping DARPA or NGA from pursuing their own AI initiatives and proving they were better than, complementary to, or just different from Cukor's. What these complaints really boiled down to is that Cukor was upending the standard way of doing things—which is to do them so slowly as to be indistinguishable from inaction. Cukor was introducing unexpected competition into the Department of Defense, and he was ready to take the flak that came with it.

Cukor's peculiar vendor selection also branded him as a traitor. What about the Air Force, Navy, or Army research labs? If Cukor was going full throttle on Maven, couldn't he at least show some loyalty and contract the work to the labs or

DARPA? But Cukor had done his homework. He'd visited the labs for his study. They were doing "hobby projects." The people who worked there were smart and liked to tinker, but they had grown comfortable and complacent without a driving vision or sense of urgency. After all, they weren't in the marketplace fighting for their company's existence, like startup founders, or answering to a daily stock price and activist investors, like corporate tech executives. The labs even conceded to Cukor their stuff wasn't useful. And finally, Cukor had twenty-five years of hard-earned experience of what worked and what didn't. He wasn't about to be steamrolled into picking less than the best.

Although the bureaucracy certainly tried. Every day, Cukor would wake up, log into his classified email, and see at least one nasty email berating him and his approach. For Cukor, this constant noise was more often a source of amusement than alarm. It just fueled him and his team to succeed. In many ways, the criticism was an indicator that the Maven team must be doing something right.

This isn't to say working with technology companies was always easy. Google, famously, pulled out of Project Maven after thousands of employees protested the company's work with the US military. Google simultaneously was working on Project Dragonfly, a censored version of its search engine purpose-built for China. Evidently, helping the CCP to repress the Chinese people gave Google fewer qualms than helping Uncle Sam to take out terrorists. (You can read more about that fiasco in *The Technological Republic: Hard Power, Soft Belief, and the Future of the West* by our colleagues Alexander Karp and Nicholas Zamiska.)

The volatile political environment posed an additional challenge. In 2017, venture capitalists hadn't yet decided that defense tech was cool. The vibe shift hadn't yet occurred. Donald Trump had just been elected president and introduced restrictions on immigration from countries linked with terrorism, which his enemies promptly labeled the "Muslim ban." Now here came Colonel Cukor (a California Democrat, not that it mattered) pitching AI to defeat Islamic terrorists in the Middle East. It was unpopular.

Lesser souls may have been discouraged by these difficulties, but not Cukor. The work continued, despite plenty of bad publicity and nasty emails. Cukor's Marine mentality saw him through the program's earliest and darkest days. Marines assume everything breaks. And in no-fail missions, even one backup isn't enough. So Cukor had two companies backing up Google. One was Palantir. With Google out, Palantir became the main effort. There was also a silver lining to Google dropping out: it helped to clarify which companies were on board with the mission and which weren't. Google's exit created an opening for Cukor to enlist Amazon and Microsoft, both of which were only too happy to contribute product and engineers to the effort.

Cukor ran Project Maven like a technology startup. Within ninety days of launch, Cukor had operational AI in a combat zone in East Africa. The program then shipped new products or features every ninety days according to its sprint schedule. Companies were kept in a state of continuous competition, a dynamic Cukor referred to as "horseracing." Because Cukor had set up a flexible contracting vehicle (more on that later), vendors were quickly onboarded—or offboarded—based on performance. While it may have appeared wasteful to pay many companies while only using a subset of their capabilities, it was ultimately cheaper to evaluate performance and allocate resources on a rolling basis as more information emerged. Duplication is a virtue in no-fail missions when your backup and your backup's backup might not cut it. It was a lesson Cukor had learned as a Marine.

Notoriously, the technology built in military labs and other research and development (R&D) centers more often resembles science projects than battle-tested weapons of war because it is never employed (and, hence, critiqued) by users in the field. Determined to avoid this fate, Cukor made the mantra of Project Maven "field to learn." Much like a tech company, Cukor wanted his team continuously shipping product to users, getting their brutal feedback, and course correcting as necessary. In the early days, the minimum viable product wasn't great. As the Modern War Institute at West Point reported, teams from a naval special warfare group "were not immediately impressed with the algorithms' performance but said they could see their potential." That was OK. The point was to expose the product to actual, operational conditions, to get it to fail, and to learn.

More mature versions of Project Maven show things like AI targets updated in real time on a common operating picture—dots on a map. But in the words of an early Maven engineer, that dot on a map is a "snowflake on the tip of the biggest iceberg you've ever seen." Any assumptions you have about the Department of Defense's digital infrastructure in 2017 are almost certainly too rosy. For starters, there was no data with which to train the AI models. This may seem impossible. After all, by 2017 drones had collected an estimated 700,000 hours, or eighty years, of footage from key geographies. The problem? Video footage took up so much space it would immediately fill up local servers, and it wasn't retained or stored. To quote the Modern War Institute again:

> Early in Project Maven, data engineers would buy multi-terabyte hard drives, mail them to operational units, and request that the units download their richest data sets for transport.... At any given point, the team had fifty or more hard drives slinging around the globe, coming and going, being downloaded and uploaded, and being painstakingly transferred between silos. Every step of the process required direct human interaction.

Classification posed another problem. AI developers at leading technology companies did not have the security clearances needed to access classified video footage. Cukor didn't have time to wait and see if his engineers in San Francisco liked to smoke weed on the weekends. He had to find a way to legally declassify the video footage, or there would be no Project Maven. So, Cukor wrote a memo for Work to declassify the data. He then built a team of engineers specially commissioned to review the footage, declassify it where appropriate, and make it available for training unclassified AI models on the Secure Unclassified Network.

Then the data had to be labeled. Initial labeling categories for Project Maven started out relatively simple—think "person, vehicle, or motorbike." Eventually, they got more complex, but each label class required roughly 10,000 labels. Humans manually produced the vast majority of the labels, a slow and arduous process. Today, image-segmentation models use AI to automate labeling, but that technology didn't exist in the early days of

Project Maven. (Even AI labeling requires manual, human validation and quality control.)

The lack of cloud infrastructure was one of the biggest challenges. Ideally, engineers would train and improve their algorithm on an unclassified network, push the algorithm to a classified network once it was ready, and then deploy it to users around the world. Software updates would happen simultaneously. In software lingo, there would be continuous integration and continuous delivery of capability. Project Maven got there eventually, but it did *not* look like that in the early days. There was no classified cloud infrastructure for Maven to use. Although "cloud" conjures an image of data disconnected from hardware, AI cloud computing requires massive data centers and racks of powerful graphics processing units (GPUs).

Cukor became the chief advocate in the Pentagon for classified cloud infrastructure, but these things take time, even in ideal circumstances. The resistance was massive. The information-security people thought that AI would blow up the networks and tried to stop Cukor. As a stopgap measure, Cukor had to run a lot of the Maven work on-premises. This means the AI had to be trained and deployed locally, versus run in the cloud at a location many miles away. On-premise deployments require a lot of hardware and are very expensive for the government and industry. Complicating matters further, no military deployments had the infrastructure for an AI model to run on a server. As a result, Cukor's government employees had to buy GPUs and fly them to various forward operating bases for installation.

These were just a fraction of the never-ending obstacles that easily could have halted Project Maven in its tracks. They show why heretical leadership is so critical to making unorthodox projects successful. By his own admission, Cukor "worked as if it were World War III in ten months," a statement that will be corroborated by anyone who worked on Project Maven. Cukor was a machine, working insane (caffeine-free!) hours, heedless of time zone. He used his 6 a.m. commute to the Pentagon for continuous phone calls with his lead engineers and members of his team. Friday evenings were reserved for rigorous, hours-long meetings with engineers critical to a sprint. It wasn't unusual for them to go until 10 p.m. One Palantir employee said Cukor didn't take lunch breaks and was never seen eating. He also had the unique ability to shift seamlessly from microdetail to the 10,000-foot view. One minute, he was critiquing the accuracy of a label on a frame of full-motion video; the next he was navigating policy on the Hill.

A focus on constantly shipping new product was as much a strategic choice as it was about field-to-learn. Cukor used momentum from "this massive flame front of projects" to overwhelm the "reluctant and resistant services." They couldn't mount an effective opposition in part because Project Maven was "just jamming things in gracefully, one at a time, over and over and over."

There is no field-to-learn without willing and able end users, so Cukor hunted for operational champions in the field. It was harder than it sounded. Although Cukor was showing up with the money and the technology for operational testing, a risk-averse culture and loyalty to programs of record pervaded the military. People were reluctant to be associated with a novel, unknown AI effort led by an unpredictable colonel. Cukor first tried working with the Air Force, but found that "they're not allowed to do anything creative...They're not ever thinking about disrupting their programs of record because they're all told not to. And so, I thought I had some champion in the Air Force, but then a Manchurian switch would flip on in their head, and they'd start talking like robots to me." As for Cukor's own Marine Corps, he had some champions at a very senior level, but high turnover meant execution suffered, and the Marine Corps fought at a much smaller level.

Cukor eventually found traction with the Joint Special Operations Command (JSOC), which became Maven's first user. Choosing JSOC as a test user was playing the game on the hardest difficulty mode for the most important mission. Special operations units operate almost exclusively in high-risk, covert environments with demanding requirements.

JSOC was hugely valuable, but Cukor concluded that executing his vision for Maven required an even bigger, conventional force: the Army. Cukor had his eye on the Army's 18th Airborne Corps, based at Fort Bragg. Known as "America's Contingency Corps," the 18th Airborne is recognized for its ability to rapidly deploy anywhere in the world, often serving as one of the first responders in crisis situations. Its officers were fresh out of combat: many had served in the most elite special forces units and were now assuming division- and corps-level commands. A few meetings and product briefings later, Cukor had a partner with the 18th Airborne Command. Not everyone was immediately enthusiastic. The commanding general of the 18th, Michael "Erik" Kurilla, was initially a skeptic. He was partial to the Army's existing solutions, the Automated Information Discovery Environment (AIDE) and Augmented Reality Sandtable (ARES). AIDE and ARES purported to perform a similar function to Maven. If Maven was better, it would need to prove it in combat. And Kurilla knew something about combat.

While a lieutenant colonel in Iraq in 2003, Kurilla ran headfirst into a firefight in the streets. The riveting account was captured firsthand by writer and photographer Michael Yon. Kurilla was shot multiple times. With injuries to both legs—including a shattered femur—and an arm, Kurilla rolled into a firing position (Yon called it a "crazy judo roll") and continued to shoot. Kurilla kept firing and giving orders until the medic was able to subdue *Kurilla* by pumping him with an extra dose of morphine.

Needless to say, General Kurilla had high standards. Maven earned its spot, and Kurilla would go on to be one of Maven's biggest proponents, including in his next job as commander of US Central Command.

Because Cukor narrowly scoped Maven rather than creating a master plan with thousands of requirements, the effort was able to scale from a limited intelligence workflow—automating the detection of targets in video feeds from drones—to an all-purpose AI operating system. The progress was swift and remarkable. After computer vision, Cukor added a natural language processing workflow so that Maven could exploit documents—an intelligence bonanza. Then, as the United States' strategic priorities shifted from the Middle East to China and the Indo-Pacific, new data sources like satellite imagery were integrated and new AI detection models were added without having to completely redesign the system. Soon, the AI-nominated targets were backed by many different data sources, from classified sensors to publicly available information. Additional workflows were built to manage targets at scale across their lifecycle, from nomination to execution. Machine-to-machine connections were enabled to allow Maven to communicate with weapons systems and send confirmed targets directly to artillery. With each new feature, Cukor came closer to realizing his *Operate to Know* vision of fusing intel and operations.

Cukor worked tirelessly to create a transition path for Maven and find it a forever home. In 2023, Maven transitioned out of USD(I&S) and landed with NGA as a program of record. Although NGA is an intelligence agency, Maven didn't get pigeonholed as an intelligence solution when it transitioned. As of this writing, it is used by almost every Combatant Command, the Joint Staff, the individual services, and NATO.

One of the best unclassified descriptions of Maven's revolutionary impact comes from a report by Emelia Probasco of the Center for Security and Emerging Technology:

> Using MSS [Maven Smart System], the 18th Airborne has demonstrated an ability to match the performance of the time-critical targeting cell in Operation Iraqi Freedom [OIF], a targeting cell that is widely viewed as the most efficient in U.S. military history. What is even more impressive, however, is that the 18th Airborne achieved this milestone with roughly 20 people in its targeting cell, whereas the OIF cell benefitted from more than two thousand staff members.

In short, Maven made the soldiers working in the targeting cell a hundred times more effective.

The Iron Dome of Pentagon Bullshit

Everything about how Cukor ran Maven put a target on his back. He infuriated the acquisition community, which is a powerful enemy in the Pentagon. Ultimately, the firestorm of criticism triggered a series of unfounded but unrelenting IG reports that would harry Cukor until his retirement. Some of the details that follow may seem obscure, but they're essential to understanding the bureaucratic inertia and pettiness that hold our military back.

When Cukor launched Maven in 2017, the government still bought software like it bought hardware. This posed a problem. The phases of a hardware program are research, development, test, and evaluation (RDT&E), followed by production and sustainment. Costs are very high initially, and then they decline. The Department of Defense treated software the same way. It paid a lot up front for a systems integrator to build software, then it paid very little when the software went into production for patches and minor security upgrades. Software was treated as a static, finished product once it entered production.

Here's the problem: software (at least, good software) is not static. It's constantly improving, yet the cost is relatively flat across stages of development, which is why you pay a recurring subscription for commercial software instead of a large, upfront fee. This insight is the basis of the software-as-a-service model, and it enables constant improvement of the product. Development, testing, and production of software happen simultaneously, all the time. Understanding this, Cukor made the heretical argument to Congress that Maven should be procured as a continuously evolving capability, with a similar cost over its lifetime. Cukor procured software using Broad Agency Announcements (BAAs), a flexible contracting vehicle that categorized software as RDT&E. Although this categorization wasn't perfect, the BAA allowed the program costs to reflect how software was developed and deployed and allowed Cukor to make frequent changes to the product while it was in production.

Cukor would soon run into other problems with categorizing software as RDT&E. The department's general posture is that if the US government is paying for R&D, it should own the intellectual property (IP) that results from that work. The problem is that despite the categorization of the contract vehicle as R&D, Maven wasn't paying for commercial companies to perform R&D. When Palantir or Microsoft or Amazon showed up on day one of their work with Maven, they showed up with products that had decades and billions of dollars already invested. The R&D was already done. Yes, that product would get fine-tuned during the program and the companies would learn from the government's mission and data, but fundamentally, the government was paying for software, not R&D. To Cukor, the government's obsession with owning IP was an "overstated matter" more likely to harm the companies, and therefore national security, in the long term. As Cukor correctly notes, "If you [the company] can't monetize this after working with us, then what's the use of doing this? Why would you hand over your IP ever?"

To be clear, the companies did not own the government's data and were not free to, say, sell a terrorist-targeting algorithm to China. International Traffic in Arms Regulations (ITAR) were in place, and the government's interests were protected. But a company that built a deep learning algorithm maintained the IP to its proprietary model weights. For Palantir, this meant that we retained the IP to our core platform while giving the government rights to Maven-specific logic configured on top of it.

Safe to say, Cukor's approach was correct. Almost a decade later, Maven remains the best example of a robust ecosystem of leading commercial technology companies working with the government. Unfortunately, Cukor's view on IP remains in the minority. It was heretical then, and it's heretical now. For this heresy, Cukor was cast by his enemies as acting against the interests of the government. "I was considered to be just a horrific human being.... There's a whole class of people in the government that will go to their grave hating me because I would not compromise on this topic: platform IP belongs to the vendor, configurations on top are the customer's."

What happened next is almost hard to believe, if you know little about how the government operates: Cukor was punished for being too effective at his job. He was very good at rapidly getting money for Project Maven because he knew how acquisition worked and because his program was delivering. What's more, he viewed acquisition as a form of "maneuver warfare" and never underestimated its importance as a source of continuous, rapid change to solve the most difficult problems.

In the Pentagon, the easiest way to attack someone is to accuse him of stealing money and issuing contracts illegally. For almost the entirety of Cukor's time running Maven, a vicious stream of anonymous complaints were filed against Cukor. Some of these complaints were fueled by personal vendettas. It was a clear abuse of the process, but each allegation was treated with the utmost seriousness. Cukor was forced to face off against his mostly faceless opponents with little more than a heavily dog-eared copy of the Federal Acquisitions Regulation (FAR), the bible for procurement law and regulations. It had a permanent spot on his desk.

One day, the under secretary—Cukor's boss—received an anonymous, five-page letter with a litany of terrible accusations against Cukor: he was corrupt, with bags of government money in his house that he used to buy expensive cars. He was wining and dining people to get contracts to move faster. His use of BAAs was illegal. He was setting himself up for a plush job after Project Maven. He had created a command environment that did not respect rank. (To this charge, Cukor pleads guilty: "I had some very strong captains that would happily tell off a colonel or general if they were wrong. We had a climate of moving fast and getting things done.") Worst of all, the letter alleged, Cukor was illegally harboring a family of foreigners in his basement. This last, fantastic allegation came about because Cukor sponsored the (very legal) immigration of exceptional foreign mathematicians.

Cukor explains why he was a target: "You just have to understand this: when one group of people in the Pentagon get ahead of everybody else, the natural reaction is to kill that thing and get everyone back in line. That's the Pentagon." One is reminded of the Soviet Union, where the central government suppressed exceptional individuals who threatened the state's uniformity and control. Everyone was doing exceptional work, which meant no one was.

Cukor told his boss the allegations were patently false and demanded the identity of his accuser. But his boss insisted on a full investigation. An Army officer was hired to investigate Cukor. This was a bad omen. The Marines and the Army have a long-standing rivalry that became even more acrimonious when the Army advocated abolishing the Marine Corps during the reorganization debates in and immediately after World War II. Harry Truman, partial to the Army, famously said that the Marines "have a propaganda machine almost the equal of Stalin's."

The Army officer published his investigation, but the best he could find, in his opinion, was that Cukor had not properly enforced rank, thereby creating a command climate that the

Army officer said was anti-military. There were no allegations of criminal conduct. What he "found," essentially, was that Cukor let his captains loose and didn't enforce niceties—hardly fireable offenses. And what about the crazy allegations of money laundering and human smuggling? The Army officer didn't have the skills to look into these matters, so he recommended that the Naval Criminal Investigative Service (NCIS) do it instead.

At this point, Cukor's ordeal turned from tragedy to farce. When an NCIS investigator showed up at Cukor's 1,400-square-foot home in Northern Viriginia, where he lived with his wife and four kids, there were no bundles of cash, fancy cars, or illegal immigrants in sight (although there were a few modest vehicles, all with more than 100,000 miles). The investigator left in disbelief. How had Cukor managed to support all these people on a government salary in such a small house?

That the NCIS found no incriminating evidence further enraged the establishment. Their options dwindling, they seized on a final chance to attack: Cukor's retirement. After thirty years of exceptional service, Cukor had announced his intention to exit. Because of the baseless allegations, he knew there was no path for advancement. But instead of letting Cukor retire in peace, his critics went for his rank, threatening to demote him to lieutenant colonel!

At this point, any confusion on your part is excusable. Shouldn't the Marine Corps be fighting for the person responsible for bringing AI to the Department of Defense? One of its own? Cukor finds the suggestion quaint. No, "the institution is always more important than the individual. We all know this; we sign up knowing this." And Cukor was now associated, however baselessly, with money laundering, luxury cars, and undermining national security. He underwent two years of soul-crushing IG investigations that never really ended.

Cukor's critics eventually gave up their campaign to take his rank, but he still suffered one final indignity on his way out the door. The last conversation that Cukor had before exiting the Pentagon was with the IG, who made clear that while Cukor was walking free today, the investigations would stay open for years. They could come after him at any point during that window.

In 2022, after Cukor had retired, the Office of Inspector General finally published an unclassified but redacted version of its findings, "Evaluation of Contract Monitoring and Management for Project Maven." The sanitized report contains no findings of fraud or impropriety. The primary conclusion is that Project Maven was indeed run "in accordance with FAR, DFARS [Defense Federal Acquisition Regulation Supplement], Defense Grant and Regulatory System, and contract requirements." The worst the IG could find is that the "AWCFT did not document its approach to monitoring by formalizing the reporting metrics, processes, and procedures for monitoring and managing Project Maven contracts." Cukor disputes even this one minor, critical finding. If you bother to read deeper in the report, it supports Cukor's claim, too. Maven "actively monitored contract deliverables using AWCFT-developed reporting, metrics, processes, and procedures to meet Project Maven objectives," and it scheduled "frequent and transparent programmatic reviews." The IG admitted that monitoring and management techniques for AI and machine learning "are not captured in current procedures and best practices that are used by the DoD acquisitions community." If only the IG applied such scrutiny and thoroughness to *outcomes,* rather than process. We should all be a little more concerned with whether a program actually works and a little less concerned with whether bureaucrats are checking the right boxes along the way.

The IG did, begrudgingly and in its own way, admit that Project Maven worked. It explained that documentation was needed, or else "future DoD acquisitions related to this complex, rapidly-moving technology may not benefit from the AWCFT's monitoring and management lessons learned." In other words, the IG criticized Maven for making it harder for other programs to learn from its example! The IG doesn't write reports like this. It's the equivalent of going before the Spanish Inquisition and coming away with a gold star for good behavior.

By the time the report was published, Cukor had already been driven out of the military. He'd had several chances for promotion, but because of the litany of accusations against him he couldn't even be on the list of potential candidates. By the time his name was cleared, it was too late. What type of people do get promoted? Per Cukor:

> Those that ascend are a rare breed: they've figured out how to survive in an environment where people can log any complaint against them and start investigations that jam up everything. This often results in a risk-averse senior leadership who avoid controversy at all costs. And the IG process is an unfortunate reality that favors the status quo and instills institutional complacency.

By contrast, Cukor had relentlessly pushed a contrarian AI agenda. People didn't like it when a colonel ran through their organization at breakneck speed, delivering new technology via real-word experimentation, unorthodox contract terms, and vendors far outside the Beltway.

As Cukor recounts this vendetta, he does so without bitterness. There's passion in his voice, but no anger. There's no victim mentality. It's actually kind of weird. Most people would, understandably, be bitter. Cukor attributes his equanimity to his Marine stoicism. He knows what's right and what's wrong. "There are many of us like that in the military. That's why you have people who literally jump on hand grenades. They'll do anything because it's what's right." What's more, the bad actions of others were often a source of motivation. This is the reason he was able to continuously deliver Maven even while these investigations were ongoing. After the fact, people on Maven were shocked to learn he'd been under investigation for more than two years, because it hadn't altered his focus or output one bit. One engineer said that Cukor so effectively shielded the team from the politics that he had a nickname for him: the "iron dome of Pentagon bullshit."

Project Maven was the culmination of Cukor's military career. Fighting for better intel methods and technology, fighting for Legacy to get police intelligence on the insurgencies in Iraq and Afghanistan, fighting against non-performant programs such as DCGS—all of these experiences trained him to bring a revolutionary AI effort to the military when the cards were stacked against him. Significantly, Cukor was in his seat for five years, long enough for it to count. Too many talented officers are rotated in and out of their positions every two years. How many potential Mavens has the military lost due to constantly rotating personnel policy? Cukor is also a prime example of why you can't separate the role of creating requirements from the role of delivering capabilities: designer and builder must work together. Much like Rickover built and then operated nuclear submarines, Cukor created the specifications for the AI solutions he wanted to exist, coordinated them, and then built them.

Cukor insists that while he and his team accomplished something exceptional with Maven, it need not be the exception. There are many others like him out there, just waiting for a chance and a climate that doesn't presume they're guilty until proven innocent. In many ways, Cukor views himself as a typical Marine: he came from a humble background, imbibed the service's values, and put his training to good use.

Perhaps most important, Cukor is living, breathing proof that herculean effort and selfless service are still possible in government—even in as flawed and sclerotic an institution as the Pentagon. We think of titans like Rickover as existing solely in a bygone and inaccessible age. Cukor shows that isn't true, either. Cukor had a book about the Yazidis, a basement office, and a righteous fire burning within him. That was enough for him to revolutionize the Pentagon and the way we fight wars forever.

CHAPTER 4

American Prosperity Is National Security

With great anticipation, Lieutenant Bernard Schriever waited his turn to take off while the plane in front of him sped down the runway. Then he watched with horror as the plane lifted into the air and erupted in a fireball, instantly killing its pilots. Schriever and his fellow Army Air Corps officers weren't locked in combat in a foreign land. It was February 1934, and they were delivering the mail in Cheyenne, Wyoming.

Schriever lived to tell of the Airmail Scandal, of which this deadly accident was a part. Many others were not so fortunate. In just over two months, sixty-six planes crashed and twelve people died following FDR's decision to yank the contracts for airmail delivery from the private sector and foist the mission onto an unprepared Army Air Corps. He made the rash decision after the big airline companies were (falsely) accused of monopolizing routes. They'd been awarded large contracts by the Postmaster General, who sought to make the system more efficient with the creation of a few major air mail routes. But it was bad optics to dole out contracts only to the biggest airlines.

It didn't matter that smaller airlines were unable to offer competitive prices or commensurate capability to fulfill the routes. An investigating Senate committee called the big company executives, including William Boeing, profiteers who were "publicly posing as patriots."

The 1934 Army Air Corps was completely unprepared for the task it received. There wasn't much military flying to be done during the Great Depression and interwar period. Pilots like Schriever flew four hours a month in outdated planes, some of which had seen action in World War I. Unlike civilian aviation, many of the military's planes didn't even have two-way radios or navigation aids for bad weather.

Tragedy ensued. The winter of 1933 to 1934 was one of the worst on record, the Army Air Corps had inadequate technology, and the pilots were unaccustomed to flying at night and in bad weather. Lieutenant Schriever's friends died because they hit a power line. They were too green to know they should scope out the runway on foot before taking off for the first time. Other pilots crashed into mountains.

The US Army Air Corps struggles to deliver mail during one of the worst winters on record (1934).

The Airmail Scandal was an early example of how the military suffers when American industry suffers. The government punished private companies; as a result, the mail didn't get delivered and good men died. Too often, antagonism has been the default state between government and industry, limiting the military's ability to underwrite American prosperity.

Thankfully, the Airmail Scandal was not the end of Schriever's story. Over the next thirty years, he became a four-star general in the Air Force and the father of the ICBM, a story explored in detail in Chapter 10. We have Schriever to thank for the hundreds of hardened, underground siloes dispersed across the United States housing the missiles that deterred the Soviets at the height of the Cold War. Schriever's ICBM program was the military-industrial complex at its most brilliant.

It functioned, in part, because Schriever drew the right lessons from what he had observed decades before. Of all the services, the Air Force worked most effectively with the innovative private sector during the Cold War. Schriever was scarred from seeing the Army Air Corps go it alone during the Airmail Scandal. The experience was a warning against the overconfident belief that the government didn't need the private sector to deliver the best technology for the US military.

Further, the Department of Defense internalized the positive and unique role it could play as a buyer of frontier technologies, capable of taking a longer view than industry. The early market for Silicon Valley's integrated circuits in the 1960s was dominated by the Apollo program and ICBMs. Eventually, the commercial market for chips completely dwarfed the value of government contracts. However, those early government customers provided the essential validation that helped the United

States to dominate the early global chips market, creating economic power that cycled back into military power. The symbiosis was real.

Perhaps these events seem like ancient history. But the Airmail Scandal and Schriever's successful deployment of ICBMs illustrate one of this book's most important themes: American prosperity is national security. The US defense enterprise—the military, Intelligence Community, and defense contractors—protects us from foreign enemies who wish to destroy us and our way of life. Less obvious, but no less important to our national security, are innovative commercial companies, spanning strategic industries from AI to shipbuilding, that make up what we call the American industrial base. The Department of War thus has an obligation *and* an incentive to encourage commercial companies that are both highly profitable and highly productive (good luck having one without the other). Their fates are entwined. When a company's products are competitive in the rough-and-tumble of the commercial market, it's a strong indicator they'll be competitive on the battlefield, too. Helping those companies to succeed, and inviting them to work with the government, is the best way to generate a technical edge over our enemies—while making Americans safer and more prosperous.

Today, we are witnessing the results of the Pentagon's failed experiment to divorce military production from the broader commercial economy. In this chapter, we trace the history of this long and troubled experiment. We cover a Senate committee that tried to nationalize weapons manufacturing in the 1930s by painting industrialists as "merchants of death." We look at how the government hobbled the aircraft industry between the world wars, but reversed course in time for World War II to forge the arsenal of democracy. We conclude by examining the modern drone industry, which is mostly centered in China—even though drones were an American invention. America's ability to re-establish deterrence depends on the Department of War's willingness to embrace capitalism as an engine of innovation.

Nye, Neutrality, and Nationalization

National security and capitalism have a complicated relationship. Many people believe, viscerally and emotionally, that it is wrong to make money from selling weapons, period—without considering who is buying the weapons and for what purpose. This simplistic belief has led to all sorts of crusades to tie the hands of defense companies.

In America, the most notorious example was Senator Gerald Nye's 1934 Special Committee on Investigating the Munitions Industry, an effort initially supported by FDR. The senator from North Dakota was a progressive Republican with a showman's streak. He grilled hundreds of executives on how their pursuit of profit supposedly caused the meat grinder that was the Great War. The Nye Committee, as it was informally known, set the tone for subsequent clashes between the US government and private industry.

By portraying the major producers during the Great War as "merchants of death," the Nye Committee was laying the groundwork for nationalization of the defense industry. Its members explored the "desirability of creating a Government monopoly in respect to the manufacture of armaments and munitions and other implements of war." Although almost twenty years had passed since the war, the Nye Committee used the tailwinds of the Great Depression and war clouds in Europe to try to prove that industry incited the Great War and was on track to start another. Above all, Nye and his colleagues were politically motivated to stoke isolationist sentiments and keep the United States out of any European conflict.

Senator Nye's hearings lasted from 1934 to 1936. Underpinning the Senate investigation was an almost Marxist-sounding question: should industry be allowed to profit when providing goods and services to the government? American giants like General Electric, General Motors, and Bethlehem Steel were hauled before Congress to answer allegations of wartime profiteering. The most famous hearings saw the DuPont brothers raked over the coals for "excess profits"—their company supplied 40 percent of the gunpowder used by US allies. At the time of the hearing, the DuPont Company received just 1 percent of its revenue from military contracts.

The hearings produced thousands of pages of reports but fell short of producing evidence of a conspiracy among arms makers and their financiers to foment the Great War. They nevertheless had great propaganda value. Nye's assistant counsel for the hearings was an ambitious young staffer named Alger Hiss, later revealed to be a Soviet spy. During the hearings, Hiss, in partnership with Nye, undermined America in plain sight. It's hard to think of a more effective way to neuter America prior to World War II than nationalizing some of the most productive sectors of the economy (during the Great Depression, no less!). Yet that was precisely the recommendation in the Committee's final report:

> The Committee majority recommends Government ownership of facilities adequate for the construction of all warships by the United States Navy Department, also all gun forgings, projectiles, and armor plate, and of facilities adequate for the production of powder, rifles, pistols, and machine guns necessary for the United States War Department.

Nye and his communist counsel asserted that the government could produce ships more efficiently than the private sector. (Master industrialist Henry Kaiser would humble such notions just a few years later when he supercharged production of Liberty ships.) They further argued that wartime mobilization, should it ever be needed, would be a breeze. The government could simply carry it out "in the same way it is now proposed to do [with nationalization]." Americans at the time agreed—82 percent supported a ban on corporations selling arms.

While the Nye Committee failed in its broader goal of nationalizing the defense industry, it succeeded in inspiring some of the most notable—and harmful—legislation of the 1930s. The Neutrality Acts were a series of laws passed in 1935, 1937, and 1939 that codified the isolationist sentiment whipped up by the Nye Committee and others. US companies were prohibited from selling arms or extending loans to foreign nations at war—including beleaguered allies, such as the United Kingdom.

It's one thing to want to stay out of conflict. It's another thing to hope that by plugging our ears and closing our eyes, we can shield ourselves from the storm of war. Once FDR understood that the Nye Committee was emphatically focused on the latter, he withdrew his support for the hearings. But the damage was done. His arguments for ending the Neutrality Acts and aiding the Allies against Nazi aggression failed to move a substantial portion of the US public until World War II was well under way.

Taking Flight

The Nye Committee perfectly captures the heavy-handed and moralistic way that government treats industry, but it is far from the only example. The government's treatment of the nascent aircraft industry before World War II is another example, and arguably more damaging to national security. The Airmail Scandal was just the tip of the iceberg.

The mythos surrounding the Wright Brothers, Amelia Earhart, and successful mass production during World War II stands in stark contrast to the reality of the aviation industry before World War II, which was plagued by poor policies and dysfunctional relations between the government and manufacturers. The Army and Navy remained tepid—even hostile—buyers right up until the outbreak of war. In partnership with Congress, they turned the screws on manufacturers. During the interwar years, industry subsidized the military for both the development and production of aircraft, losing money along the way. In return, manufacturers were deprived of their IP rights and accused of corruption and inciting past and future conflicts. Acquisition law was so punitive toward aircraft manufacturers as late as 1939 that firms were convinced of a conspiracy against them led by the auto industry. There was no conspiracy, just the government's deep-seated skepticism that money-making firms were compatible with the national defense.

Unlike other companies, aircraft manufacturers could not be accused of "excess profits" during World War I, and their business fundamentals remained poor throughout the 1930s. A commercial aviation market barely existed. Instead, companies existed largely at the whim of the Navy Department and War Department, often their only customers. Rather than nurturing this important infant industry, the government took advantage of its bargaining power to pursue a procurement process that separated design from production and prioritized the lowest price at the expense of the best value.

Here's how it worked. Firms responded to government specifications with paper designs and the estimated cost to build prototypes. The government selected a handful of firms to build those prototypes and compete in a fly-off. The government then acquired the design rights to the winning firm's prototype. Firms consistently lost money on prototyping in the hope of making a profit on the production contract—but there was a catch.

The government then held a *separate* competition to determine which firm(s) would produce the winner's prototype. Production competitions were almost solely based on price. This put the firm with the winning prototype at a huge disadvantage: it needed to amortize its design costs, so its production bid inevitably came in higher. To make matters worse, the firm that won the contract for production received just the winner's prototype; it had to reverse engineer the blueprints, a recipe for disaster.

These penny-wise but pound-foolish competitions resulted in terrible manufacturing and business failures. Glenn Martin developed an excellent MB-1 prototype bomber for the Army at a loss during World War I. In 1919, Martin was selected to build a small run of its bomber along with three additional firms that had underbid on the production contracts. The bombers from the four firms turned out completely different. Martin was so put off by the fiasco that he suspended the bomber's development and did not deal with the Army again until 1931. Versions of Martin's story played out across the industry. In 1919, Curtiss won the production contract for fifty of the Orenco D, a standout pursuit aircraft developed by a separate firm. Curtiss botched production so badly the planes were deemed too dangerous to fly and were scrapped. Meanwhile, the company that had developed the plane went out of business.

Separating design from production was a short-sighted acquisition strategy. It degraded the incentives for firms to invest their own money in innovative aircraft designs while encouraging firms to submit artificially low bids to manufacture the aircraft. The government was paying less than the full cost for a prototype, and then it paid less than the full cost for production. Industry was subsidizing the government on both ends! This may seem like a great deal for the taxpayer—but only temporarily. It was unsustainable for industry to operate unprofitably. More important, it resulted in our aviators getting bad, possibly dangerous, products.

Not everyone was blind to the military's broken procurement process. In 1919, Secretary of War Newton Baker advocated a more farsighted procurement program for military aircraft, telling Congress that "it cannot be expected that industry will long engage in an unremunerative line." Some ten years later, Rear Admiral William Moffett, then director of the Navy's Bureau of Aeronautics and the man credited with introducing the aircraft carrier, sang a similar tune. In the words of historian Jacob Vander Meulen:

> For him [Moffett] the distinction between design and production was meaningless and an obstacle to procurement.... Still worse for naval aviation in Moffett's view was the tendency of price competition to deter aggressive innovation.... He felt procurement laws dishonored the government.

Although price competition on manufacturing orders was the default, loopholes allowed "negotiated contracts," where a contracting officer could award the manufacturing contract to the firm with the winning prototype without a full competition. Moffett pushed for the use of negotiated contracts whenever possible, but the extreme risk aversion of contracting officers prevented their regular use.

Widespread distrust of big business making money off defense got in the way of rational national security policy. The aircraft industry became a scapegoat in the 1930s and was subjected to several high-profile congressional hearings, including the Nye Committee. Private capital from stock issuances buoyed the industry through the Depression years when the government was barely buying aircraft and the commercial market tanked. It also allowed the government to continue to buy aircraft below cost despite its ongoing and destructive policy of not recognizing the design rights of manufacturers. But this influx of private capital put a target on the aviation industry when some executives, like William Boeing, made a lot of money. Attacks on the industry continued.

The Navy, to its credit, had the self-awareness to recognize it was exploiting industry—but it was perfectly happy for the exploitation to continue. When Congress held a hearing about supposed excess profits in the aviation industry, Rear Admiral

Ernest King, the new chief of the Bureau of Aeronautics following Moffett's untimely death in an airship crash, proudly boasted that industry averaged just 4 percent profits on its naval business, while airframe manufacturers were often in the red. King opposed nationalizing aircraft manufacture at the Naval Aircraft Factory because "contractors always bear the losses." Assistant Secretary of the Navy H.L. Roosevelt, a relative of the president, amplified this point by explaining that the government was getting the best of both worlds: it didn't have to provide any "tangible consideration" to the aircraft manufacturer, but it received the full benefits of the latest innovations in private design. "Without further compensation to the designer, [the government] has the right to make, to have made for its use, and to use any number of aircraft embodying the design." Congress had come to the hearings hoping to show how rich industry was getting. Instead, the hearings exposed the harm caused by its own policies.

The Nye Committee piled on a few months later, accusing companies that exported aircraft of pulling the country into war. No such evidence was uncovered, and the European export market kept US aircraft manufacturers alive during the 1930s, when the US government wouldn't.

Congress's inability to prove that aircraft manufacturers were merchants of death did not end its attacks on contractors. In 1934, Congress, led by the powerful Congressman Carl Vinson, passed the Vinson–Trammell Act to accelerate naval shipbuilding and grow the fleet (Vinson now has an aircraft carrier named after him for his efforts). The bill wasn't meant as an assault on industry, but in a concession to the isolationist political climate, the bill's sponsors included new restrictions on contractors. In particular, the bill required that government plants complete 10 percent of aircraft work and placed a 10 percent profit limit on all Navy contracts above $10,000. If a contractor won a contract and executed it with a greater than 10 percent profit margin, it was forced to return excess profits. What's more, profits were computed before federal taxes, so actual profit limitations were lower.

The IRS was responsible for auditing contracts and collecting excess profits, but it didn't specify in advance what counted as acceptable costs. This imposed huge uncertainty on industry. Donald Brown, president of Pratt & Whitney, commented, "This of course means only one thing. The contractor will not know his profit or loss until the contract is audited by the IRS." Contractors could not apply the losses from one contract to the profits on another in the hope of evening out profits and losses over time. Most painfully, writes Vander Meulen, "losses on development contracts could not be recovered in production contracts because the Treasury had simply decided that that was forbidden." Of course, auditing enforcement required massive government resources, not to mention the time that firms spent filling out paperwork and itemizing costs. Leroy Grumman complained that these regulations were transforming his aircraft business into a compliance shop.

Ultimately, profit limitations on industry were redundant—few aircraft companies were making money to begin with. During a three-year period from 1934 to 1936, manufacturers averaged 71 percent losses on Navy development contracts and 3 percent profits on Navy production work. Martin consistently lost money on military contracts during the 1930s, and Curtiss Wright earned only $5.8 million in contracts compared to $25.6 million spent on aircraft development from 1937 to 1941. Boeing lost 28 percent on only $2.2 million in sales in 1938 and produced the B-17 at a loss well into World War II. The cutthroat business of aircraft manufacturing was sustained in its early years mainly by the enthusiasm of entrepreneurs drawn to the inherent appeal of flight.

Aircraft procurement policy during the interwar years is a story of the aviation industry suffering—and national security suffering right along with it. The United States entered World War II with inferior fighters. The bombers held up well, but this was due mainly to commercial innovation in passenger transport that was then applied to bombers. America's aviation success in World War II was about mass production more than superior technology. Self-defeating policies that harmed manufacturers made sure of that.

The Production Czar

How did the US aircraft industry transform from an anemic shell in the 1930s to a mighty pillar of the arsenal of democracy in the 1940s, capable of outproducing the combined output of the Axis powers? The answer is that when its back was against the wall, the government treated commercial industry like a vital partner rather than a mark to be squeezed, and accepted that companies could even make money during the war. Arthur Herman provides the definitive account of these events in his excellent book, *Freedom's Forge: How American Business Produced Victory in World War II.* As we mentioned in Chapter 1, President Roosevelt announced in 1939 that the United States would make 50,000 planes a year to supply the Allies via Lend-Lease. Yet merely announcing an ambitious goal does not make it reality. Industry, and in particular an industrialist named Bill Knudsen, had to muscle FDR's vision into reality.

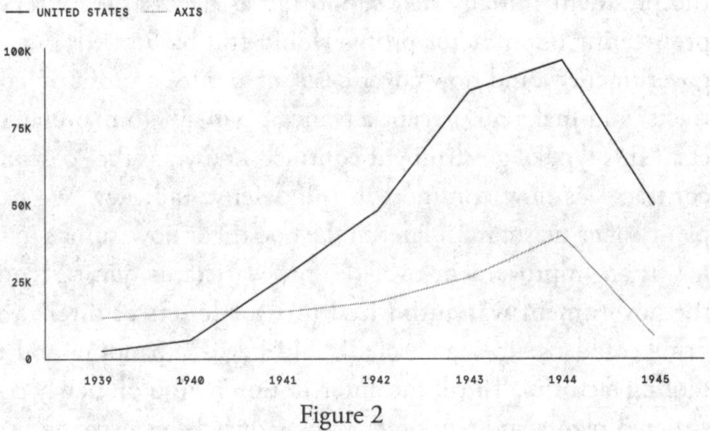

Figure 2

The Danish immigrant came from humble origins. Formerly a shipyard worker and bicycle maker, Knudsen was a self-taught engineer, and an excellent one at that. He worked at Ford and then General Motors, where he helped to develop modern mass production. Out of pure patriotism, in 1940 he left a well-paying job at General Motors to join the wartime industrial mobilization effort. At the recommendation of Bernard Baruch, FDR's close friend and advisor, Knudsen became one of the first "dollar-a-year men" and moved to Washington to lead the Office of Production Management. He brought a much-needed capitalist ethos to FDR's White House and soon became known as the production czar.

One of Knudsen's first actions was to get FDR to repeal or change self-defeating policies that a nation can only afford during the luxury of peacetime. Once war breaks out, priorities snap into place and policy quickly changes from what *feels* good to what *works*. Knudsen succeeded in suspending or repealing three such luxury policies. First, he convinced FDR to work with Congress to suspend Vinson–Trammel, a policy the president initially had supported as necessary to prevent profiteering. Contractor profits would still be limited, but the government would now cover costs, guarantee a profit on contracts, and make 30 percent advance payments to manufacturers. (This type of government contract, known as the "cost-plus contract," is now common in the defense industry. We have plenty of criticism for it later in the book. For now, suffice to say it was an improvement over the pre-war status quo.) Second, the government was authorized to issue letters of intent that firms could use to secure credit and begin expanding and retooling factories. Third, the amortization period on newly constructed plants and equipment was reduced from sixteen years to five, which allowed manufacturers to write off their investments within a reasonable time period. Some of these policies were criticized as too favorable to big business, but they were essential for the voluntary participation of private industry in the wartime mobilization effort.

Many, including Senator Harry Truman, believed the dollar-a-year men represented a gross conflict of interest for the government, but barring them would have drastically slowed down national mobilization. Take Knudsen, for example: the man ruled the automotive industry. He was not only friendly with every major player but also knew how warm their production lines were at any given moment. When the Army desperately needed a supplier to make what would become the M3 tank, Knudsen called up K.T. Keller at Chrysler. Keller agreed in part because he knew his old boss, Walter Chrysler, had great respect for Knudsen. And Knudsen wanted the M3's engine built not by Chrysler but by Continental because the company had fallen on tough times and had a dormant plant in Detroit.

After Knudsen's call with Continental's president, the company was in the business of Army engines. Knudsen's relationships generated goodwill and trust that enabled these big decisions to happen quickly. Other dollar-a-year-men did the same, expediting contracts to the most capable companies.

When Knudsen retired in 1945, President Truman wrote him a letter praising his "organizational genius in transforming our peace-time industry into a vast war machine." It was a kind gesture toward a man whose service on behalf of his country was not always appreciated. In 1942, Knudsen had been fired from his position as chairman of the Office of Production Management when FDR decided to dissolve the organization without notifying Knudsen. This firing came right on the heels of Knudsen pulling off the near-impossible: he had exceeded FDR's ambitious 1941 production goals by extending the right incentives for companies to build new factories and retool old ones. It was only at the direct intervention of Secretary of Commerce Jesse Jones and Under Secretary of War Robert Patterson that Knudsen was commissioned as a three-star general in the Army just days after he was fired. He remains the only civilian ever to receive such a commission. Knudsen approached his new role with equal gusto, leading production of the B-29 Superfortress, the world's biggest bomber—and first nuclear bomber.

America's production engine was so effective at supplying not just the United States but her allies (in all, some $50 billion in Lend-Lease aid) that at the Tehran conference in 1943, no less a communist than Stalin toasted "American production, without which this war would have been lost."

The forging of the arsenal of democracy during World War II is more remarkable when contrasted with the anti-business sentiment of the Nye Committee less than five years before. If Nye had his way, Chrysler and Continental wouldn't have made the M3 tank, Pontiac wouldn't have made the 20 mm Oerlikon antiaircraft gun, and a trio of American car companies wouldn't have designed and mass-produced the Jeep. Kaiser Shipbuilding wouldn't have churned out dozens of aircraft carriers, vastly outproducing the Axis. It took a patriotic industrialist and a president willing to set aside his prejudices against business for America to fulfill its potential as a production powerhouse.

DJI Should Not Exist

The drone industry is the modern counterpart to the aviation industry of the twentieth century. Both attracted passionate, optimistic entrepreneurs enamored with flight and a new paradigm of waging war, even in the face of a skeptical and generally uninterested government. Both industries saw private companies commit serious R&D dollars to build a product that had neither a proven government nor commercial market. And both industries had restrictions placed on private ownership of IP.

That's where the similarities end. While the story of the aviation industry had a happy ending, the story of the commercial drone industry so far is tragic: a single Chinese firm, DJI, has a chokehold on the industry, with more than 90 percent of the global consumer market. It wasn't until 2019 that Congress banned the Pentagon from buying Chinese drones. It would take another five years before similar legislation extending to the rest of the federal government passed in the 2024 National Defense Authorization Act.

Many heretical and heroic figures populate the early drone days, but there was no Knudsen equivalent, no titan of industry who was given the opportunity to quickly and decisively shape government policy toward the industry. There was also no watershed drone procurement moment akin to FDR calling for

50,000 planes, finally reversing the fortunes of an innovative industry hungry for real work. As a reminder, FDR issued his clarion call *before* Pearl Habor and America's formal entrance into World War II. The domestic drone industry never received such a call despite the evident need for a "Lend-Lease" moment in Ukraine.

China's DJI should not exist. The drone was a Western—specifically an American and Israeli—invention. The US Air Force deployed primitive drones in Vietnam, while Israel developed drones shortly after the 1973 Yom Kippur War. The first highly capable, high-endurance drones were developed in the United States during the late 1980s and early 1990s through commercial R&D.

We have Abe Karem, an Israeli immigrant, to thank. Karem was a true believer in drones who initially built remotely piloted vehicles (RPVs) in Israel to sell to the Israel Defense Forces (IDF). When the IDF proved a fickle customer, Karem moved to America in 1980 and became yet another idealistic engineer running a garage startup in California—except in this case, DARPA eventually swooped in and gave him a crucial injection of cash. Karem's prototype, named Amber, had long, thin wings and a high fuel ratio for endurance, a satellite dish in the nose for navigation, and a go-kart motor and propellor for propulsion. Amber was an odd duck, but it was also a revolution in reliability and endurance.

When Congress slashed the budget for RPVs in 1987, Amber was caught in the crossfire. Despite heroic efforts by Karem to find a mission and a buyer for his drone, his company ran out of money and went bankrupt in 1990. The six surviving prototypes were mothballed in a government warehouse in the desert, like the Ark of the Covenant in *Raiders of the Lost Ark*.

It seemed for a while that Amber was a technology ahead of its time, until Karem's inventions were rescued from oblivion by two other inventors, Neal and Linden Blue of General Atomics. The Blue brothers had been working in parallel on a drone that could serve as a "poor man's cruise missile." Their drone was primitive, so when they heard that a more capable craft was on the market, they bought it on the cheap.

Amber was reborn, with a new owner and a more intimidating name: Predator. Early drones were licensed by the government under the Advanced Concept Technology Demonstration program to show their utility in military contexts. General Atomics deployed the first Predator drones as part of a $31.7 million contract in 1994. The United States seemed poised to dominate this market, just as it had the market for microprocessors and other revolutionary technologies.

By the early 2000s, however, the drone market had shifted significantly. This was not (yet) a shift from the United States to China, but a shift from private US innovation to government-driven IP development. The Department of Defense's contracting process required contract holders to transfer IP they developed during their performance of the contract to subsequent contract holders.

This policy is standard practice for major weapons systems, and there is clear logic behind it, but it also shifts the incentives for commercial development. Government rules negating private ownership of such IP kept drone technology inside the military's walled garden—and out of the commercial market. The result was an enormous reduction in commercial R&D spending on drone technology because firms couldn't easily recoup the value of that risky effort. There was no diversified customer base to amortize R&D spending. American businesses often decry China's technology-transfer policies, which force them to give away valuable IP to access the Chinese market. The Pentagon's technology-transfer policies are just as bad for commercial innovators.

Heavy-handed regulation hasn't helped. Bad policy from the Federal Aviation Administration (FAA) prevented commercial companies from conducting beyond visual line of sight (BVLOS) operations for drones, which allow operators to control drones without being able to see them. This capability has countless commercial uses, such as large-scale infrastructure inspections, agricultural monitoring, and delivery services. While BVLOS operations introduce additional challenges to avoid collisions, the FAA's blanket prohibition cut the commercial market off at the knees and set innovation back many years.

Finally, arms-control laws under ITAR crushed any chance of an export market for the builders of military and commercial drones. While American companies shouldn't be selling drones to countries like Russia, ITAR rules didn't allow alternative markets to emerge even among US allies. In the run-up to World War II, allied markets proved crucial for fighters like the Curtiss P-36 Hawk and the North American P-51 Mustang. It was France and the United Kingdom that provided the procurement dollars and battle-tested feedback that helped US aircraft manufacturers to become competitive in a global market.

The US drone industry never got such a boost. Linden Blue, CEO of General Atomic Aeronautical Systems (GA-ASI), a subsidiary of the company he co-founded decades earlier, explained the lasting ramifications of such poor policy in 2024:

> Within GA-ASI's own export market, poor US Government (USG) policy and sluggish bureaucratic decision-making has opened the door for competitors like China, Turkey, and Israel to win

> important international customers. Sales lost to these competitors while we waited on some USG action means less funding available for re-investment into R&D and modernized manufacturing infrastructure.

And so, despite an estimated $29 billion in government spending on unmanned aerial systems between 2001 and 2013, no commercial market emerged. The result is that Americans are poorer, American drones are less capable, and China is in control of the global market. This was a choice, not an inevitability. America built and deployed the Predator and Reaper drones to great military and intelligence success. America would have been first to the commercial market if it hadn't robbed itself of the opportunity.

Abe Karem with photographs of his creations (2025).

Merchants or Missionaries?

The government often preaches that private companies selling to the military should live like missionaries, willing to turn the minimum profit necessary to keep their business alive to serve the public interest. Company leaders who deviate from the missionary script are accused of being merchants of death eager to price gouge the government irrespective of the national security implications.

Most of the men and women who make up the defense industry are, in fact, missionaries in their love of country and their excitement about frontier technology. As we've seen, pioneering aviation companies in the early twentieth century forged ahead, despite considerable hardship and risk, because they wanted to achieve the age-old dream of human flight in America. Civilian Lockheed test pilots died or were severely injured while testing aircraft like the SR-71 Blackbird and F-22 Raptor. The World War II–era arsenal of democracy had a high human cost: the Bureau of Labor Statistics reported two million disabling industrial accidents per year between 1942 and 1945. Arthur Herman reports that 189 senior executives at General Motors dropped dead on the job during the war.

Patriotism persists despite the Department of War's routine hostility toward the very firms that are delivering the weapons on which the military depends. The US government is a notoriously difficult customer. There are far easier ways to make money. Many companies keep trying anyway. The fact that these companies are public spirited is not a reason to starve them of funds or ensure that their profit margins are as slender as possible. If anything, it's an argument for ensuring that they can succeed as profitable commercial companies, capable of scaling, innovating, and growing. In any case, it's a mistake to think the public good and the marketplace are always in conflict. The profit motive is an amazing engine of innovation that makes society richer and safer. Bill Knudsen, Abe Karem, and countless other innovators came to the United States because it's the land of opportunity, which is a more tasteful way of saying "you can get rich here!" Their work on cars, airplanes, drones, and much else have made us all immeasurably better off.

From a purely practical perspective, the United States has long since passed the point where government shipyards, armories, and national labs can take leading roles in weapons production. Deep partnership with industry is necessary. President Eisenhower's 1961 Farewell Address is a favorite in some quarters for its warning against the "unwarranted influence" of the "military-industrial complex." This warning feels especially powerful coming from Eisenhower, a war hero who, unlike Nye, did not have an obvious incentive for political grandstanding.

Viewed in isolation, however, Ike's warning is missing critical context. In the preceding paragraph, Eisenhower states:

> Until the latest of our world conflicts, the United States had no armaments industry. American makers of plowshares could, with time and as required, make swords as well. But now we can no longer risk emergency improvisation of national defense; we have been compelled to create a permanent armaments industry of vast proportions.... We recognize the imperative need for this development.

In other words, Eisenhower wasn't warning about the existence of the military-industrial complex; he was warning about its potential for undue influence, a distinction often lost. By 1961, the United States was firmly ensconced in a position of global influence, but it had also acquired formidable enemies. Deterring and defeating the Soviet Union would not be possible without the private sector.

It's clear that American capitalism and the American military need each other. There is no private sector and no prosperity without the safety and security delivered by America's brave men and women in uniform. Similarly, those same men and women deserve the very best that capitalism can deliver. The government should let it deliver.

CHAPTER 5

Breaking the Pentagon

In *The Fast and the Furious*, Ja Rule's character tells Paul Walker's character: "It's not how you stand by your car. It's how you race your car. You better learn that."

Today the Pentagon is standing by a very expensive car. To use the industry lingo, it's an *exquisite* car. But the entire system is geared for standing still and looking impressive, when what really matters is whether we can race. Speed is the critical variable that separates winners from losers, in business and on the battlefield. For too long, we've been moving painfully slow.

The figure below, from Bill Greenwalt and Dan Patt's paper "Competing in Time," gives a historical view of how long it took to bring a new product to market in military aviation, commercial aviation, and the automotive sector.

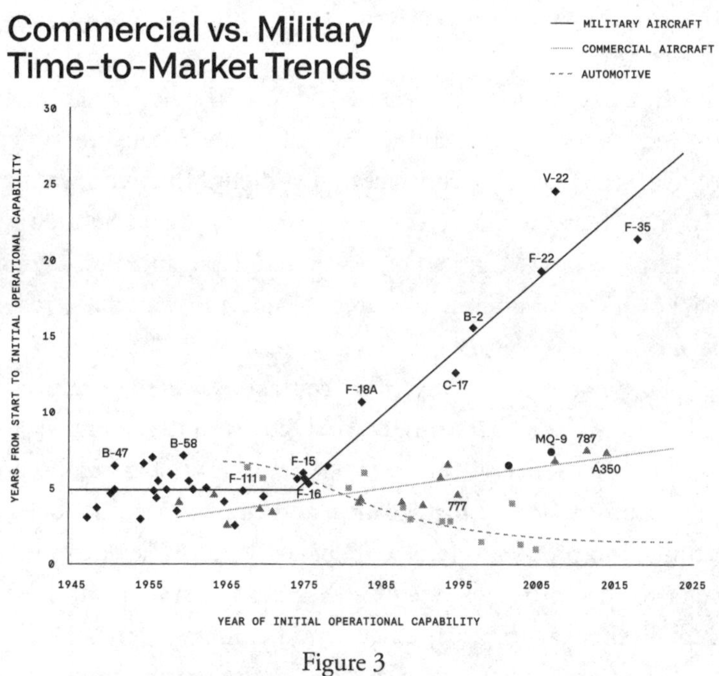

Figure 3

This is a visualization, above all, of speed. On the commercial side, time to market increased slightly for aircraft and decreased for cars. But on the government side, time to market absolutely exploded, diverging from the commercial sector in the 1970s and never looking back. The F-35 took more than twenty years to achieve initial operational capability—and it wasn't even the slowest of the bunch. The troubled V-22 Osprey took nearly a quarter-century to enter operations.

In technological terms, twenty-five years might as well be an eternity. Twenty-five years ago, Windows 2000 was the state of the art and the world was breathing a sigh of relief after Y2K. If your procurement cycle takes a quarter-century to complete, that means by default you're fighting today's war with yesterday's army.

In the two decades after World War II, the United States moved fast. Very fast. Military aircraft projects took an average of five years from first contract to first flight. The trend was similar for other systems. It took five years for Bernard Schriever to build the Atlas, Minuteman, Thor, and Titan missiles. Hyman Rickover's first nuclear-powered submarine was delivered in fewer than seven years. The list goes on.

So what went wrong? The Pentagon started breaking in 1961 when the Department of Defense and Congress embarked on a series of centralizing "reforms" that attempted to give planners greater insight into, and control over, the defense acquisition process. (Here, we're using the term "acquisition" to refer to the entire lifecycle of a weapon or a system, from concept all the way to procurement and fielding.)

The primary outputs of these reforms are new acronyms and endless delays. When we wrote this in early 2025, the acquisition process started with JCIDS (Joint Capabilities Integration and Development System), a years-long process that created the requirements for a new system, whether an air superiority fighter or a pistol. Then, via PPBE (Planning, Programming, Budgeting, and Execution), the Pentagon incorporated that new system into its budget and Congress authorized and funded it. That process added three years (plus another half year, since Congress can't pass a budget on time). Only then, with money in hand, could the Pentagon initiate the contract. As the system progressed through development, testing, and fielding, defense contractors and program managers complied with the 5000 series, which are directives that include process-intensive milestones and performance reviews against requirements conceived years ago. Recent reforms (discussed in Chapter 13) are trying to streamline this process, notably by eliminating JCIDS, but the basic structure remains.

On average, it took seventeen years for a system to work its way through the dark triad of JCIDS, PPBE, and the 5000 series. At the end of this process, the military theoretically had a shiny new weapon or platform to use on the battlefield. Then our troops got to find out whether it really worked.

Behind these reforms are would-be reformers—well-intentioned patriots who wanted American supremacy to persist, but whose actions often had unintended consequences. We'll look at the stories of three individuals: James Forrestal, the first secretary of defense, who was put in the difficult position of unifying the department with minimal authority to do so; Secretary of Defense Robert McNamara, the former Ford executive who brought business school management methods and data-driven analysis to defense acquisition; and Deputy Secretary of Defense David Packard, the Silicon Valley titan who tried to bring the dynamism of a successful technology company to a stunted bureaucracy.

Today, the procurement labyrinth built by would-be reformers in the military and Congress tries to minimize risk to programs but paradoxically maximizes risk to mission. The Department of War must respond to time-consuming oversight requests, while coloring within the lines of its original cost baseline and authorization parameters, lest it be accused of wasting taxpayer money or acting unaccountably. Congressional appropriators cling to their influence and control over defense spending, often micromanaging small sums in a nearly trillion-dollar budget. Speed is sacrificed on the altar of control. And we don't get any of the other things the reformers wanted, either. The main variables these reforms were designed to control are cost, schedule, and performance. Famously, cost has ballooned. Schedules have been blown out. And quality has been undermined by delay in a world ruled by Moore's Law and constant change.

To fully understand the counterintuitive arguments that we make in this book, it's necessary to look back at attempts to fix the Pentagon that ran amok. There is no time to repeat the mistakes of the past.

Defense Acquisition Process Over Time

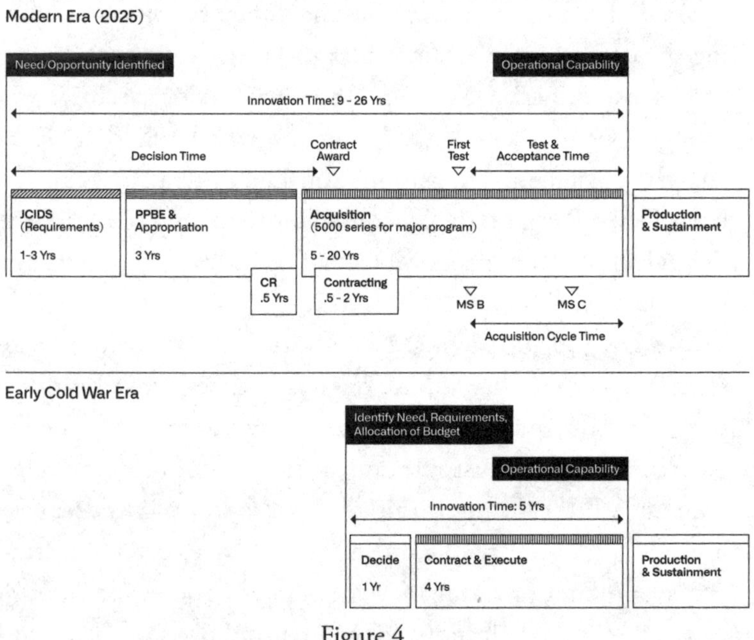

Figure 4

James Forrestal, the Reluctant Centralizer

World War II was a time of barely controlled chaos. The Department of War (that is, the Army) and the Department of the Navy operated independently, coordinating procurement and logistics on a voluntary basis. They went head to head for funding and resources, without a centralizing secretary of defense to coordinate efforts. This reality inevitably bred rivalry. Interservice competition was so intense that it was only at President Truman's command in 1948 that the Navy finally agreed to be housed under the same roof as the Army. That roof was the Pentagon, built during the war for the express purposes of improving readiness and coordinating mobilization.

Even before World War II ended, many were eager to bring a semblance of order to a defense apparatus they thought was crippled by duplication and inefficiency. As a senator and then vice presidential candidate, Truman advocated consolidating America's defense into one department and complained that defense procurement was "a dreary succession of wastes, duplications, and ugly conflict."

This kicked off a contentious—at times philosophical—debate about how to organize defense. The debate was resolved with the 1947 National Security Act, which, among other things, created the National Military Establishment (renamed the Department of Defense in 1949), established the civilian position of secretary of defense, and at long last created an independent Air Force. The act was a tremendous feat of centralization, but it would be more than a decade before the secretary of defense had any real authority.

It's worthwhile to briefly revisit the debate that produced the 1947 act. A version of it rages today: to what extent can one legislate efficiency and joint operations? Is it possible to eliminate duplication without compromising innovation and competition? How much centralization is too much? The answers to these questions are upstream of national security.

James Forrestal was the leading opponent of centralization. Ironically, he would also become the first secretary of defense. While Forrestal wasn't responsible for subsequent acquisition regulations, he left behind a structure upon which they could be grafted. Forrestal was a highly respected figure who adeptly served as under secretary of the navy for most of World War II before becoming secretary of the navy in 1944. He was responsible for all naval procurement and industrial mobilization. During the war, the biggest fleet the world had ever seen took to the seas. It did so in large part thanks to Forrestal.

While the Army favored centralization, the Navy resisted. For one, it had more to lose. The Navy feared losing its air component (the Bureau of Aeronautics) and its ground component (the Marine Corps). (These fears did not come to pass.) More broadly, the Navy didn't want to play second fiddle to the Army. It had operated with autonomy for so long that being subsumed into one department risked its very identity and esprit de corps.

As a Navy partisan, Forrestal was partial to these views, but he was also able to articulate an anti-unification argument that transcended what could be viewed as petty or parochial concerns:

> My chief misgiving about unification derived from my fear that there would be a tendency towards over concentration and reliance on one man or one group direction. In other words, too much central control—which I know you will agree with, is one

> of the troubles with the world today. A lot of admittedly brainy men believe that governments, history, science, and business can be rationalized into a state of perfection.

Forrestal didn't believe that a "state of perfection" was possible. He was extremely skeptical of efforts to unify decision-making and remove the healthy friction and dissent of competing ideas in a decentralized organization. Forrestal's views were also informed by his successful career on Wall Street leading a prestigious investment bank. He'd seen many an M&A deal fail to deliver the promised synergies and efficiencies that looked so good on paper.

Perhaps unsurprisingly, Truman's first choice for secretary of defense was not the man who so vocally opposed centralization. But when Secretary of War Robert Patterson declined the position, Truman turned to Forrestal. The patriot agreed to step up.

Forrestal was unable to stick to his guns for long. During a contentious budget debate in 1948, he appealed for more authority to fulfill the president's wishes. Truman wanted to aggressively cut defense spending, but the services were battling for the biggest slice of the first-ever integrated budget. Under the National Security Act, budgeting was a straightforward process, although this didn't mean it was easy. Truman set a budget ceiling of $14.4 billion, the amount to be requested from Congress. The services independently prepared their budgets; for 1950, they collectively proposed a whopping $29 billion. It was up to Forrestal to reconcile the discrepancy.

Navigating the politics of the situation with minimal authority and a rank equivalent to the service secretaries was frustrating. Forrestal soon requested greater powers for the secretary of defense, and a version of his recommendations came to pass with the 1949 amendments to the National Security Act. The service secretaries were downgraded from cabinet-level positions to subordinates of the secretary of defense, who became the "principal assistant to the President in all matters relating to the Department of Defense." Centralization was well under way. Notably, the amendment did not give the secretary of defense much control over the budget. That would come later.

Forrestal, however, was not around to see any of these changes. The bitter budget disputes and interservice rivalries had broken the man. Truman pressured him to resign, and Forrestal's mental health deteriorated. He developed paranoia—while on vacation, he believed the beaches were bugged and everything he said was being recorded. Then, just two months after his resignation, Forrestal committed suicide by jumping from the sixteenth floor of Bethesda Naval Hospital on May 22, 1949.

It was a tragic end to a brilliant life. Forrestal had eagerly signed up to be one of the first naval aviators during World War I, he'd excelled in a stressful and lucrative Wall Street career, and he'd carried the burden of building the Navy during World War II when many executives dropped dead from the stress. Perversely, it was wrangling the defense bureaucracy that was Forrestal's undoing.

Nevertheless, after the passage of the 1949 amendments, Truman was triumphant: "We finally succeeded in getting a unification act that will enable us to have unification, and as soon as we get the crybabies in the niches where they belong, we will have no more trouble." But unification (centralization) had only just begun. Forrestal's early warnings would start to sound prescient from beyond the grave.

Robert McNamara, the IBM Machine with Legs

After Sputnik lit up the night sky in 1957, it prompted a crisis of faith among Western elites, who questioned whether the Soviet Union's model of top-down planning produced superior results. While President Eisenhower generally resisted moves toward a centralized security state, he felt compelled to address the need for "better integration" during his January 1958 State of the Union address. Turf wars were a problem: "To end inter-service disputes requires clear organization and decisive central direction." Achieving this would necessitate a "reorganization" that could "assume with top efficiency and without friction, the defense of America."

The changes that Eisenhower advocated were soon formalized in the Department of Defense Reorganization Act of 1958. The command structure changed: the service chiefs were mostly removed from the operational chain of command in lieu of unified and specified commands (the precursor to today's combatant commands). And for the first time, the secretary of defense was endowed with the legal means to exercise firmer control over the budget and programs—and therefore over the services.

It may seem strange that there was a big push for centralization during the golden age of defense innovation, but Sputnik and the Cold War led to a relentless push for rationalization and efficiency. Congress, in particular, viewed overlapping efforts as wasteful, even though such efforts produced the fighters, missiles, and other systems that made this a golden age.

The important thing to highlight about the 1958 act is that it gave the Office of the Secretary of Defense (OSD) a real role in acquisition. Previously, acquisition—broadly defined to mean everything from preparing a budget to executing a program—was left to the services. Secretaries of defense certainly tried to exercise control over the services, as when Defense Secretary Louis Johnson cancelled the aircraft carrier USS *United States* in 1949. But this sort of unilateral action and the furor it provoked (the event to this day is known as the "Revolt of the Admirals") were exceptions that proved the rule: the secretary of defense was meant to coordinate, not administrate and operate.

Despite the enhancements set in law by the 1958 act, it took a secretary of defense like Robert Strange McNamara to fully put them into effect. Where Forrestal had been reluctant to grab the reins of power, McNamara seized them with gusto.

Robert McNamara could have been designed in a lab for upper management. His résumé was impeccable and remarkably modern: Phi Beta Kappa at Berkeley, Harvard Business School, a brief stint at the accounting firm Price Waterhouse, then back to Harvard Business School as the youngest member of faculty.

During World War II, McNamara turned his considerable brainpower to airpower, performing statistical analyses to determine why the United States' strategic bombing campaign was faring so poorly. He found that the unusually high abort rate on missions had a simple cause: fear. General Curtis LeMay's response to the report, as head of the Army Air Forces' strategic bombing campaign, was simpler still: he threatened to court-martial anyone who turned his plane around. The abort rate plummeted. McNamara's analysis also found that high-altitude conventional bombing was inaccurate. "Bombs Away"

LeMay responded with low-altitude fire bombing, to devastating effect.

During the later years of the war, McNamara performed these studies under the auspices of the government's Office of Statistical Control. The bright, young, and heavily credentialed employees of this office would form the nucleus of McNamara's team in the years ahead. They were known as the "Whiz Kids."

After the war, Ford Motor Company recruited McNamara and nine other whizzes to turn around its struggling operation. It was a bold and, again, modern experiment in management science. Before the Whiz Kids, Ford's leaders were men who had literally built the company, working their way up from the factory floor. Most didn't have college degrees. The Whiz Kids brought a level of polish and rigor to the C-suite that it had never known. McNamara became convinced through his work that large, ailing bureaucracies could be invigorated and modernized with modern methods, namely methodical, data-driven, top-down planning. For example, McNamara set up a market research organization at Ford. The data suggested there was a market for cheaper cars. With McNamara's input, Ford introduced the economical Ford Falcon, a commercial success. McNamara was credited with the company's financial turnaround and postwar expansion. Eventually he was elevated to president—a remarkable feat for someone whose last name wasn't Ford.

McNamara's process optimization came at the end of the US automotive golden age, before Detroit came under increasing pressure from Japan. Ford could sell every car it made—the company was limited only by how much it could produce. McNamara's methods were a good fit for this one-sided problem, but his approach had little applicability to the Department of Defense or even to the auto industry a few decades later.

McNamara was Ford's president for less than five weeks before President Kennedy asked him to assume control of the largest bureaucracy in the world, the Pentagon. For a Whiz Kid, it was the opportunity of a lifetime. McNamara threw himself into the work.

Secretary of Defense Robert McNamara with his characteristic slicked side part and wire-rimmed glasses (1964).

Today, McNamara is best known for his unsuccessful attempt to scientifically manage the Vietnam War, but his reforms to defense acquisition were no less consequential—and arguably more damaging. The Planning, Programming, and Budgeting System (PPBS) that McNamara introduced (renamed PPBE in 2003, which is how we will refer to it going forward) remains a pillar of how the Pentagon buys and fields technology.

PPBE is one of the principal reasons why procurement is slow and monolithic, betting heavily on a handful of exquisite, preordained programs as the future of war—with few alternatives if those programs fail.

Of course, that wasn't what McNamara thought he was doing when he set out to reform the Pentagon. He was a patriotic Whiz Kid who thought he was "rationalizing" a chaotic bureaucracy through centralized decision-making, systems analysis, and detailed program budgeting. But he was wrong. Process only works when it serves the principal. Even if McNamara's methods suited him, it was insane for the establishment to allow them to persist, zombie-like, decades after McNamara was gone.

In some ways, McNamara's failures in Vietnam and defense acquisition were two sides of the same coin—they were attempts to reduce the complexity of the universe through stovepiped analysis that could produce a magic-bullet solution to every problem. In Vietnam, the "McNamara Fallacy," as this mindset became known, led notoriously to the use of body counts as a proxy for success. Meanwhile, in the Department of Defense, "efficiency" was the watchword, and it became an end in itself—at the expense of flexibility and optionality.

McNamara used the 1958 act to mold the position of secretary of defense into one that "establishes the primacy of technical process," as James Roherty writes in *The Decisions of Robert McNamara*. McNamara's analytical approach received critical support from the RAND Corporation. Founded shortly after World War II to retain technical talent for the government, RAND's statisticians, economists, and mathematicians produced recommendations on national security issues, from the space race to nuclear deterrence. McNamara identified these experts as kindred spirits. Much as Ford had acquired Whiz Kids wholesale after World War II, so McNamara acquired a block of RAND employees to be *his* Whiz Kids.

The king of the RAND Whiz Kids was Charles Hitch. A Rhodes scholar and fellow Harvard man, Hitch served as RAND's chief economist for more than a decade. In 1960, during the end of his time at RAND, Hitch dreamed up PPBE in his seminal work, *The Economics of Defense in the Nuclear Age*. PPBE shared DNA with the industrial efficiency processes that McNamara had implemented at Ford. McNamara quickly installed Hitch as the Department of Defense's comptroller and assistant secretary of defense, identifying PPBE as the missing mechanism required to impose order on the department. While "comptroller" hardly conjures an image of someone who shapes history, Hitch was critical to implementing McNamara's vision and forever altering how technological innovation does (or does not) happen in the department.

Prior to 1961, the budget process was pretty straightforward. The total defense budget was divided among the services, and each had a budget ceiling. Within that ceiling, there was great flexibility in how money was spent. A department's budget was a laundry list of line items, but with no great specification. For example, in 1956, the Army had a single line item of $713 million, around $23 billion today, for "Support Vehicles." If there was money left over from a line item, it was easy to transfer that money to, say, "Ammunition." But to McNamara and Hitch, such an approach was haphazard and unbecoming of an organization the size and stature of the Department of Defense.

PPBE was meant to tighten things up by strictly relating military requirements to fiscal resources. McNamara's staff sought to optimize decision-making through comprehensive analysis of the trade-offs and implications associated with different courses of action. This led to an explosion of detail. Today, the defense budget has more than 1,700 line items. Almost 40 percent are funded at less than $20 million. PPBE also introduced a rigidity that makes it difficult to move money as priorities change and new technologies emerge. It empowered the OSD and Congress to dictate exact amounts of money for specific programs years in advance, eliminating the discretion to shift funds rapidly in response to facts on the ground, such as new threats or the unexpected failure or success of a certain program. Imagine if your grocery list and budget had to be set years in advance and if one week beef was on sale at the store, you couldn't automatically use the money you saved to purchase something else. Today, Congress and OSD would never cede control to the Army to determine how to spend large amounts of money on "Support Vehicles." And that is what this is about—control.

PPBE culminates in the Future Years Defense Program, a five-year projection for forces, personnel, and funding. It was originally called the Five Years Defense Program, which bears an uncomfortably close resemblance to the five-year plans of the Soviet Union. The resemblance is more than superficial. Bill Greenwalt explains the link between the new budget method and socialist planning:

> This [ideology and management] approach, now deeply engrained in defense management culture, process, law, and regulation, is based on the concepts of scientific management that were once fashionable in the Soviet Union and at the vanguard of the 1950s U.S. auto industry before it was outcompeted by Japan in the 1970s. Centralized,

> predictive program budgeting, management, and oversight were then thought to be superior to the trial and error and messiness of time-constrained, decentralized experimentation and the seemingly wastefulness of having multiple sources rapidly prototyping potential solutions.

This dated, top-down approach still haunts us today. Everyone, including the Russians and the Chinese, has given up on communism except for Cuba and the Department of War. The Pentagon runs a centrally unplanned process with neither the supposed advantages of a planned economy nor the (far superior) advantages of a free market.

Analysis Meets Reality

McNamara dismissed creativity, competition, and spontaneity in favor of systems analysis. This was the primary method the Whiz Kids used to make rational decisions about tradeoffs by performing one-to-one comparisons across different technologies. Supposedly, this method produced answers to important questions, such as: Should the United States buy more bombers or more missiles? Was the Army's ground-based continental air defense system more valuable than buying more interceptor aircraft for the Air Force? According to Assistant Secretary of Defense for Systems Analysis Alain Enthoven, OSD's civilian analysts were the perfect people to answer these questions because the "whole military ethos, conditioned by rank, hierarchy, and discipline, conflicts with the ideas of intellectual independence and objectivity." Only the Whiz Kids could "ask the hard questions" and make recommendations via "a more rational and objective process." Enthoven was a Whiz Kid himself, of course.

The systems analysis performed by the Whiz Kids was reviled throughout the Pentagon, and it quickly drove a wedge between the civilian OSD and the uniformed leadership. General Thomas D. White, retired Air Force chief of staff, growled that the Whiz Kids were "pipe-smoking, tree-full-of-owls type of so-called 'defense intellectuals.'"

OSD's decisions were conveyed via Draft Presidential Memoranda (DPM), a McNamara special. The dreaded DPMs were equipped with detailed cost-effectiveness calculations to support the Whiz Kids' strategy and force structure decisions. OSD acquisition history describes DPMs as the "central and culminating feature of PPBS." McNamara's ability to materialize a calculation for any decision earned him the nickname "IBM machine with legs."

The fact that McNamara and his Whiz Kids were obsessed with crunching data was not the problem in itself. We can hardly say otherwise, working at a company that helps customers to make decisions using their data. The problem is that the Whiz Kids' data was often detached from reality, and the Whiz Kids themselves were so far from ground truth they didn't know they were often building castles in the air.

We see this in the tech world today. Many companies dangle lavish perks to keep engineers parked in Silicon Valley offices, but as one of us (Shyam) repeatedly tells employees and external audiences, you're not going to have your good idea eating strawberries in Palo Alto. Instead, Palantir pushes its engineers into the field with customers. This is known as our This is known as our Forward Deployed Engineering (FDE) model, which now has spawned countless dupes at other companies that have recognized the danger of building in a vacuum. The FDE model is the best way to know if the things we're building are of any use at all. Intelligence is only part of the equation. Undoubtedly, the Whiz Kids were smart, just as the engineers in Palo Alto are smart—but they were on an island far away from the rest of the building, and further still from the grunts wading through rice paddies in Vietnam.

The fundamental problem with McNamara's studies was that they were usually performed on systems that had not yet entered development. This raises the question of where the assumptions and data were coming from, and if they were anything other than educated guesses. From the perspective of uniformed personnel, they were coming from the equivalent of Silicon Valley engineers eating strawberries. Admiral Hyman Rickover, never one to mince words, had this to say toward the end of McNamara's tenure: "The social scientists who have been making the so-called cost-effectiveness studies have little or no scientific training or technical expertise; they know little about naval operations.... Their studies are, in general, abstractions.... [W]e are unwise to put the fate of the United States in their inexperienced hands." Rickover's comments cut to the heart of the issue. The Whiz Kids thought analysis could trump experience. The uniformed personnel knew that good analysis flows directly from experience.

All this analysis was, at base, an attempt to achieve certainty about the future instead of embracing the uncertainty inherent in technological development. One of the most harmful manifestations of this fruitless quest was long requirements documents. In 1964, the request for proposals for the C-5A military transport aircraft was 1,287 pages. To prepare the bidders for the grueling contest, the program manager jokingly sent Lockheed, Boeing, and Douglas wooden swords and encouraged them to commit *seppuku* with the note, "Why wait?" The firms in turn sent back 60,000-page proposals, which, laid end to end, would have been ten times longer than the runway that the massive plane needed to take off. The culture of acquisition had changed dramatically in a short period of time—less than ten years earlier, the specifications for the F-4, a Navy fighter, had been just two pages.

The man who had managed car production efficiencies in such detail now tried to do the same for cutting-edge weapons. This led to high-profile procurement failures, famously the Tactical Fighter Experimental (TFX), a multirole fighter-bomber. As McNamara fought to avoid wasted work, he over-specified contracts and limited competition.

The TFX, which would become the menacingly named F-111 Aardvark, was an early and prominent victim of McNamara's "efficiency" philosophy. When McNamara became secretary of defense in 1961, the Air Force and Navy were independently pursuing new aircraft. The Air Force wanted a high-speed, long-range strike aircraft for deep penetration missions. The Navy wanted a carrier-based fighter that could fire air-to-air missiles to intercept far-off enemy aircraft. McNamara saw this as a prime example of duplication and a prime opportunity to apply the Ford approach of commonality to create a multiservice fighter-bomber, stating: "The essential operational requirements of the two Services could be met with one plane and...a great deal of money could be saved in that way." If only it were so simple.

Combining the planes' requirements in Frankenstein fashion produced a design of dubious technical feasibility. The Air Force needed the plane to fly across the Atlantic on a single tank of fuel and achieve supersonic speed at low altitude. The Navy needed the plane to operate from aircraft carriers and carry a heavy payload of powerful air-to-air missiles to defend carrier battle groups. The resulting design employed a novel, swing-wing technology to accommodate these very different flight profiles; the wings could be forward for heavy payload missions and swept back for higher-speed, longer-range missions.

The ill-fated F-111 Aardvark, a victim of Pentagon micromanagement.

The design that haphazardly emerged for the F-111 satisfied neither the Air Force nor the Navy, and by 1966, the F-111 was in serious trouble. Engine stall problems were the main culprit, caused by disruptions in airflow through the engine. The problem was exacerbated by the aircraft's variable-sweep wing design. In 1967, two test pilots died from a double engine failure. The Aardvark had a bad rap before it ever went into production.

To correct the engine stall problems and other issues, McNamara instituted weekly, Saturday program meetings with senior civilians to hold the contractor, General Dynamics, accountable. He gave the turnaround effort the unfortunate name "Project Icarus." Incredibly, McNamara often excluded the program managers from these meetings, limiting military involvement in fixing a plane that military men would fly (in sidelining the voices of uniformed personnel, he was nothing if not consistent). Struggle sessions were held, but solutions were elusive. Still, McNamara remained wedded to the unreasonable 1963 requirements. Any deviation in performance, he believed, was akin to letting the contractor off the hook.

It's understandable why a program office—or in this case, a micromanaging secretary of defense—would want a contract executed as written, but it's another thing entirely to enforce a bad contract. The F-111 was supposed to be the most technologically sophisticated fighter-bomber the United States ever made. No one knew if the plane could be built at all. Despite the huge technical uncertainty, the contract set performance expectations up front and did not allow adjustments based on new information learned during development. In seeking predictability, McNamara invited the worst kind of chaos, as real-world flight data collided with an unyielding bureaucracy.

In 1968, the Navy convinced Congress to terminate further Navy involvement in the F-111. By that point, McNamara, the biggest bulldog for the plane, was gone—shunted by LBJ to a position as head of the World Bank. As it happened, the Navy had been working on an alternative in the background, proving again the value of "duplicated" work. It was able to award Grumman a contract for the F-14 Tomcat in 1969. The Navy would get the fighter it wanted all along, plus some star-spangled American propaganda when the plane stole the show in *Top Gun* seventeen years later. Meanwhile, only the Air Force's F-111 variants went into production. None of the promised commonality or economies of scale materialized.

For every program that McNamara tried to will into existence, there were several he was happy to cancel. Thomas McNaugher sums up the record well:

> For the Air Force, it was cancelling the Skybolt ballistic missile, stopping the B-70 bomber, and deferring the Advanced Manned Strategic Aircraft. For the Army, it was his downgrading of the Nike-X antiballistic missile system. For the Navy, it was his insistence upon developing a carrier version of the Air Force F-111, and cutting back on construction of nuclear attack submarines.

Cancelling programs that no longer work is not a problem. But there's an irony here that seems to have flown right over McNamara's head: he had the option to cancel programs because multiple programs existed in the first place. The services' hated "duplication" and "inefficiency" had produced hardware alternatives that he could choose between. After McNamara's departure, canceling programs would be much harder because fewer alternatives existed. Today, the US military is stuck with many "forever programs" that don't make sense but that can't be canceled because no alternative exists. It is hostage to countless single points of failure.

There is one final layer of irony. One of McNamara's biggest goals was to hold contractors accountable and decrease their leverage. However, by canceling programs and encouraging big, joint projects in the name of efficiency, he limited new starts and competing alternatives—which gave the few companies that did win contracts even more leverage.

We're hard on the man, so it's worth being clear: Robert McNamara was neither dumb nor evil. He was a patriot who devoted much of his life to public service and to wrestling bureaucracies of staggering size. But by centralizing power and chasing efficiency as the end goal, McNamara corrupted his legacy and burdened the Pentagon with PPBE, a maze of requirements, and endless five-year plans.

McNamara brought central planning to the Department of Defense. Central planning only makes sense if you believe in the power of the planner, yet our whole system is set up to reject that there are special people; it treats people as interchangeable, and it treats process as forever. The Chinese learned from Soviet failures that the right leader, not the right process, is what matters. Meanwhile, the biggest change to PPBE in the past sixty-plus years is one letter in the name.

David "Fly Before You Buy" Packard

Our final would-be reformer is David Packard, the innovative co-founder of Hewlett-Packard who came in to shake up the

Pentagon. Packard served as deputy secretary of defense from 1969 to 1971. He then returned to the Pentagon in 1985 to lead the blue-ribbon Packard Commission.

Packard left a complicated legacy. He's been called the "father of fourth-generation airpower and one of the founding fathers of modern acquisition policy." His prototyping competitions produced no fewer than four novel aircraft that the United States still flies. Along the way, he inadvertently added a mound of process to the mountain that McNamara had already created. Packard's two stints at the Pentagon and the reforms they produced are stories of an unstoppable force meeting an immovable object. The result of the collision was stalemate.

Even as a child, Packard was the antithesis of McNamara. Where the latter had been exacting, the former was experimental. He had an innate love of tinkering, whether with radios or explosives that permanently disfigured his thumb.

Packard attended Stanford University, which is where he met his eventual co-founder, William Hewlett. In 1939, the pair founded HP in a small garage in Palo Alto with an initial capital investment of $538 (no, we're not missing any zeros—seed rounds looked different back then). The company's first product was an audio oscillator, an electronic test instrument used by sound engineers. One of HP's first major customers was Walt Disney Studios, which used its equipment for the film *Fantasia*. Over three decades of Packard's leadership, HP grew into one of the world's leading technology companies. In 1969, he resigned as CEO and joined the Nixon administration.

Philosophically, Packard differed most from McNamara in his embrace of uncertainty in innovation and technological progress. As deputy secretary of defense, he used competitive prototyping to bring optionality back to the Pentagon. An implicit feature of prototyping is that not all prototypes will be successful. Some—maybe all—will be unsuccessful, but the information gained from the experiment is less expensive than committing to a single system before any work has been done. And Packard didn't just want to prototype the weapon of the contractor that had won the proposal. He wanted to select *multiple* contractors for the prototyping phase to increase competition and approximate market dynamics.

Packard immediately did away with McNamara's obsession with paper studies and lengthy requirements documents. His 1970 memo, "Policy Guidance on Major Weapon Systems Acquisitions," reflected Silicon Valley principles. Process for the sake of process was out: "[requests for proposals] for the development stage should be carefully reviewed to eliminate demands for reports, documentation, and work tasks which are not absolutely necessary." Further, people mattered: "put more capable people into program management, give them the responsibility and the authority and keep them in their jobs long enough to get the job done right." We wholeheartedly agree.

Packard believed prototyping deserved a dedicated pool of money. He approached Congress and asked for $67.5 million above what had already been authorized, specifying that the money should not be skimmed off the services' existing budgets. Senator Thomas McIntyre (D-NH) summed up the conventional view—and certainly one McNamara would have agreed with—when he said, "I am a little concerned with all of the 10,000 projects you already have, you ask the services to go back and dream up 12 or 15 more. Why do you have to go out and find these new deals…?"

Like Forrestal before him, Packard would have to explain why thoughtful duplication can produce innovation. In the end, he received just $12 million for the prototyping efforts. But Packard was about to demonstrate just how far a small sum of money can go when spent well.

The hallmark acquisition of Packard's time was the Lightweight Fighter (LWF) program. The fly-off, between the General Dynamics YF-16 and the Northrop YF-17, crowned General Dynamics the winner for what became the F-16 Fighting Falcon. (The loser did alright, too. Northrop's design matured into the F-18 Hornet, the Navy's workhorse fighter for decades.)

The LWF competition made history for its heresy. The Air Force already had a new fighter, the F-15 Eagle. In pushing Congress to back the LWF, Packard was creating intra-service competition inside the Air Force. The establishment, which included both Congress and the Air Force, did not want a new fighter that would threaten the F-15. Second, in supporting the LWF, Packard was backing the so-called Fighter Mafia led by John Boyd. This group of Pentagon insurgents, which advocated highly maneuverable aircraft capable of dogfighting, was widely hated for challenging the bulky, multirole aircraft of the day. Third, the LWF competition recognized the need for speed—not just for the fighter but also the associated budgeting and contracting. Eric Lofgren writes that "the LWF contracts accomplished a four or five year journey in just seven months." Finally, Packard ran the acquisition largely outside of PPBE channels. When Secretary of Defense James Schlesinger authorized the plane to fly missions, the Air Force still had no formal requirement for the fighter.

The F-16 was produced at lower cost than the F-15, providing the optionality that Packard had hoped would result from competitive, potentially "duplicative" prototyping. The

Air Force bought both the F-15 and F-16 to achieve a fighting force capable of addressing a wide range of combat scenarios while managing budget constraints. In this way, Packard kept McNamara's principle of cost-effectiveness in mind, but he created a more flexible way for the services to achieve it by providing them with real options.

The iconic A-10 Warthog also emerged from a Packard prototyping competition to select a resilient airplane for close-air support missions. Northrop and Fairchild Republic went head to head in unusually realistic live-fire tests: their prototypes flew in outdoor "wind tunnels," with gale-force wind supplied by the fifteen-foot propellors of old B-29 engines, while testers shot at them with Russian weapons acquired on the black market.

Fairchild's winning design was a beast. "The Hog" features a titanium-reinforced cockpit and a custom, tank-killing weapon called the GAU-8. The Gatling-style gun, built by General Electric, fires 3,900 30 mm rounds a minute, producing the A-10's signature and terrifying *brrrt*. The A-10's standout performance came during the Gulf War, its first combat deployment. Nearly 150 A-10s flew more than 8,000 combat sorties. Five were shot down, but their effect on the enemy, physically and psychologically, was undeniable.

You might wonder: if Packard's acquisition legacy is so great, why is he featured in a chapter about breaking the Pentagon? Because, in addition to the many good things Packard did, he was also responsible for a process that added years-long delays to acquisition: DoD Directive 5000.1.

Packard approached reform motivated by the (correct) beliefs that McNamara had micromanaged acquisition to death, the services had been sidelined, and OSD and Congress should be less involved in acquisitions. In 1971, when Packard released DoD Directive 5000.1, "Acquisition of Major Defense Systems," it seemed like an invitation to return to the good old days. The concise, seven-page document largely reinforced themes he had introduced earlier about empowering program managers and reducing red tape. It's hard to argue with the following:

> Successful development, production, and deployment of major defense systems are primarily dependent upon competent people, rational priorities and clearly defined responsibilities. Responsibility and authority for the acquisition of major defense systems shall be decentralized to the maximum practicable extent consistent with the urgency and importance of each program.

But this short and sweet document morphed in the intervening years into something unholy. By the mid-1990s, after numerous revisions, the document peaked at 1,000 pages. That's a 22 percent compounded growth rate over twenty-five years—one of the few areas where the Pentagon outperforms the market. As the document grew, so did the time to market for major systems. Greenwalt and Patt show that the regulations stemming from Directive 5000.1 are the primary drivers of delays in defense acquisition. Packard, who advocated cutting acquisition regulations by 35 percent, would no doubt be appalled by what his creation has become.

But Packard isn't wholly blameless in what the document became, either. The original text stated that programs should be able to prove that their performance matches Pentagon requirements: "Programs shall be structured and resources shall be allocated to ensure that the demonstration of actual achievement of program objectives is the pacing function." Nice in theory, but in practice this meant that programs were hostage to the bureaucracy's glacial pace and (often unrealistic or irrelevant) requirements. Packard, who should've known better, codified a linear acquisition process that isn't representative of how technology develops.

Packard's 5000 series also formalized the milestone review process to evaluate programs throughout their lifecycle. In theory, this formal process gave the government chances to scrap underperforming or unaligned programs. The reality was different. Milestone reviews paved the way for decision-making by consensus and by committees far from the program itself. Just think about it: no revolutionary piece of technology ever had unanimous consensus—not the airplane, not stealth, and certainly not AI. Ironically, Packard got the idea for milestone reviews from his time at HP. The other half of the company, Hewlett, was responsible for go/no-go decisions for new projects. But the differences between this process and the government's couldn't have been starker. The HP process was just one individual, and a remarkable one at that. It was the opposite of decision-making by committee.

Packard's management mantra from his 5000 memo did not come to pass. Program managers were neither empowered nor retained long enough to deliver revolutionary technology. Instead, Congress and the Pentagon bureaucracy latched on to the part of the memo that introduced process, namely, review boards and milestones. And that's why program execution, to this day, takes anywhere from five to twenty years. It's the unintended legacy of a seven-page memo that grew up to become a 1,000-page monster.

The Joyless Quest for Jointness

Packard returned to the Department of Defense in the 1980s for another crack at reform. In 1986, the Packard Commission published its recommendations in *A Quest for Excellence.* One issue dominated all others: how to promote a joint force. Packard's report informed the Goldwater–Nichols Act of 1986, which introduced significant organizational changes. For reasons we'll cover shortly, the act did little to improve the weapons acquired or used by the joint force. So, a new process—the joint requirements process—was layered on to try to fix what Goldwater–Nichols had not. By then, Packard had retired from the Department of Defense, and there was a new crop of runaway reforms that were as misguided as the ones that had come before.

Jointness, or the ability of the different branches of the military to cooperate and work together, is essential to success in war. For as long as we've had multiple armed services, we've had interservice rivalry, parochialism, and calls for jointness. These issues came to a head with Operation Eagle Claw and Operation Urgent Fury in the early 1980s. Operation Eagle Claw was an attempt to rescue Americans held hostage by Iranian terrorists. It ended in fiery catastrophe when a Navy helicopter collided with an Air Force transport at a desert rendezvous point. The need for better coordination and standardization—for jointness—was apparent. Eight US servicemen paid for the lesson with their lives. Just three years later, the invasion of Grenada via Operation Urgent Fury exposed similar problems. While the invasion was a success, each branch of the military had operated under its own command structure; the Army and Navy essentially ran separate missions. There were incidents of friendly fire, and incompatible radios resulted in Navy jets attacking the wrong targets.

These problems were the impetus for Goldwater–Nichols. The act streamlined the chain of command by placing the service chiefs in an advisory role. They would no longer have operational control over their forces in the field. Instead, combatant commanders would control those forces, reporting directly to the secretary of defense. Goldwater–Nichols brought needed clarity to the chain of command for joint operations. The (relatively) smooth execution of Operation Desert Storm proved that. But Goldwater–Nichols, like prior reforms, had an unintended consequence for acquisition: it divorced the buyers of technology from the users. Today, the combatant commanders generate the demand for things they need, but it's the services that are responsible for buying those things.

JCIDS, the joint requirements process that emerged after Goldwater–Nichols, was intended to fix the disconnect between what combatant commands needed and what the services were supplying. A version of JCIDS has existed since 1991, and it has been through several iterations since. JCIDS exists to ensure that capabilities produced by the services advance the "joint" force and US strategy rather than parochial interests, and that those capabilities are interoperable across the services. In practice, JCIDS has added another layer of complexity and delay. The failures of JCIDS are documented in another paper by Greenwalt and Patt, who found that it takes 852 days, on average, for JCIDS to validate a joint requirement. That's 2.5 years of bureaucratic wrangling *before* a program has entered the PPBE process.

The validated joint requirement is the holy grail of the JCIDS process. It's a stamp of approval that means—in theory—a capability gap has been identified and resources will be directed to meet it. Instead, the joint requirements process creates rigid system specifications in a vacuum. The JCIDS process starts when the services and combatant commands each submit their priorities. These are the inputs to JCIDS. Because only the services have budget, the combatant commands have little sway. Requests are then reviewed by the Joint Staff gatekeeper, a process and position that has devolved into a paper-pushing and box-checking exercise. Incumbents and insiders weaponize this "hidden curriculum of requirements" against upstarts that don't know how to play the game. Projects can be delayed months by a single adverse comment.

Despite these delays, proposals usually limp along to validation, for essentially political reasons. The services need each other to validate their proposals, so there is a strong incentive to go along to get along. Perhaps worst of all, JCIDS's legalism often comes at the expense of technical feasibility: "With no dedicated technical assessment capability within the Joint Staff and no incentive to constrain requirements to achievable parameters, the process validates performance specifications that engineering analysis would quickly reveal as impossible." (Readers may be reminded of McNamara's improbable F-111.) In other words, the quest for a "joint" force has produced requirements for planes that don't fly and guns that don't shoot. Only bottom-up, iterative testing in the real world uncovers what is possible and produces true interoperability.

Jointness doesn't come from a joint-requirements process—plenty of successful programs prove it. Take Cukor's Maven: in use by every service and almost every combatant command, Maven is, by any definition, a successful joint program. It did eventually become a program of record, meaning it went through the gauntlet of JCIDS. But this happened years *after* Maven had proved its worth in the field. By necessity, Cukor had to reverse-engineer the process because the process was broken.

The most important projects aren't dreamed up by Whiz Kids and planners. America's cultural strengths are fundamentally creative and improvisational. The requirements process ensures that we play to our weaknesses. In a fight, no one cares about the requirements document. The only requirement is winning. And winning requires engaging in the messy, overlapping, seemingly wasteful process of building in the real world.

The Need for Speed

These Pentagon reforms, like so many government initiatives, are proof that good intentions are not enough to produce good results. More than a half century of centralizing reforms have not given bureaucrats the ability to see into the future and control military innovation; quite the opposite. Some of the most iconic platforms and weapons of the twentieth century, including ICBMs, the Jeep, the aircraft carrier, the four-engine bomber, and radar, were developed in the "Wild West" before these reforms existed. More recent successes, like stealth technology, unmanned aerial vehicles (UAVs), and AI, emerged and were initially procured outside the normal acquisition process. Today's process encourages participants to deliver what is asked for, and no more. True innovation delivers what is needed before soldiers know they need it.

But the most fundamental problem is that the current acquisition process just takes way too long. If this chapter has demonstrated anything, it's that speed—not money, not process, and certainly not "requirements"—is the determining factor in innovation. Speed means fewer wasted manhours, less overhead, and longer service life for new systems. Palantir would gladly accept half the money for a contract if the government could deliver the money twice as fast. The US government must close the cash chain to close the kill chain.

Forrestal, McNamara, and Packard tried to tame the Pentagon. In the next chapter, we'll meet a Pentagon leader who took a different approach, emphasizing speed and flexibility in responding to adversaries. His insurgent approach delivered game-changing technologies that helped the United States to dominate the battlefield for decades, even while the Pentagon continued its descent into dysfunction.

CHAPTER 6

The Last Supper and the Great Schism

In 1957, the Soviet Union launched the first artificial Earth-orbiting satellite, Sputnik 1. It may as well have been the hammer and sickle streaking across the sky, the way Washington and many Americans reacted to this first. Edward Teller, father of the hydrogen bomb, proclaimed it a "greater defeat for our country than Pearl Harbor." The USSR had beaten America into space with ministries, central planning, and state-owned enterprises. Many wondered if the Soviets had the superior strategy in the Space Race.

While the Soviet space program robbed the United States of a great distinction, Americans answered with their own, incredible first.

No, we're not talking about the Moon landing.

On August 19, 1960, the United States recovered the first capsule of exposed film from a spy satellite in outer space. It was a critical milestone for the top-secret CORONA project after three challenging years of development.

Today, we take for granted that satellites digitally downlink data to ground stations, but there was an epic era in reconnaissance when that wasn't possible. Instead, CORONA satellites orbited the Earth for a few days, snapping pictures, before discharging and deorbiting a forty-pound film capsule, complete with retro-rockets and parachutes. The falling capsule was then intercepted mid-air by an elite crew of Air Force pilots turned meteor catchers. Fairchild C-119 and Lockheed C-130 transport aircraft were retrofitted with specialized hooks and winches to capture the parachutes attached to the descending film capsules. Much like fighter pilots score an "ace" when they shoot down five or more enemy aircraft during aerial combat, pilots supporting CORONA fiercely competed to retrieve five or more film capsules in mid-air. It was a high-wire act in the sky, and the stakes were war and peace.

While this may sound like the harebrained plot from a cartoon, it was among the saner alternatives to figure out the true number of Soviet ICBMs. The United States needed to know if the "missile gap" was real, but the USSR had locked down the Iron Curtain, forbidding overflights. As a result, Eisenhower was forced to turn to moonshot technologies that could either stealthily return the needed information about the USSR or render the prideful Khruschev too ashamed to admit his country's airspace was being repeatedly violated.

The predecessor to CORONA was the equally implausible Project Genetrix, a reconnaissance program that launched more than 500 spy balloons during one month in 1956. (You thought the Chinese were the first to use spy balloons?) The program didn't return much actionable intelligence because Mother Nature frequently steered balloons off course, and the Soviets and Chinese began to intercept the balloons.

Both programs were vying to be a more trusted alternative to the U-2 spy plane, which could soar at 70,000 feet on massive wings. Eisenhower was increasingly wary of authorizing U-2 overflights of the Soviet Union, believing it was only a matter of time before one was shot down deep in Soviet territory. His trepidation was justified when exactly that happened to Francis Gary Powers in 1960, causing an international incident. Powers survived the crash, and Khruschev exploited the situation to maximally humiliate the United States.

When the first CORONA film was recovered just three months later in August 1960, it couldn't have come at a better time. Over 12 years of operations, 145 CORONA flights returned 165 capsules containing 866,000 frames of film. The photos proved there was no missile gap and put the United States in a strong negotiating position during the 1961 Berlin Crisis. The success of CORONA demonstrated to President Nixon that satellite reconnaissance could be trusted as a verification method for the Arms Limitation Treaty, a product of the Strategic Arms Limitations Talks. To quote the National Reconnaissance Office, itself a product of CORONA: "The United States of America, confronted by the problem of a closed society, was once blind, but now it could see."

Who was responsible for this intelligence coup?

Naturally, the CIA (with Air Force assistance), but also a host of innovative commercial companies. Lockheed was the prime contractor in charge of building the satellite buses, but Eastman Kodak developed the high-resolution photographic film and General Electric made the reentry vehicles that contained the exposed film cannisters. General Mills—yes, the cereal company—was the lead contractor on Genetrix.

This was the great American industrial base in action: a deep bench of American companies whose goods could be found in grocery stores and military depots alike. Contractors during that era served both civilian and government customers. Before the fall of the Berlin Wall, only 6 percent of defense spending went to defense specialists—so called traditional contractors. Most of the budget went to companies that had both defense and commercial businesses. Chrysler made cars and missiles. Goodyear had an aerospace subsidiary that invented synthetic aperture radar. The list went on.

Major Weapons Systems Acquisition Budget: Share by Industrial Base Category

● DEFENSE SPECIALISTS ● AEROSPACE & DEFENSE COMPANIES ● COMMERCIAL COMPANIES Serving defense & many other markets

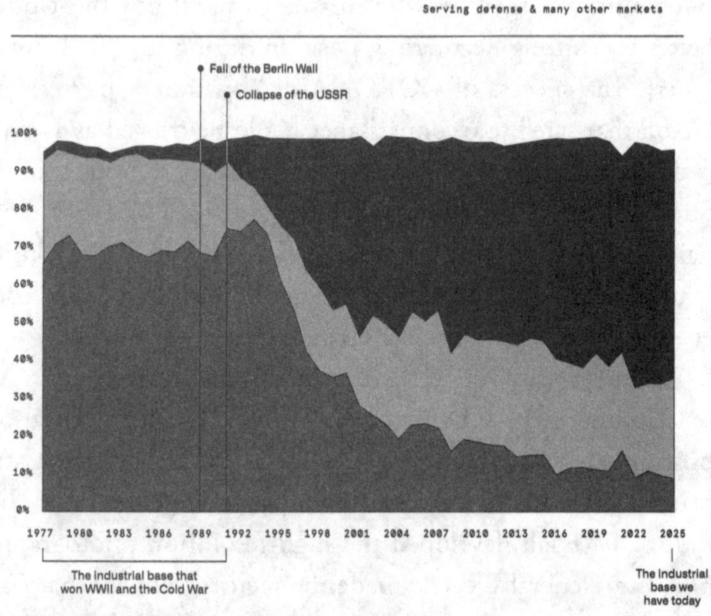

Note: "Major weapon systems" includes MDAPs and some additional spending, not the entire procurement and research, development, test, and evaluation budget.

Figure 5

But today, that 6 percent has ballooned to 86 percent. When Pentagon officials talk about the defense industrial base, they aren't talking about the dynamic, commercially focused companies that supplied the military once upon a time. They're talking about a shrinking number of contractors, most of which live and die by their ability to get defense dollars.

The point to emphasize here is that the American industrial base was once filled with dual-use *companies*, not necessarily dual-use products. Today, investors and builders fixate on whether a product can serve the defense and commercial market. But many vital defense products have no other purpose but to defend the country and attack our enemies; you will never find anti-ship missiles on the shelf at Home Depot. It's still important for such things to be made by dual-use companies, which can apply the knowledge and resources they use to serve the commercial market to improve defense products. Sherwin Williams and Quaker Oats operated bomb-loading plants during World War II. They had no experience with ordnance, but they "knew the fundamentals of mass production and good business management," in the words of military historians Harry C. Thomson and Lida Mayo. We need great companies that can leverage the lessons of the private sector to defeat our enemies.

So how did the military go from being supplied by hundreds of highly competitive commercial companies to a handful of lumbering specialists? As we will see, the Pentagon became a very unattractive customer. Companies were forced to adapt in one of two ways. They could either transform into specialists, only capable of doing business with the government, or take their talents and disruptive engineers elsewhere—namely, to the parts of the economy that still resembled American capitalism. Most did the latter.

The Entrepreneur

One man, William Perry, was at the center of the transformation from an American industrial base to a defense industrial base. He was also one of the few to understand the unfolding catastrophe. At every phase in his career, in the public and private sector, he tried to stop it. The momentum was too great, but Perry nonetheless serves as a model for how to accomplish great things when the deck is stacked against you. He worked both within and around the system as the situation demanded, delivering remarkable technologies to offset the Soviets' numerical superiority and usher in a period of unrivaled American power. Most important, he left us with the tools and lessons to rebuild the American industrial base.

Perry came of age at the tail end of World War II. He eagerly enlisted as a pilot, but the war ended before he could complete training. After an honorable discharge, he reenlisted, this time in the Army Corps of Engineers, where he was shipped to occupied Japan. The mathematically inclined Perry was tasked with making high-precision topographic maps of areas that had been destroyed by bombing. Surveying the rubble of Okinawa and Tokyo changed him. Although these places had "only" been targets of conventional bombing, Perry viscerally felt the civilization-ending possibilities of nuclear weapons in a way he hadn't before.

But Perry was also eager to experience the normalcy of postwar peace. Thanks to the GI bill, he earned a PhD in mathematics from Stanford and then went to teach at Penn State. Normalcy—real or contrived—did not suit Perry. The nuclear threat pulled him back to national security, this time as a defense contractor.

Perry's first job after academia was with Sylvania Electronic Products in Mountain View, California, a company squarely in the American industrial base. Sylvania manufactured vacuum tubes and fluorescent lights. During World War II, its vacuum tubes were used in proximity fuze shells. Perry worked at the company's defense subsidiary, Electronic Defense Laboratories (EDL), which made ground receivers to intercept and analyze telemetry signals from the Soviets' ICBM tests. The tests were a prime opportunity to leverage EDL's technology and uncover the performance capabilities of the missiles.

Perry became the foremost expert in analyzing data from Soviet missiles, on loan from EDL to the Pentagon as a consultant. He was soon in the thick of the action. As photos from U-2 flights and CORONA satellites were developed, Perry was among the select few tasked with piecing them together. During the Cuban Missile Crisis, Perry helped to prepare a daily report for the director of the CIA containing information on the missiles the Soviets had deployed off our coast.

Then as now, frontier technologies and national security crises were great catalysts for entrepreneurship. Perry was ready to be a founder and bring signals intelligence (SIGINT) into the digital age. At EDL, SIGINT was done with analog receivers, but Perry saw a different future, with computer companies like Hewlett-Packard and semiconductor companies like Intel leading the way. Perry's employer, the world leader in vacuum tube manufacturing, was like a buggy whip maker at the dawn of the automotive age. It was about to get crushed by a digital wave that few saw coming—but Perry did.

So, in 1964, Perry took the leap and founded Electromagnetic *Systems* Laboratory (ESL). Like EDL before it, ESL was in Silicon Valley before it was the Valley. As CEO for thirteen years, Perry succeeded in disrupting how SIGINT was analyzed. ESL quickly became the best at what it did, building a successful book of business with three letter agencies. It was the first organization—public or private—to use digital computers for SIGINT.

No truly great company was ever started solely to make money. ESL was no exception: "We were undertaking a business," Perry recalled, "but more deeply, we were embarked on a mission, and that mission was the overriding factor." Perry's employees felt the same way he did. At the time, there was no venture funding available for companies that couldn't say who their customers were. So ESL was entirely capitalized by its employees and founders, who bought equity in the company. Many used their life savings to do so. They believed in the mission that strongly.

Giving equity to rank-and-file employees was another first that Perry and ESL can claim (a compensation model now used by many startups and technology companies, Palantir included). Per Steve Blank, an early ESL employee, Perry modeled the company's culture after Hewlett-Packard, with one key difference: "Unlike HP, which had restricted stock ownership to the founders and top management, Perry made sure everyone at ESL had stock." Perry was a prophet before his time. It would be a recurring theme in his career.

Perry's Smart Weapons

By 1977, it was clear that the United States couldn't rely on nuclear weapons as a substitute for conventional forces. The First Offset strategy had served its purpose, but now America's adversaries had nuclear arsenals of their own. Meanwhile, the Soviets had an advantage in the sheer mass they could throw into a fight rapidly in Europe. The nightmare scenario was the Soviet Red Army rolling through Germany's Fulda Gap with an overwhelming conventional army—think Nazi Germany's Operation Barbarossa, or Napoleon's campaigns, but in reverse.

In an era of "malaise" and Vietnam Syndrome, President Carter and Secretary of Defense Harold Brown had no appetite to increase the size of conventional forces to match the Soviets. It would be up to Perry to square this circle. He had just been hired as the under secretary of defense for research and engineering (USD(R&E)), essentially the foremost technologist of the United States. Perry had the ideal background and remains a good model for the USD(R&E) position: a successful, technical founder with deep exposure to national security challenges.

During Perry's four-year tenure, he would demonstrate that being a founder does not—in fact, *must* not—end upon leaving the private sector. Perry approached every day inside the Pentagon with a wartime founder ethos. This is how the United States figured out a strategy to offset the Soviet's conventional military power.

Perry believed that new technologies could revolutionize the balance of power in the Cold War, much like computers revolutionized the analysis of SIGINT. In just three months, Perry generated an offset strategy that detailed how the United States would make up for the loss of its nuclear advantage without having to fight the Soviet Union "tank for tank, missile for missile." Perry identified stealth technology, GPS, and precision-guided munitions as tools that could diminish the need for mass and provide an asymmetric advantage over the Soviets.

Deploying these technologies together would allow the United States "to be able to see all high-value targets on the battlefield at any time, to be able to make a direct hit on any target we can see, and to be able to destroy any target we can hit." This approach may sound familiar to readers who've served in uniform. Today, the Department of War's priority warfighting concept is Combined Joint All Domain Command and Control (CJADC2, which is no less a mouthful). The goal of this concept is to connect every sensor to every shooter, creating an integrated battle network. CJADC2's technology is new, but its goals aren't much different from Perry's crisp articulation of the Second Offset almost fifty years ago.

The Silicon Valley entrepreneur was evident in Perry's actions. The procurement system was broken, and Perry didn't have time to fix it. So, to implement the Second Offset quickly, he hand-picked the most important programs and did end-runs around the traditional and slow PPBE process. Perry wasn't the first to identify the new technologies that would form the Second Offset; however, he turned these technologies from science projects into a fully funded defense strategy that could be operationalized at scale. This was the public-sector equivalent of building a unicorn. And he did it in large part by leveraging the American industrial base. The technology underpinning stealth, smart sensors, and smart weapons all depended on the digital revolution happening in industry.

Lockheed's Ben Rich earned the title "father of stealth" for developing the world's first stealth aircraft (which you can read about in Rich's excellent memoir, *Skunk Works*), but Perry poses a worthy challenge to that title. After witnessing an incredible demonstration of the Lockheed stealth prototype—a DARPA project—in 1977, Perry did whatever it took to get a stealthy fighter-bomber operational as quickly as possible. The Air Force wasn't interested in stealth because it competed for funding with its existing efforts on electronic countermeasures. Perry didn't care. He made the Air Force raid funds from its other programs to get the resources necessary. Perry admitted that circumventing the typical, PPBE acquisition process "must be used sparingly." But it got results. Within five years, the F-117 Nighthawk was operational.

It was a similar story with GPS, which started as an experimental program led by the Aerospace Corporation in partnership with the Air Force. GPS was excluded from the fiscal year 1980 budget and well on its way to termination, even though four GPS satellites were already in orbit. Perry intervened, restoring funding for an expanded constellation of sixteen and eventually twenty-four satellites. GPS gave America a generational lead in precision-guided munitions and reconnaissance. The smartphone in your pocket exists thanks to this technology, as well.

With long-range cruise missiles, Perry forced the Air Force and the Navy to work together. He required both services to allocate their entire cruise missile funds to a single special committee that would oversee the work—and he put himself in charge. Unlike McNamara, though, Perry allowed the development of other missiles to continue. We got the Tomahawk and the Air Launched Cruise Missile (ALCM) as a result. As the authors of *The Politics of Naval Innovation* conclude: "Without Dr. Perry's direct intervention, expeditious and fiscally efficient development of the cruise missile would not have occurred." Technological innovation requires authoritative founder personalities, and Perry was that founder for the Second Offset. The obstacles that Perry encountered could not simply be pushed on middle management. They required accountability and action from the top.

To secure freedom of action, Perry designated many of the Second Offset initiatives as secret "black" programs. He did this to minimize the number of gatekeepers, particularly the money-movers in Congress, who might otherwise have ensured that the strategy was never implemented. Classification with a cudgel wasn't the most elegant (or accountable) strategy, but it was extremely effective. The lesson we should take away isn't that more programs should be classified, but that more process, red tape, and delay should be removed from all programs, whether highly classified or not.

Perry ripped through the Pentagon during his four years with the attitude of a wartime general—or a tech founder. Perhaps the founder quality that Perry embodied most was what we call the primacy of winning. With limited time as USD(R&E), Perry had to make a choice: he could either attempt a top-to-bottom reform of defense acquisition, or he could implement the Second Offset on a timeline that mattered. Perry understood that winning required speed and prioritization: "Rather than giving my time and energy to reforming the entire acquisition system, I chose to work around it for the most urgent programs: the Stealth programs, the cruise missile programs, GPS, and several of the smart weapons programs." Failure was not an option. Perry played to win.

William Perry explains one of his high-tech programs as under secretary of defense for research and engineering (1978).

The success of the Second Offset strategy is best understood by comparing it to state-of-the-art technology just a few decades earlier. During World War II, the average circular error probable (CEP)—the estimate of where a bomb will land with 50 percent confidence—was 1,200 feet. It often required hundreds of bombers and thousands of bombs to take out a single target. These numbers improved during the war, but that improvement occurred because bombers started flying at lower altitudes while escorted by fighters. Just how much better were Perry's smart weapons than the dumb bombs of World War II? The Gulf War delivered the report card: the CEP was just ten feet. That's a more than hundred-fold improvement, owed almost entirely to the Second Offset. Stealthy platforms and GPS-guided munitions packed with miniaturized electronics won the day.

Air & Space Magazine summed up the ramifications of this new paradigm: "no longer did airmen have to plan for how many aircraft were needed to destroy each target; now it was about how many targets could be destroyed by a single aircraft." The most impressive Gulf War stats came from the F-117. The stealthy attack aircraft flew only 2 percent of missions but took out 40 percent of high-value targets, striking Iraqi communications and air defense targets in and around Baghdad. Precision strike remained a near monopoly of the United States for decades.

The Last Supper

In 1993, Perry returned for an encore at the Pentagon, this time as deputy secretary of defense. Where Act I was marked by rapid development of new and exciting technology to offset the Soviets, Act II was markedly less fun. The Berlin Wall had fallen and the Cold War was over—in large part thanks to the technology and strategy that Perry had developed—but the new, unipolar moment presented its own set of challenges. Americans, not unreasonably, wanted a peace dividend. Defense spending was slashed. This time, the Clinton administration challenged Perry to maintain a defense industrial base with dramatically fewer dollars. Perry was again asked to square a circle.

Perry and his boss, Secretary of Defense Les Aspin, decided to host a meeting that would become known as the Last Supper. Around 25 executives from the major defense companies were invited to the Pentagon for dinner, where they learned that the Pentagon didn't plan to fund the surge capacity and overhead needed to support all the companies present. Perry gave a slide presentation detailing how the reductions would affect industry. For example, five companies were producing ships, but the Department of Defense could only afford to support two.

Norm Augustine, then CEO of Martin Marietta, provides one of the only firsthand accounts of the infamous dinner. Per Augustine, Perry told the executives, "We expect defense companies to go out of business, and we will stand by and watch." In Augustine's words, companies could either "integrate, disintegrate, or disappear." Indeed, Martin Marietta survived the Last Supper by merging with Lockheed Corporation to create Lockheed Martin. Controversially, the costs of the merger were subsidized by the government, which was using every tool at its disposal to incentivize industry consolidation. In his usual, colorful language, then-Representative Bernie Sanders referred to the arrangement as "payoffs for layoffs."

The tidy narrative around the Last Supper goes like this: the Cold War ended, and with it, the Reagan defense buildup. Presidents Bush and then Clinton cut defense to issue a peace dividend. Then, Perry's Last Supper caused mass consolidation in the defense industrial base, from dozens of companies to only five. Today, these five contractors—Boeing, General Dynamics, Lockheed Martin, Northrop Grumman, and RTX (formerly Raytheon)—receive the majority of contracts from the Department of War. Collectively, they are known as the defense "primes." The result of this consolidation is lack of competition, soaring prices, and stagnating innovation. We are now ill equipped to fight and win one war, let alone multiple.

This narrative is essentially true, but incomplete for reasons we will explore in the next section.

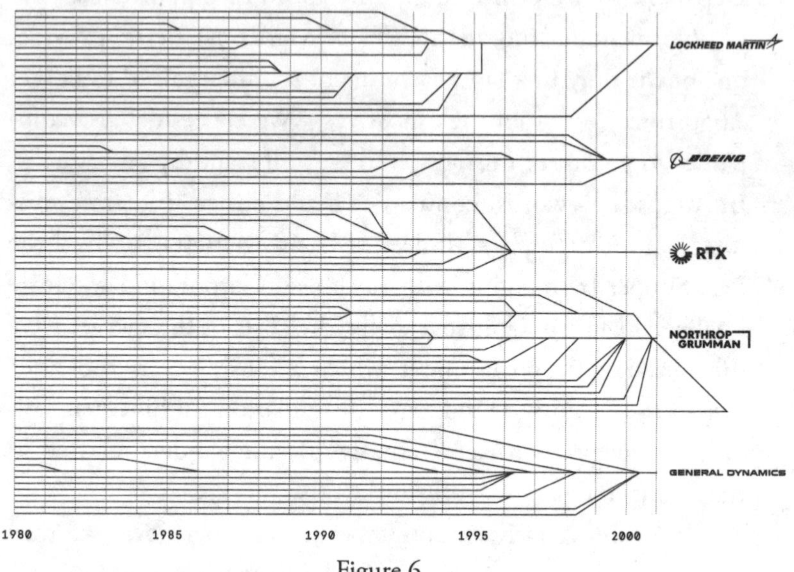

Figure 6

The Great Schism

The most important consequence of the Last Supper wasn't a reduction in competition, but what we call the Great Schism: the decoupling of commercial innovation from defense. In a defense industry rocked by turmoil, the "American industrial base" of the Cold War became the pure-play "defense industrial base" of today. Amid budget cuts, consolidation, and increasingly arcane defense-specific regulations, dozens of companies had to decide whether to stay in the defense game. For most companies, it wasn't a particularly difficult choice. The grass and the money were greener in the booming commercial market of the '90s, so it made sense to go all-in on commercial and get out of government work altogether.

In fact, the Pentagon had ceased to be an attractive customer long before the Last Supper and even before the collapse of the Soviet Union. As one report put it: "During 1985–1988, ten of DoD's top 60 prime defense contractors either acquired, or were acquired by, others in the industry." The '80s are remembered as a capitalist golden age. Not so much in the defense industry. Adding to the "reforms" of the previous decades, the Department of Defense implemented a series of damaging policies during the 1980s—such as limiting companies' ownership of IP, reducing profit percentages, and requiring companies to invest in special tooling—that made it harder to do business with the government. It consolidated its power and control over suppliers, even while other parts of the economy were being set free.

It was increasingly difficult for dual-use companies (previously just thought of as companies) to exist. Goodyear sold its aerospace subsidiary to Loral in 1987; Ford did the same in 1990. Loral experienced success in civilian telecommunications, so it decided to leave the defense industry behind, too, selling its defense assets to Lockheed in 1996. One year later, Texas Instruments sold its storied military electronics business to Raytheon. The Great Schism was accelerating. For all the caricatures of greedy defense companies making too much money, the reality was that most firms couldn't make enough money in defense to satisfy their fiduciary responsibilities to shareholders.

The companies that stayed in the defense business tended to be the ones that didn't have a choice, whether because they were too dependent on the Pentagon as a revenue source, because they couldn't hack it in the marketplace, or both. Gradually, these companies merged into the five prime contractors we know today, and they became more insular, to boot. The defense industry slowly drifted away from the much larger commercial world, until it was an island unto itself, inhabited by exotic creatures adapted to its peculiar environment but unfit to live on the mainland.

As an increasing share of defense spending went to defense specialists, we ended up with a risk-averse and homogeneous defense industry, more concerned with keeping its share of the pie and keeping the customer happy than with risky bets and moonshot ideas. The remaining companies embarked on a journey of intense cost cutting, acquisitions, and adoption of the newest acronym-soup management techniques. Activity-based costing (ABC) and just-in-time inventory (JIT) were prioritized over long-term investments and innovation. Company strategy focused on maximizing share buybacks and dividend payments.

Unsurprisingly, these conditions were kryptonite to crazy founders and innovative engineers. Consolidation bred conformity. Would Glenn Martin recognize Lockheed Martin today? What about Vannevar Bush and Raytheon? The government's stranglehold over how products should be built and the financialization of the defense industry didn't leave room for founder culture.

One of the only new defense companies to be "founded" in the 1990s perfectly reflects this shift. TransDigm emerged from a rollup of the aerospace industry. There was no bold technologist or founder behind this company, no "Bob TransDigm"—it was the private-equity firm Kelso & Company that successfully executed this strategy before passing the company on to Odyssey Investment Partners and then Warburg Pincus. TransDigm didn't develop innovative new manufacturing techniques. It acquired companies, cut costs, and increased prices as they became the only supplier that made certain critical components for aircraft. Technological engineering was out. Balance sheet engineering was in.

The companies that chose to remain in the defense industry largely did so with the understanding they were forgoing commercial opportunities. Perry's Last Supper was thus a formalization and perhaps acceleration of a trend already underway, rather than a causal event.

The Law the Pentagon Loves to Break

To his credit, Perry saw the Great Schism happening before his very eyes and tried to stop it. Among his many gifts to the nation, which include stealth and GPS, was a 1994 bill called the Federal Acquisition Streamlining Act (FASA), which ordered the government to buy more commercial technology. By this time, Perry was the secretary of defense (he replaced Aspin, who was "asked" to retire after the Black Hawk Down catastrophe in Mogadishu).

FASA was an elegant solution to the complex problem of a broken defense procurement system. As we've seen, Perry was clear eyed about how the Pentagon operated and how difficult it would be to fix. In fact, he'd thought about tackling acquisition reform while serving as USD (R&E), but decided it was too big a task to take on and would prevent him from implementing the Offset Strategy. So he put it off. Perry was so pessimistic about sweeping reform that he remarked that the financial system in the Pentagon was "probably beyond fixing."

FASA was not a silver bullet, but it did address one of the root causes of the Great Schism: specialized acquisition processes. Most people have heard stories of outrageous government waste, like $650 hammers or toilet seats. Those absurdities are not usually the result of contractor price gouging, but of highly specialized defense requirements that bar the Pentagon from just buying a hammer at Home Depot. FASA mandated that the Department of Defense buy commercial items when possible. It went further, too. The legislation tried to force the Pentagon to embrace American commercial business as the default, not the exception.

FASA and subsequent related statutes created what is known as a "preference for commercial products and services." But the language is, in fact, much stronger than a preference. The statute requires that government agencies, to the maximum extent practicable, define their requirements so that they can be fulfilled by commercial products and services. The statute requires government purchasers to undertake preliminary market research and then use the results to determine whether commercial products or services are available that: (1) meet the agency's requirements, (2) could be modified to meet the agency's requirements, or (3) could meet the agency's requirements if those requirements were modified to a reasonable extent. FASA sets a high bar if an agency wants to build a custom product on the taxpayer's dime.

For Perry, the problem of ignoring the commercial economy transcended procurement. Reversing the Great Schism was a matter of national security and economic prosperity, critical to ensuring that the United States could meet its "military, economic, and policy objectives in the future." It's no coincidence that the individual who spearheaded legislation for commercial buying was a successful entrepreneur who built a business around rapidly changing commercial technology. Perry wasn't just sympathetic to the private sector. He was shaped by it. His firsthand experience formed a deep conviction that tearing down what he referred to as the "Chinese firewall" between commercial and defense procurement processes was essential: "[My] passion for this goal was my principal reason for returning to DoD."

As the Great Schism deepened, Perry did everything in his power to stop it. It wasn't enough. Decades later, FASA may be the most violated law in the land. In 2016, when Palantir sued the government (and won), the case rested on a FASA violation. A decade later, the situation has not improved. The government competes with the private sector when it should enable it. The Department of War, the Intelligence Community, and their favorite contractors regularly waste taxpayer money trying and failing to build solutions that exist in the commercial market. Frequent violations of FASA serve as a reminder that while legislation matters, culture and incentives often play an equally important role.

And it's the Department of War—as the only customer in the defense market—that overwhelmingly determines culture and incentives. Reuniting the American industrial base, commercial and defense, is an existential issue. If the Pentagon continues down a specialized path that excludes the commercial economy, it will continue to undermine American power and degrade the country's industrial capacity. At the root of the problem is the Department of War's monopsony. We explore this in the next chapter.

CHAPTER 7

Monopsony: The Original Sin

What does the Lockheed Electra—the twin-engine, propellor-driven passenger plane made famous by Amelia Earhart and *Casablanca*—have in common with the SR-71 Blackbird, the faster-than-a-speeding-bullet, titanium spy plane?

The answer, besides the fact that they both have wings and fly, is that they were designed by the same engineer: Clarence "Kelly" Johnson, father of Lockheed's Skunk Works and the most legendary aerospace engineer of all time.

Kelly was an engineering prodigy. He got his start at Lockheed right out of the University of Michigan, where he had tested Lockheed plane designs in the university's wind tunnel. His first act as a junior employee was to inform his boss that the plane he had tested on campus—a plane that the company pinned its hopes on—was unstable in all directions. This was a bold way to start his career, but Johnson's boss was wise enough to take this criticism in stride. He ordered Johnson back to the wind tunnel to fix the problem, which Johnson ultimately did by giving the plane a double vertical tail. That plane ultimately flew as the Electra, one of the most iconic and commercially successful passenger aircraft of the prewar period. Singlehandedly, the plane transformed Lockheed from a startup fighting for its life into a going concern.

The outbreak of World War II transformed Lockheed into the aerospace giant it is today. It was during this period that Johnson started Skunk Works, a super-secret, tightknit unit set up with such speed that it initially worked out of a circus tent.

The unit's mission was to help the United States to catch up in jet aircraft. The War Department gave Lockheed 180 days to build a prototype; Skunk Works delivered in 143. The P-80 Shooting Star streaked over European skies in the final days of the war.

Kelly was able to deliver this plane ahead of schedule due to his forceful personality and several features unique to Skunk Works. As Kelly's protege and successor, Ben Rich, wrote in the classic book on the secret unit, Lockheed underlings viewed Kelly "with the knee-knocking dread and awe of the almighty best described in the Old Testament." He had a razor-sharp mind, he did not suffer fools lightly, and he invited only the best of the best under his circus tent. He was also an organizational genius who insisted on tight control of Skunk Works' operations. For decades, Skunk Works was Kelly's personal fief. Head count, budget, and—crucially—outside meddling were kept to a minimum. When the Air Force and the CIA tried to assign minders to Skunk Works to oversee its increasingly classified and consequential projects, Kelly battled their demands to a bare minimum. He knew that more oversight meant more delays, which would be bad for business and bad for the country.

It was thanks to Kelly's insistence on control, accountability, and excellence that Lockheed created some of the most important (and spectacular) aircraft of the Cold War, from spy planes like the U-2 and SR-71 to stealth attack aircraft like the F-117 Nighthawk.

When Kelly Johnson died in December 1990, his country was at the peak of its economic and military power. The United States was marshalling strength for Operation Desert Storm, in which several Skunk Works aircraft played vital roles.

Skunk Works founder Kelly Johnson poses with the U-2 spy plane.

But even at the zenith of American military power, during the final years of his life, Kelly fretted that the freewheeling qualities that had made Skunk Works a success were being stifled by red tape, gatekeeping, and risk aversion. "I fear that the way I like to design and build airplanes one day may no longer be possible," he wrote in his autobiography, published in 1985. "It may be impossible even for the Skunk Works to operate according to its proven rules at some point in the future. I see the strong authority that is absolutely essential to this kind of operation slowly being eroded by committee and conference control from within and without."

Rich shared these concerns, describing explosions in head count and oversight on military aviation projects. Just 240 people from industry and government developed the F-117, he wrote. A decade later, "more than 2,000 Air Force auditors, engineers, and official kibitzers" were involved in the development of the B-2 bomber. "What are they doing? Compiling one million sheets of paper every day—reports and data that no one in the bureaucracy has either the time or the interest to read." Generating documents to maintain the illusion of progress and control had become an end in itself. The problem wasn't one program. Rich reported encroachment all over, as armies of uniformed inspectors descended on assembly lines and more and more programs were deemed classified and hidden behind the government's veil of secrecy.

Bureaucratic overload posed an existential threat to enterprising engineers and innovative organizations like Skunk Works. Kelly designed more than forty airplanes during his career. Rich's fingerprints were on more than twenty-five. But as Rich pointed out, today's aerospace engineers are lucky to work on a single airplane. Reflecting on the SR-71, defense analyst Eric Lofgren wrote, "Imagine if the Lockheed team had to do all of today's documentation for the SR-71. It is difficult to imagine the program succeeding for less than $1 billion per unit, if it could succeed at all."

Kelly and Rich's concerns about overregulation, overclassification, and government encroachment are real. They are among the most visible symptoms of a distorted defense market where a single, overbearing and controlling customer (the Department of War) uses its market power to absorb and reshape the sellers in its control. This market structure, known as a "monopsony," explains how once-freewheeling and innovative defense contractors were transformed into lumbering leviathans, glorified state-owned enterprises molded in the bureaucratic image of their government customer. Monopsony is the root cause of defense dysfunction, and the logical result of all the centralizing and controlling "reforms" we have learned about to this point.

In this chapter, we'll learn what a "monopsony" is, why the defense market suffers from this debilitating condition, and how it has made defense development less about building the next SR-71 and more about compliance, requirements, and paperwork. We'll look at why the big defense companies are rarely competitive in commercial markets, much to the detriment of our national security. What stands between us and the dizzyingly innovative American industrial base of Kelly Johnson's day is a long list of peculiar policies found only in the Pentagon.

The Disease of Monopsony

Our defense industry is chronically ill from the disease of monopsony. Readers are probably familiar with "monopoly," a situation where a single seller supplies an entire market, giving it enormous power to raise prices and hurt buyers. In a monopsony, a single buyer has all the power, forcing sellers to conform to the buyer's demands. As the sole buyer of defense products and services, the Department of War faces no competition. It is a monopsonist as a result of decades of centralization and "reforms" like the ones discussed in Chapter 4.

At first glance, you might think this arrangement would be good for taxpayers. If the government has ultimate leverage over its suppliers, then it can dictate contract terms, pricing, and requirements to get the best possible deal. That's a win for good government, right? Not exactly. Consider what happened to another American monopsony, a company called Walmart.

Walmart once had a virtual monopsony in the retail industry. Like the Pentagon, it had immense purchasing power and thus dictated terms to suppliers, including price points, delivery schedules, and product specifications. Companies of all kinds made the trip to Bentonville, Arkansas, where Walmart is headquartered, with fear and trembling. They knew a contract with Walmart could put their products on thousands of store shelves—but that they were essentially at the company's mercy regarding the terms. Suppliers often had little choice but to comply with Walmart's demands due to the sheer volume of business the retailer represented. While this enabled Walmart to offer low prices to consumers, it placed considerable strain on suppliers who faced slim profit margins and stringent requirements. Additionally, Walmart's focus on cost-cutting often led suppliers to outsource production to countries with lower labor costs, contributing to the offshoring of manufacturing.

Because Walmart's strategy focused on squeezing suppliers on price rather than encouraging innovation, Walmart was blindsided by the rise of another retail giant—Amazon. Walmart is now one-third the size of its biggest competitor. Could the same fate happen to the Pentagon's monopsony? Could an innovative rival sneak up on us while we're sleeping?

A single buyer stifles competition and market dynamics, when instead we should be trying to approximate market dynamics in defense. While it's true that unique features of the defense industry prevent an unrestricted free market—defense companies should not be able to sell to, say, China or Russia, even though it would technically lead to greater competition in the marketplace—there are still many opportunities to put capitalism to work. We shouldn't be beholden to the monopsony. During Kelly Johnson's heyday, Lockheed and Skunk Works sold airplanes to a variety of customers, not just the Air Force. The Intelligence Community, not the Department of Defense, was the customer for some of Johnson's most iconic airplanes. The U-2 and the SR-71 that Kelly dreamed up had their origins at the CIA. While the Air Force eventually operated these unconventional planes, it was uninterested in doing so during the critical development period when uncertainty was great. If the Air Force had been the sole buyer in the market at that time, we might never have gotten the planes in the first place.

The most harmful effect of the monopsony, though, is how it molds the industrial base in its own image. The five defense primes reflect this dynamic. As we will see, dealing with a monopsony means sacrificing much of the freedom and focus required for innovation. That's in fact what happened to a lot of once-great companies. To repurpose a line from *The Dark Knight:* you either die a startup or live long enough to see yourself become a prime.

Cargo Cult Management: The Financialization of Defense

The monopsony's fixation on control and tedious regulation has made working in the national interest bad business, suitable only to risk-averse investors who are addicted to dividends and buybacks—a luxury only affordable at the end of history. That's not how the most dynamic parts of the American economy operate—only the dying parts. Working with the monopsony as a defense contractor is so unappealing that Ball Corporation (the manufacturing company that once made the famous glass jars) stopped making satellites to focus on beer cans instead. That is depressing.

If the Last Supper was financial winter for the defense industry, the past twenty-five years have been another story entirely. A Pentagon report analyzed financial performance from 2000 to 2019 and found "the defense industry is financially healthy, and its financial health has improved over time." Indeed, over that time period, the defense sector outperformed the S&P 500 on most metrics, including total shareholder return, return on assets, return on equity, and cash flow return on net assets. But this performance came at a price to innovation. While cash paid to shareholders in dividends and share buybacks increased by a massive 73 percent from 2010 to 2019 versus the previous decade, the amount that defense contractors spent on R&D *declined* from a paltry 3.6 percent of revenue to an even worse 3.1 percent (for comparison, Palantir spent 18 percent of revenue on R&D in 2024, which is par for the course for publicly traded technology companies). As we'll cover shortly, even the small amount that defense contractors spend on R&D isn't comparable to what the traditional private sector spends because of perks and quirks specific to the defense industry.

Decreased spending on R&D is the exact opposite of what you'd expect from a healthy sector, which should be plowing profits into new products. Lockheed Martin, for example, paid $3.1 billion in dividends in 2024, while spending just $1.6 billion on R&D. In short, despite improved financial performance from the lean times of the '90s, we've seen an aggressive continuation of the financialization of defense, incentivized by a monopsonistic Department of War. Share buybacks and dividends to pump a stock price have replaced superior products and engineering leadership as the markers of a strong and healthy defense contractor.

How could anyone seriously describe our defense sector as healthy? We'll run out of critical munitions within a week of a major conflict, it's taking longer to modernize the ground leg of the US nuclear triad than it took to build it, and our supply chain is hopelessly dependent on China. Somewhere along the way, financial performance diverged from product performance, and we fooled ourselves into thinking they were the same thing. Maybe we shouldn't be surprised that a bureaucracy that incentivized financialization now takes those metrics at face value as proof of health.

Our industrial base is suffering from what could be called "cargo cult management," and nobody on the inside seems to realize it. During World War II, the United States used islands in the Southwest Pacific as military bases. The indigenous Melanesians watched in awe as big metal birds carrying all sorts of supplies and cargo magically materialized whenever the soldiers were marching and signaling toward the sky. When the war ended, so did the magic cargo. Local chiefs tried to summon the cargo by engaging in the same rituals they believed caused the cargo to appear in the first place. They cleared the forest to look like landing strips and made wooden replicas of airplanes and control towers. The Americans and their Coca-Cola did not reappear.

In cargo cult management, a company's leadership uses financial metrics as the definition of success, instead of the actual criteria of success: building great products, solving real problems, and delivering value. This focus can lead to perverse decisions, like underinvesting in R&D or over-relying on contractors, that boost the share price in the short term but destroy the ability to innovate in the long term. Today, defense companies are satisfying their shareholders, but they are not healthy by the only measure that matters: the military getting the best possible innovation at the best prices.

The Department of War and Congress are not blind to the incongruence. They're frustrated that financial performance isn't translating to product performance. Former Secretary of the Navy Carlos Del Toro accused shipbuilders of "[goosing] stock prices through stock buybacks, deferring promised capital investments, and other accounting maneuvers...rather than making the needed, fundamental investments in the industrial base." Similarly, politician Rahm Emanuel proposed banning stock buybacks for defense firms that fail to meet their performance and cost commitments. Their frustration is justified, but the problem won't be solved until we address the heart of the issue.

How to Kill Capitalism

The Department of War can either berate the primes, or it can be the change it wants to see in the world. It is the monopsony buyer. It dictates the solutions it gets and the terms of delivery. Many of its policies have produced welfare-addicted primes that look more like state-owned enterprises than the innovative, founder-driven companies of the Cold War. Specifically, there are three unnecessary, socialist policies that have destroyed the dynamism of the marketplace in defense: cost-plus contracting, reimbursed R&D, and spreading around contracts.

Despite the barrage of criticism that cost-plus contracting has received over the years, we still don't hate it enough. As the name implies, cost-plus contracts reimburse the contractor for expenses incurred and then typically pay the contractor a fee on top of that. The fee may be a guaranteed rate of profit, usually around 10 percent, or it may be based on performance incentives. The problem is that markets work based on price, not cost. When a consumer buys an iPhone, he doesn't ask Apple for a bill of materials—but the Pentagon does this when it buys a jet. The Department of War's preferred cost-plus contract encourages waste, fraud, and abuse, since the only way to make more money as a contractor is to find a way to spend more money in your costs. The fundamental underpinning of our capitalist system is that better, faster, and cheaper will win. With cost-plus, there is literally no incentive to invest in innovations that reduce price because they won't increase profit—those innovations are likely to *shrink* profit. Cost-plus is a one-way ratchet for things to get more expensive and never cheaper.

If you've ever done a home remodel, you're likely to have experienced the adverse effects of the cost-plus contract. There's a reason it's hard to find someone who is happy with the cost, schedule, and performance of their last remodel. It's an industry notorious for overbudget projects with late delivery, all thanks to cost-plus.

There is an alternative to cost-plus: the much simpler and straightforward firm-fixed-price contract. The contractor assumes the risk by committing to deliver goods or services for a set price, regardless of what the contractor's costs end up being. There is an obvious incentive to keep costs low, so that the contractor can make higher profits.

If these features are so obvious, why do the Pentagon and the primes twist themselves into knots arguing for cost-plus contracts and against firm-fixed-price contracts?

Let's steelman the cost-plus contract. The Department of War argues that this type of contract is required where the scope of work involves big uncertainties and technical challenges, making it difficult to estimate costs accurately in advance. There isn't a commercial analogue to an aircraft carrier that can serve as a cost baseline. By agreeing to cover the costs, the Department of War encourages contractors to undertake innovative and ambitious projects essential to the security of our nation without the fear of incurring significant financial losses.

Maybe cost-plus contracts are the right way to buy aircraft carriers, but they are the wrong way to buy 95 percent of things—including most ships. Years ago, Palantir completed a pilot project with a major American defense contractor to improve its performance on a shipbuilding contract. Unfortunately, the pilot project failed. Why? The product we provided saved the shipbuilder (and the taxpayer) money, but the shipbuilder had no incentive to save money. Under the Pentagon's standard cost-plus contract, the company would have to give back any money it saved using Palantir's software when the contract was put up for competitive bidding upon recompete. The company had more to gain from spending more money. So it made the obvious choice, even though it meant fewer ships at greater cost to the taxpayer.

The ability to price value is a crucial skill. You could say it's the only skill that matters for a person in charge of buying weapons for the military. But with cost-plus contracts, emotions interfere with rationality. The Pentagon would rather pay more money to a company making a lower profit margin than pay less money to a company making a higher profit margin. While Senator Nye is six feet under, emotional policies targeting "merchants of death" reverberate beyond the grave.

The existence of SpaceX decimates the argument for cost-plus, which robs any reward for going faster or developing innovative approaches. SpaceX reduced launch costs by 90 percent.

That simply isn't possible in a cost-plus domain. In fact, NASA estimated the cost of developing the SpaceX rocket at $4 billion. SpaceX did it for under $400 million. Cost-plus is the reason that defense costs grow faster than inflation and don't result in compounding price performance decreases. You would think monopsony would at least lead to "everyday low prices," like it did with Walmart. But when the government does monopsony, it's expensive. The government is simply bad at managing and predicting the cost of innovation. The Pentagon's motto could be "everyday astronomical prices." And those astronomical prices might not even get you into space without Elon giving you a lift.

Launch Cost per Kilogram

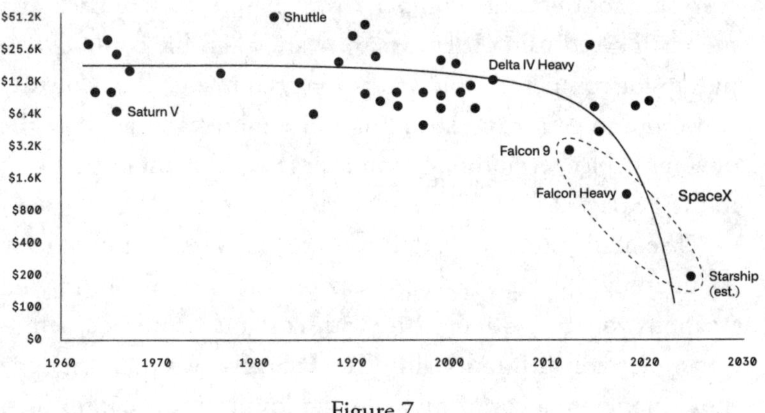

Figure 7

Because the cost-plus machine functions on a cost basis, just about every expense is billed to the government. Egregiously, this includes independent R&D. Despite the name, there's nothing independent about it, and it isn't real R&D. The primes get direct reimbursements for their R&D as allowable, indirect expenses on their cost-plus contracts. In other words, American taxpayer dollars subsidize the R&D of defense contractors so they can gamble with house money. If the Pentagon wants innovation, companies must have skin in the game. Apple didn't charge you for its failed self-driving car in your last iPhone purchase. Contractors shouldn't be able to charge you when their lab experiments run amok, either.

The primes are so subservient to government that often they're not willing to work on product innovation unless they've been fed the requirements. Long gone are the days when Lockheed expended serious internal funding on stealth before there was any real interest from the government. For the most part, the primes are working on incremental improvements to products squarely on the government's roadmap instead of blazing their own trail. This is not the path to true innovation. As Henry Ford noted, "If I had asked people what they wanted, they would have said faster horses." The "Mother, may I?" culture is the antithesis of innovation.

To be fair, if the Department of War is going to reimburse contractors for R&D, it has every right to dictate what gets built. But that shouldn't be a game the government wants to play. It imposes a ceiling on American excellence and creativity. Bob Noyce, then co-founder of Fairchild Semiconductor and future co-founder of Intel, refused government-funded R&D for this very reason. Ninety-five percent of Fairchild's customers were military, but Noyce declined most R&D funding because he wanted to stay in control of his roadmap and, consequently, the future of his company. He worked hard to ensure that his company would not be captured and corrupted by the monopsony, and he never let more than 4 percent of his R&D budget come from government contracts. That fact helps to explain why Fairchild and later Intel grew to be successful companies in the commercial sector, not just in defense. Private R&D in the commercial world far outstrips government R&D. The 1960s are over. Contrary to what the Defense Acquisition University claims, defense contractor R&D is not "a key source of innovation."

When we had an American industrial base, contractors proved they were perfectly capable of investing their own funds and using their own discretion to produce innovation. During World War II, Boeing made the legendary B-17 bomber with privately funded R&D. There was no requirement for a four-engine bomber. Similarly, North American Aviation (NAA) produced the iconic P-51 Mustang even though the US military wasn't interested. It was only after the aircraft's stellar performance with the British Royal Air Force that the US Army Air Forces did an about-face. NAA ended up producing 15,000 of the fighters.

Finally, the Pentagon is known to spread contracts around based on its suppliers' financial need, rather than merit. Per Lockheed's Ben Rich: "The open secret in our business was that the government practiced a very obvious form of paternalistic socialism to make certain that its principal weapons suppliers stayed solvent and maintained a skilled workforce." He alleges that Northrop won the B-2 contract and edged out Lockheed because Northrop needed the work. Similarly, author William D. Hartung argues that Lockheed beat out Boeing to win the C-5A military transport aircraft because Lockheed had a factory in Georgia that was running out of work, while Boeing had a large backlog of aircraft orders. Even at Palantir, a software company, we've heard government customers say they don't want to award us a contract because our software is already prolific and other companies should get a chance.

If the Department of War insists on spreading out contracts according to financial need, it shouldn't come at the expense of top performers. If a firm with a worse bid needs the work to survive, the government should award an additional contract to the firm with the best bid. Once you deprive companies of the opportunity to win on merit, the negative side effects—to the warfighter and to a company's incentive to innovate—will far outstrip any meager benefits produced in the name of equity.

Given these extraordinarily generous policies, the question isn't how the primes outperformed the S&P 500 from 2000 to 2019, it's how could they *not?* It's impossible for them to lose money on a cost-plus contract, their R&D is reimbursed, and contracts are spread around to keep production lines warm.

And yet, viewed from another perspective, the primes are terrible businesses with unit economics worse than some pizzerias. Operating margins are around 11 percent, and they are valued at just 1.5 to two times revenue in the equity markets. Meanwhile, technology companies are regularly valued at ten times revenue or more. Investors do not value the primes as technology companies—a scathing indictment given that Americans are supposed to believe that our defense industry will provide technological overmatch against adversaries on the battlefield. The emperor has no clothes.

Financials aside, there's one piece of data that reveals everything we need to know about whether defense companies are as "healthy" as claimed: their performance in the commercial market. War is far more ruthless than capitalism, red in tooth and claw, yet our defense companies have repeatedly shown they can't handle the pressure of the market without government coddling. For example, many of the government's leading IT services companies get 95 percent or more of their revenue from the government.

Why don't these companies serve a commercial market? Because they can't compete. After tailoring their business to the eccentricities of the defense market, these companies have become the corporate equivalent of exotic, flightless birds on secluded islands—curious to study, in the interest of science, but completely unfit for life on the mainland. As defense analyst Thomas McNaugher puts it, "one wonders if a nation that stakes its security on technological advantage wants to rely on firms that are in the defense business only because they have nowhere else to turn." The monopsonist Department of War selfishly molded a base of companies that could cater to its eccentricities and desires. In doing so, it rendered those companies unfit for the wide world beyond its island. The result is a national security crisis.

A Prime Is Born

During the golden era of the American industrial base, plenty of companies served both the commercial and defense markets. In 1958, the top twenty-five defense contractors had less than 40 percent of their business in defense. By 1975, they decreased that number to less than 10 percent. Ironically, the companies that became today's prime contractors for the most part did *not* have large commercial businesses. They tried to rectify this between the 1960s and the 1990s, but their efforts to penetrate non-defense markets mostly resulted in defeat and surrender. The Last Supper and the Great Schism underscored their failure. It's worth looking at some of these efforts in detail.

Raytheon was co-founded by Vannevar Bush in 1922 initially to serve the consumer electronics market. Its first product was a gaseous rectifier tube that improved the efficiency and reliability of home radios. During World War II, Raytheon manufactured the UK-invented magnetron, a microwave-generating electron tube crucial in radar. Raytheon then pioneered shipboard radars used during the Battle of the Atlantic.

Although Raytheon is credited with inventing the consumer microwave shortly after the war, by 1964 more than 80 percent of its business was with the US government. When Thomas Philipps became CEO, he set out to address the fact that "the government business is too volatile to stake all one's hopes on"—an ironic statement, given the many defense policies that are designed to limit volatility. One of Philipps' many diversification plays was to expand into computers with the creation of a Data Systems division, formed in part by acquiring Packard-Bell's operations. But by the 1980s, it was clear that Data Systems was uncompetitive in what had become a cutthroat market. Raytheon sold Data Systems to Telex in 1984.

Maybe construction would be a better fit. In 1986, Raytheon acquired Yeargin Construction Company. The acquisition was part of an aggressive diversification quest that included everything from a publishing house to a laundry business. The construction strategy also didn't pan out. Defense analyst Harvey Sapolsky notes that "[the acquisition] proved to be an expensive mistake because defense is like no other business in its forgiveness of cost overruns and time slippages: Raytheon could not manage construction and environmental cleanup projects, even for government customers, the way it was used to managing defense projects." As the twenty-first century dawned, Raytheon waved the white flag. It doubled down on defense after all. Goodbye to the publishing house, home appliances, heating and air conditioning, commercial laundry, and semiconductor businesses. Hello, monopsony.

Grumman's history looks similar. Once founder Leroy "Roy" Grumman retired from the iconic aerospace company in the

1960s, the company floundered. The Grumman responsible for the Hellcat and the Apollo Lunar Module now embarked on a diversification strategy not unlike Raytheon's. Under the leadership of lawyer and financier John "Jack" Bierwirth, in 1975 Grumman expanded into aluminum body buses, garbage disposal, windmills, solar panels, and large commercial refrigerators. The bus business lost $244 million as severe cracks were found in the undercarriages, causing New York City's Metropolitan Transportation Authority to cancel the contract. George Skurla, the former president and chairman of Grumman Aerospace, was pained by the downfall of a once great company: "I saw the money come out of aerospace and go over to headquarters. There it was frittered away on fruitless diversification schemes.... All just mixing jellybeans with diamonds."

While some of these diversification efforts were surely harebrained, others should have succeeded. Skurla's diagnosis of why diversification failed underscores the challenges of selling to the monopsony for too long: "Still remains the conundrum of trying to diversify an aerospace organization focused on and exquisitely attuned to the government's procurement system. If one tries to adopt aerospace practices, which can run to gold plating a product, the hardware gets pretty expensive. This I discovered with the truck body business." In 1994, Grumman fell victim to the Last Supper; it was acquired by Northrop.

Lockheed mostly remained a defense specialist, but it did try to translate its experience in military reconnaissance satellites to commercial opportunities in telecommunications satellites. In 1975, it competed against Hughes, TRW, and Ford Aerospace for the Intelsat constellation. Not only did Lockheed lose, the financial and technical portions of its proposal were rated last. In analyzing why Lockheed struggled, historian Thomas

Heinrich wrote that "telecom satellites developed by spy satellite builders were notoriously overdesigned and expensive."

It's hard for defense specialists to establish competitive, commercial businesses once they've been shaped by the monopsony. This wasn't really an issue during World War II and much of the Cold War because there were few defense specialists and the Department of Defense hadn't consolidated power and control over suppliers. But in recent years, selling primarily to the Pentagon almost necessarily means a company is not competitive commercially.

Boeing is the exception that proves the rule. While it receives just 42 percent of its revenue from defense, by far the lowest of the five primes, its commercial business has suffered high-profile failures that say more than a stock price ever could. The 346 dead from the 737 MAX tragedies, the two astronauts stranded on the International Space Station because of faulty thrusters on Boeing's Starliner, and the door that flew off a jet mid-flight all should have served as a flashing red light on the dash for the Pentagon: one of its five primes was falling behind in the commercial market. Could it be trusted to stay competitive in defense against China? But few seem to have internalized that the two are linked: success in the commercial market predicts performance in the defense market. American prosperity is national security.

Perry intuitively grasped this idea with his FASA legislation. So did future defense acquisition czar Jacques Gansler. Writing as far back as 1980, when the US defense economy was not nearly as isolated as it is today, Gansler contemplated a law that would require less than 25 percent of a firm's business to be in defense. That may be too prescriptive, but Gansler's line of thinking is directionally correct. It should worry us that US defense primes do not have thriving commercial businesses. On average, US primes get 73 percent of their revenue from defense, while China's earn just 27 percent from defense.

Diversification is more than just a way for a company to weather the downturns of a cyclical defense industry. Market forces are healthy and produce strong companies. We must force our companies into the gladiatorial area of commercial competition. And most important, we must recognize that relying on defense-specific companies means relying on a small and stagnant part of our economy to defend the nation. That's a travesty. We should be leveraging all our most successful companies for defense, something that's only possible with an American industrial base. Defense spending is mostly insular today; it should be stimulating a much broader part of our economy.

Defense Revenue as a Percentage of Total Revenue for Select Companies (2024)

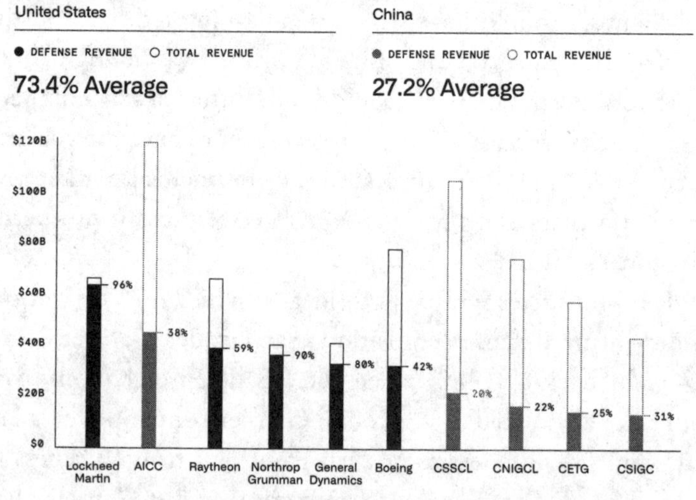

Figure 8

The primes' decision to double down on defense is first and foremost an indictment of the monopsony, which jealously and zealously oversees their activities.

Much of the monopsony's intrusiveness is downstream of cost-plus contracts. These contracts demand contractor cost data on every penny spent to ensure that prices are "reasonable." As a result, both contractors and the government spend an enormous amount of time and money to monitor, track, and audit contractor expenses. This has very real consequences and influences how companies operate. Some of the primes look more like compliance shops that happen to make airplanes, rather than airplane manufacturers.

To comply with cost-plus contracts, contractors must abide by the Cost Accounting Standards (CAS), which are defined by the Cost Accounting Standards Board. Contractors also need to comply with the Generally Accepted Accounting Principles required by the US Securities and Exchange Commission, which means they have to keep two sets of books. This is a massive barrier to entry for commercial companies that might otherwise be willing to do business with the government.

In addition to special accounting systems, companies must have an audit system capable of passing an audit by the nearly 4,000-person workforce of the Defense Contract Audit Agency. Companies log employee hours worked and categorize every penny spent. Even this is insufficient. Companies must also provide certified cost and pricing data across the entire supply chain for any procurement of $2 million or more. L3Harris CEO Chris Kubasik estimates that this process alone adds one to two years to the acquisition process due to the time spent auditing, reviewing, and negotiating the provided cost data. The ironic result of this vast bureaucratic endeavor to control costs? Massive and avoidable cost overruns.

There is one way to get around keeping a separate set of books, logging every hour worked, and categorizing every penny spent: becoming a "non-traditional defense contractor" (NTDC). This is a legal designation that applies to companies that are not performing contracts subject to the CAS. You can think of NTDCs as regular companies that want to do business with the Department of War but don't want to do cost-plus contracts. By market capitalization, Palantir is the most valuable publicly traded defense contractor as of April 2025. If you look at the top publicly traded defense contractors, we are also the only NTDC. Something is seriously wrong when a successful, publicly traded commercial technology company is considered "non-traditional" for refusing to build a business around billable hours. The Department of War has it all wrong—it is the primes that should be classified as non-traditional contractors. They literally look unlike any other companies in our economy.

The monopsony has created a stagnant defense industrial base that shares a lot of similarities with Europe's declining economy. A recent report, "The Future of European Competitiveness," found that "there is no EU company with a market cap over EUR 100 billion that has been set up in the last fifty years, while all six US companies with a valuation above EUR 1 trillion have been created in this period. This lack of dynamism is self-fulfilling." While America's commercial companies experience dynamism and turnover, its industrial base looks a lot like Europe's. The S&P 500 last added a defense company forty-six years ago—until Palantir's addition in September 2024. Further, of America's top eight public defense companies, only Palantir was founded in the twenty-first century. Much of the list goes back to the late 1800s and early 1900s.

Defense Companies by Market Capitalization

COMPANY	MARKET CAP	EMPLOYEES	FOUNDED
Palantir	$253,831,853,299	3,936	2003
RTX	$170,674,803,270	186,000	1934
BOEING	$139,208,265,437	172,000	1934
LOCKHEED MARTIN	$109,281,465,157	121,000	1912
GENERAL DYNAMICS	$72,707,161,509	117,000	1952
NORTHROP GRUMMAN	$70,295,972,162	97,000	1939
BAE SYSTEMS	£53,705,680,000	107,400	1979
L3HARRIS	$40,412,030,352	47,000	1926
Booz | Allen | Hamilton	$15,523,584,420	35,900	1914
Huntington Ingalls Industries	$9,140,755,333	44,000	1886

Market data as of April 30, 2025

Figure 9

Regulatory Capture and Security Theater

In the primes, the monopsony has minted loyal soldiers that carry out its program-destroying policies. The monopsony has instilled such risk aversion in the primes that they do not even need to be cajoled into pushing bad policy. We'll provide a concrete example from our line of work. There's a critical weapons system currently undergoing modernization. An industrious and forward-thinking employee from the prime contractor reached out to Palantir. The employee—we'll call him Eric—was leading the modernization strategy and knew that software would be critical to success. He felt strongly that Palantir could make a difference. Unfortunately, it took him three years of dogged work before Palantir was brought on as a subcontractor.

The first problem was clearances. This was a Special Access Program (SAP), and because Palantir was not involved in the program at inception, we did not have access to it. An SAP is a program so secret, so restricted, that the number of people who can be "read on" to it is very limited. You can have a top-secret security clearance and still not have access to any SAPs. While there are legitimate reasons to designate a program an SAP, the designation has been abused, leading to calls for reform, particularly in the space domain. As early as the 1980s, Ben Rich complained that he couldn't get his best people read on to SAPs:

> Each project had a specific quota of security clearances allocated by the Pentagon, and each clearance had to be justified by me personally and approved by the Air Force. And Kelly [Johnson], who was only coming in once a week to consult with me, was tough to justify with such tightly allocated clearance spots.

There's a real problem when Kelly Johnson himself is boxed out of problem-solving for our nation.

Eric pushed hard for us to get read on to the SAP, but it took *two years*. Even then, we were far from getting government work. This was just about getting access to the problem so Palantir could make an informed argument about how we could help. For this program, the government didn't want a company read on if it wasn't on contract, but we couldn't get a contract until we were read on. A catch-22 at its finest.

Along the way, Eric faced opposition internally from his security team, which was paralyzed by this conundrum. Even with a well-placed champion, it took two years to convince this company to convince the government to grant a read on to Palantir and a handful of other NTDCs. Savor the irony of trying to do a modernization program without any companies founded in the past thirty years.

The second problem came after we were read on and it was time to negotiate a small (less than $500,000) initial contract so we could prove our value. We would be a subcontractor to the prime, rather than contracting directly with the government. This matters because the prime controlled the type of contract it issued. Although a firm-fixed-price contract required a fraction of the paperwork, the prime's contract team had so little experience working with NTDCs that they only had internal processes for cost-plus contracts performed in compliance with the government's CAS. It took many months for us to convince the prime that we do not perform cost-plus contracts as an NTDC and are not required to comply with CAS. Eventually it agreed on a firm-fixed-price contract, but not before making us fill out dozens of forms that were not applicable to NTDCs.

The prime then had us jump through hoops to provide certified cost data. Again, NTDCs aren't required to provide such data, but the prime was so terrified of being audited and accused of wrongdoing that it imposed needless, time-consuming requirements on us. As painful as this box-checking exercise was, it was less painful than arguing we shouldn't have to provide the information because we were a commercial company. And so, three years later, we became a subcontractor and were able to start studying the problem. We made the argument to Eric, who then made the argument to the government customer, that a software demonstration would be far more valuable than yet another study. But the government just wouldn't budge.

This isn't meant to be a Palantir sob story, although you should feel bad for every NTDC trying to sell to the Department of War. Palantir is the biggest name in venture-backed defense technology. If it's this hard for us to break into SAPs, imagine what it's like for others. The only time we've promptly been read on to an SAP is when the program was fighting for its life in a true code red. That's simply not a formula for success for our most important national security programs.

We can tell a similar story with sensitive compartmented information facility (SCIF) sponsorship and access to classified networks. A SCIF is a physical location designed to handle classified information. It is obviously beneficial for a company to have a SCIF in its office: cleared employees can discuss classified programs with government visitors and understand where there are gaps, and such employees can meet with one another ad hoc to work on proposals and gameplan product development. There is further benefit to having a SCIF that has access to classified networks: employees can send and receive classified information and write classified code to build and improve the product.

Today, this process could not be more broken. Government agencies sponsor SCIF access and access to classified networks, but the process is opaque and filled with false hope. The priestly class of the monopsony decides the timeline and schedule to let a company access classified networks from its offices. Palantir has been waiting twenty years to access the top-secret network from our office despite having many contracts that are top secret. We have long since passed the point where these delays represented legitimate security concerns. While the Pentagon loves to opine about the need for "more competition," a big reason why just five primes control most weapons contracts is that they're the only ones with access behind the classified door.

It's time for the government to hold itself accountable by creating a transparent process to enable a secure and competitive industrial base. As acquisition experts Matt MacGregor and Pete Modigliani write, "Facility accreditation should be a checklist verification to make sure the pieces are in-place to prevent exposure. It should not take two years to get a SCIF at the levels needed to contribute to national security." More timely access to SCIFs and classified networks isn't just about giving other companies a real chance at winning business. It's another component of the national security crisis. If companies with great technology and a need to know can't ship code from their office, and if engineers can't have conversations about what needs to be built and who should build it, the pace of innovation slows. The cumulative effect of those delays is a matter of life and death for soldiers who need the technology to win, today.

We have plenty of criticism for the primes, but we hope it's clear that our criticism is directed primarily at the monopsony. Not only are the primes filled with hard-working, well-intentioned patriots like Eric, they are also critical to American mobilization against our adversaries. Love them or hate them, the primes control the majority of weapons contracts. They have cozy relationships with the customer and often have great discretion when subcontracting work. They have as much—and sometimes more—control than the government over new technology that gets incorporated into weapons systems. Today, the primes operate like miniature Departments of War. They operate in this manner because of the monopsony.

If America is going to mobilize, it needs to reward its most innovative commercial companies for doing business with the Department of War. In turn, the primes need to look more like the dynamic companies you'd expect from capitalist America. In the next chapter, we'll explain the role of venture capital and human capital in making this vision a reality. When the best funders and founders join forces, they create a potent combination that should be dynamite for the Department of War—and kryptonite to America's enemies.

CHAPTER 8

Building for Scale

In the final days of World War II, the Allies had German factories, laboratories, and military bases circled in red on their maps. Nazi propaganda had long proclaimed the superiority of German science and technology, a claim seemingly supported by strange *Wunderwaffen* zooming through European skies: jet fighters with top speeds of more than 500 miles per hour, ballistic missiles packed with one ton of high explosives, and the like. How much truth was there to the propaganda? What other spoils lay abandoned in mountain mine shafts and bombed-out research complexes like Peenemünde, awaiting the victors? The Americans (and the Soviets) mobilized to grab as much as they possibly could. The US effort, Operation FIAT (short for Field Intelligence Agency, Technical) ran from 1945 to 1947.

After the initial scramble for hardware and real estate, Operation FIAT was left mainly with mountains of paperwork. It prioritized creating reports from the available documentation and then publishing those reports, many of which were classified but some of which were made available to the public and leading corporations for exploitation.

The daunting task more closely resembled finding a needle in a haystack than having your pick from a buffet. Teams of experts had to select what should be copied from the hundreds of thousands or even millions of pages available at any given site. Microfilm made it easier to copy documents, but the technology also meant that reviewers were indiscriminate in assessing what was important. Miles of microfilm were boxed, shipped, and processed. The documents then had to be translated, a severe bottleneck in the age before PCs and AI. Finally, a report was written and assigned a classification designation.

FIAT was an enormous, labor-intensive undertaking. It was also a failure if you define success as rapidly accelerating new technology. Douglas M. O'Reagan, historian on the subject, concluded: "The lasting legacy of FIAT is not that it likely granted America many billions of dollars of value in technology. It is that before FIAT, FIAT seemed like a tremendously good idea to a huge array of American businessmen and policymakers; afterwards, it seemed almost silly to have bothered."

There's a reason why many people have heard of Operation Paperclip and almost nobody has heard of Operation FIAT, even though the two occurred at the same time. Operation Paperclip prioritized human capital, not documents. Wernher von Braun and his team of V-2 rocket developers were famously—and controversially—spirited out of Germany and dropped into Huntsville, Alabama. We don't need to whitewash Nazi crimes, or minimize the moral culpability of people like von Braun in the Nazi war effort, to understand it was good for

America and the world for him to end up on the right side of the Iron Curtain, helping the free world to defeat Soviet communism. Whatever your views of the man, there is no disputing von Braun's contributions to technological innovation once in America.

Von Braun first went to work on ballistic missiles for the US Army. His brainchild was Jupiter, the first successful test firing of an American intermediate range ballistic missile (IRBM). The Army knew it had hit the mother lode of technical talent. The editors of *Aviation Week* observed with amusement in 1957 that "Wernher von Braun and his able group of former Peenemünde technicians represent virtually the Army's entire technical capability in this field" and "the Army brass clings to them almost hysterically for shelter." This was a bit of an exaggeration—there was plenty of home-grown American talent waiting to build the age of rocketry. But there's no doubt that von Braun, the father of rocket science, was an ace hire and founder personality. When Sputnik forced America to set its sights higher, von Braun modified the Jupiter rocket to fit a satellite payload. The resulting Redstone rocket launched the first American satellite, Explorer 1. The newly created NASA soon poached von Braun. His career culminated with the Saturn V rocket, which enabled the Apollo missions and man's first steps on the Moon. Von Braun's work laid the foundation for modern space exploration and established him as one of the most influential figures in the history of aerospace engineering.

Wernher von Braun stands in front of the Saturn V launch vehicle days before the Apollo 11 lunar landing mission (1969).

What can we learn from the failure of Operation FIAT and the success of Operation Paperclip? We learn that innovation and progress do not live in technical diagrams, business plans, or requirements documents: they live in people, in founders. This is a lesson the American people know—we revere the Founding Fathers for a reason—but it's something the Department of War has forgotten. Today's failed programs have no easily identifiable leader. Who is the von Braun or Admiral Rickover or Gene Kranz of the Navy's Littoral Combat Ship? Nobody. And that's precisely the point.

Nowhere is the importance of founders felt more viscerally than in venture capital (VC). This chapter uncovers the secrets behind the VC industry and why its founder-driven model is so good at discovering and delivering giant leaps in technology. We'll learn from one of the incredible founders and funders at the beating heart of industry: Trae Stephens, general partner at Founders Fund and co-founder and executive chairman of Anduril. We'll explore why it is so important for government to understand the power law that drives VC outcomes if we're going to mobilize. And we'll consider how the traditional primes can adopt the lessons of VC to fix their broken business model and become more valuable—to their shareholders and, more important, to their country.

Founders and Funders

No VC firm appreciates the role of founders more than Founders Fund. It's right in the name! Founded in 2005 by Peter Thiel, Founders Fund has consistently delivered some of the top returns in the Valley. Facebook, SpaceX, Airbnb, OpenAI, Oculus, and yes, Palantir, are among some of its category-defining investments. The firm is made up of founder absolutists. If the firm's partners love a company's idea and business model but don't love the founder, they don't invest. They don't invest in non-founder-led businesses for the same reason. When Founders Fund *does* invest in a company, it always votes with the founder, its members rarely take board seats, and it stops investing when the company is no longer led by the founder. While other VC firms sometimes fire founders when the going gets tough—Benchmark's Bill Gurley removed Travis Kalanick from Uber—Founders Fund's cardinal rule is to never replace the founder. Period.

Anduril, a Founders Fund portfolio company with an unorthodox founding history, has attracted more attention than any other recent defense tech investment. Anduril was founded in 2017 by Palmer Luckey, the inventor-prodigy who sold

Oculus, the virtual reality company he'd founded as a teenager, to Facebook for $2.7 billion—only to later be fired unceremoniously for his political views.

Meanwhile, Anduril's co-founder and executive chairman, Trae Stephens, is also the biggest *funder* of the company via his other job as a managing partner at Founders Fund. As of this writing, Anduril is valued at $30.5 billion. The company makes autonomous weapons and is currently building its first hyperscale manufacturing facility, Arsenal-1, in Columbus, Ohio. (We'll return to Arsenal-1 in Chapter 11, which focuses on manufacturing.)

Trae's life and career illustrate the role that private capital and visionary founders play in mobilization. His perspective is shaped by an almost unbelievably relevant blend of experiences across the public and private sectors. While it's easy to connect the career dots in hindsight, Trae's upbringing did not suggest that he would go on to be one of the most notable defense investor-entrepreneurs of the twenty-first century.

Trae grew up in an evangelical Christian household in an Ohio town not far from where Vice President JD Vance grew up. His father was handy: in addition to building the log cabin that Trae grew up in (yes, literally), he built and maintained roller coasters at the nearby amusement park, Kings Island. His mother was a substitute teacher and librarian, and his grandpa was a pastor. As a kid, Trae dreamed of becoming an international correspondent, but 9/11 affected him in a profound way during his senior year in high school. He resolved to instead find a way to work in national security. Trae received rejection letters from the elite colleges he'd applied to, but his fortunes soon reversed—more by sheer chutzpah than luck. At his mom's encouragement, Trae booked a flight to Georgetown, his dream school and ticket into the national-security community. He waited outside the admissions office for hours until the Dean of Admissions agreed to see him. The best the dean could do was put him at the top of the wait list—and it turned out that was enough. He graduated from the School of Foreign Service with a degree in Regional and Comparative Studies of the Middle East. Everything would eventually come full circle when Trae became an adjunct professor at his alma mater.

In 2008, Trae was working in the Intelligence Community when he came across a little-known company called Palantir during a demo given by none other than me (Shyam). Trae immediately saw the potential for the company's software to completely transform his job. He tried to convince his agency to use Palantir without success. So I recruited Trae instead. There was a minor hiccup in the interview process. Trae showed up to interview in a full suit and tie, a big no-no in a Silicon Valley culture where formality stands out like a sore thumb. Fortunately, the alarmed receptionist intercepted Trae and had him ditch the jacket and tie. Faux pas aside, his interviews with the T-shirt wearing, ragtag band of misfits went well. Trae joined as an early employee and led government sales for six years before being poached by Peter Thiel to work at Founders Fund. Despite this defection, we've remained close friends. I even roasted him on his fortieth birthday (but that's a story for another book).

Peter and Trae bonded in part over their shared faith—Christianity can be pretty contrarian in Silicon Valley. When Thiel told Trae he wanted him to join Founders Fund as an investor, Trae felt he had no choice but to say yes. He didn't know what a venture capitalist was, but he did know that Peter believed he could learn. And—no surprise—Peter was right. Trae has returned over a billion dollars to Founders Fund's investors. But the path was neither easy nor obvious. Trae first tried to invest in companies working with the government. During his first year on the job, he met with hundreds of companies but found nothing compelling enough to invest in. While he did eventually pick a winner (cybersecurity company Qadium, renamed Expanse, was acquired by Palo Alto Networks for $1 billion), the company he really wanted to invest in didn't exist. Founders Fund told him to build it himself—and so Anduril was born.

Innovation Needs Customers, Not Capital

The business model of a technology company is to invest R&D dollars to produce new and innovative products. These R&D costs are amortized across a large number of customers to create affordability and scale. The customer benefits by paying a small fraction of the actual cost of development and operations rather than being on the hook to pay the company for its entire development costs.

Technology companies typically require large capital investments before they are profitable, and they may be unprofitable for many years. Palantir operated unprofitably for two decades while investing billions of dollars in R&D. SpaceX, founded in 2002, may still be unprofitable, yet today it's the most valuable private American company. Amazon was unprofitable for almost a decade, including years after it became a publicly traded company. Who provides this needed capital? If the founders are independently wealthy, they may be able to self-finance. But overwhelmingly it is VC firms that provide the capital required for founders to go and build great things.

If you only take away one thing from this chapter, it should be this: VC produces power law outcomes. A tiny number of companies generate most of the value. The power law makes venture a risky business. Most startups fail and VC firms take minority stakes in startups, so the startups that do succeed need to be massively successful. Of Founders Fund's thousands of investments, just twelve companies have returned more than 95 percent of all returns to investors. To understand how this happens, it's helpful to walk through a hypothetical: a VC firm raises a $500 million fund and targets a 4x return to its limited partners, or $2 billion. The firm's average check size to startups is $20 million, and ownership ends up being around 10 percent after dilution through multiple rounds of funding. The startups that make it big (which are likely to be just a couple or even one), must collectively be worth $20 billion for the VC firm to achieve its target returns (10 percent times $20 billion equals $2 billion).

Trae gives examples of how consistent the power law is in VC, no matter the category. He wrote in 2024:

> [Uber's] success sparked a predictable venture hype cycle, with billions of dollars funding dozens of new competitors. And yet, fifteen years later, Uber is still the dominant player. At $162 billion, its market cap is triple that of the next ten ride-sharing companies combined. At $47 billion, Coinbase's market cap is more than double the next ten crypto companies combined. At $180 billion, SpaceX's market cap exceeds that of the next twenty space companies combined. And at $1.2 trillion, Meta's market cap is more than double the next dozen social media companies combined.

The VC model works, and is hugely innovative, because it empowers founders who can generate those kinds of abnormally large returns. It's not enough to have a solid, profitable business. It must be able to scale or it's not a venture investment. American power is built on big companies delivering results at scale. From the Pentagon's official acquisition history, "[During World War II], of the 18,000 prime contractors, 100 captured two-thirds of the business and 33 almost half. General Motors led all contractors with 8 percent." Behind those big companies, you'll find founders—and lots and lots of customers who bought into those founders' visions for their products.

Yes, there is a role for small businesses, but Americans worship the small business aesthetic to the detriment of our country. The goal of our founder-driven, free-market system is for small businesses to get big. Yet too often the government incentivizes companies to stay small. The Small Business Innovation Research (SBIR) program is Exhibit A for this dysfunction. The program was established in 1982 by Congress to stimulate technological innovation and commercialize federal R&D using small businesses. That last part—commercialization—is crucial to keep in mind. A key purported aim of SBIR is to help businesses grow by giving them non-dilutive funding. The tagline on sbir.gov is "Keep your equity and IP. Change the world." Today, the Department of War awards more than $1 billion annually in SBIR funds. From 2016 to 2022, one percent of companies received 25 percent of the total awards, and 5 percent of the companies received 50 percent of the total awards.

The power law is alive and well! But government handouts are not the same as private capital, and unintended consequences abound. One such consequence is the creation of "SBIR mills," or companies that exist to rake in SBIR dollars instead of getting big. That's exactly the outcome you *don't* want if your goal is to promote innovation and commercialization. Instead, we've created mini-primes that are addicted to SBIR dollars, working on incremental science projects, and led by PhDs who lack business acumen. The government should judge its small business efforts not by how many companies it is helping, but by market-cap creation, which represents wealth and value for Americans. The point of national security is to underwrite freedom and economic prosperity. SBIR programs should measure how many of their small businesses get big, not how many programs receive follow-on funding.

And the best way for small businesses to get big—besides developing a competitive commercial business—is with real contracts to deliver real goods and services. Not with handouts. Innovation needs customers, not capital. Stephen Miran, a Federal Reserve governor, wrote that to encourage greater investment in defense, "The most powerful tool at our disposal is the federal procurement budget." We couldn't agree more. Not enough is said about the US government as customer, while too much has been said about the US government as an R&D financier.

A story from Palantir's work illustrates the point. When Palantir was founded in 2003, there was no path to working with the Department of Defense. Not a difficult path. No path. And there was exactly one path to working with the Intelligence Community: In-Q-Tel. In-Q-Tel is a VC firm that invests in commercial technologies that are relevant to national security. But this headline confuses the actual value proposition. America has plenty of capital for quality companies. A startup that can't raise money is probably not a very good startup. A deep and wide venture ecosystem is one of America's strengths. The gamechanger that In-Q-Tel provides is customers. The capital it invests is often de minimis, even if it is extremely valuable validation. The customer contracts, clearances, and commitments that In-Q-Tel furnishes are the real fuel for innovation.

America doesn't have a capital problem. In defense tech in particular, venture money is flowing fast and free to innovative startups. The top one-hundred venture-backed US national security startups have collectively raised $70 billion in private capital. Trae doubts that any of the Department of War's current initiatives to solve the non-existent capital gap via subsidized loans or non-recurring grant money are likely to deliver American dominance: "The types of businesses that suck at fundraising are the types of businesses that fail. So we're basically just throwing good money after bad, with the belief that actually these companies would be good if the VCs just understood what it was that they were doing."

Despite all of the private money flowing into defense tech, venture-backed firms have consistently received less than one percent of defense contract dollars annually since 2018—and most of that money has gone to SpaceX. One percent is a drop in the bucket and a sign that the Department of War isn't yet serious about accessing the wellspring of innovation in our economy. While Trae thinks that the percentage should be a lot higher, he is allergic to the idea that the way to get there is by spreading around money to lots of venture-backed companies. He feels that the Department of War has a legitimate critique of VC, in that investors are now agitating for a "let a thousand flowers bloom" strategy—when in reality, there are likely to be power law outcomes, just like in World War II:

> I believe there's some combination of leaning in heavily to the more competent companies that have the talent base to do the things that we want as well as picking national champions, so that we're not distributing money among the same twenty players and losing all of the economies of scale that you would get out of picking someone and going really hard in a specific vertical.

Founders Fund's own investing strategy reflects this. In the past seven and a half years, 97 percent of the dollars invested in defense have gone to Anduril.

The Great Schism has created a religion in government that is unaware or dismissive of the power law outcomes generated by power law talent. Instead, government tries to "protect" technology from the brilliant chaos of humanity through endless rules and regulation. But we can't plan our way out of our pitifully low production and delayed weapons systems—we must grow our way out of it. That's where VC, obsessed with scale, is most instructive. It's telling that the "failure résumé" of many venture capitalists isn't the startups they invested in that didn't get big—that's just considered the cost of doing business. The real failures are the investments they *didn't* make that became huge successes. When the Department of War creates processes that ensure that nothing goes wrong, it also creates processes that ensure that nothing can go right, and it condemns us to mediocrity—or worse.

In VC, it's standard to have a weekly partner meeting where partners review the investments under consideration and vote on whether the firm will make the investment. Founders Fund doesn't do this. Per Trae, "Oftentimes, when you have process in the way to get a deal done, you tend to make a lot of mediocre investments because you have a confirmation bias.... Well, if it's made it this far, maybe it's good enough for at least a small check." That sort of thinking produces mediocre outcomes, with a lot of companies that do well enough to return the initial investment to the VC but that are nowhere close to being rocket ship investments. Trae admits that Founders Fund probably has the same number of "dogs," investments that don't work at all, as other funds, but it has a bigger number of companies that succeed because Founders Fund eschews consensus-driven decision making. The Department of War could learn a thing or two.

VC is hard. Only the top 25 percent of firms outperform the S&P 500. Fortunately, we don't need the Department of War to play venture capitalist. We need it to lean into where it has a competitive advantage—awarding contracts to the companies with the best products. America doesn't have a capital problem, and that's a privileged position for the government to find itself in. It just needs to be a smarter customer.

Talent Is Not a Commodity

The Department of War's go-to contracting method, the cost-plus contract, is the death knell of VC-funded companies. As explained in the previous chapter, cost-plus contracts reimburse contractors for their costs and typically apply a fixed profit percent on top, usually around 10 percent. With this arrangement, no matter how far a company scales, it will never be able to generate high enough margins to pay for its R&D and outrun its fixed costs. Profit remains proportional to cost, rather than increasing with scale or efficiency improvements. As a result, companies benefit from scale (more dollars spent, more workers employed, and so on) but do not benefit from *economies* of scale. They have no incentive to become more efficient or innovative—in fact, the incentive runs in the opposite direction.

This is why the primes are not valued like technology companies. They may be viewed as "safe" investments, but they are not—and cannot—be growth investments. The nature of defense contracting does not allow it. Consequently, VC firms will not want to invest in companies that do a lot of business with the Pentagon if the only way for those companies to make money is via cost-plus contracts.

One of the defining features of cost-plus contracts is their treatment of individuals as standardized inputs. Proposals require companies to bid a certain number of engineers; those engineers are then bucketed into categories with different hourly labor rates, like "senior engineer" or "junior engineer." But for the most part, contracts treat engineers like commodities by valuing their time equally. The problem is that talent is not a commodity—it's precious and spiky. Likewise, founders are not commodities. Wernher von Braun was a generational talent. He was a hundred times better than the replacement-level "director of engineering" at a legacy defense company today. Talent isn't uniform, and it doesn't scale linearly. Cost-plus contracts ignore those facts of life.

In the commercial world, technology is viewed as cheap and people as expensive. Companies will spend virtually unlimited sums to poach game-changing engineers, while squeezing every penny out of their products to remain competitive. Look no further than the red-hot AI talent war. In 2024, Google spent

$2.7 *billion* to win back former employee and AI genius Noam Shazeer. Meta went on an aggressive hiring spree in July 2025, offering salaries of $200 million or more to the world's best AI engineers. But in government, there is a perverse inversion where people are viewed as cheap and technology is viewed as expensive. This is why many government contracts staff hundreds of people to perform software or integration services when the same work could be performed by good technology and a team of ten crack engineers—only faster and better.

At Palantir, we've had government customers and prime contractors ask why we can't perform cost-plus contracts and log billable hours, like everyone else. Just use QuickBooks, they say! This request fundamentally misunderstands the problem: cost-plus is anathema to our business model. Yes, we are technically capable of adopting software that would allow us to perform cost-plus contracts, just like we're technically capable of flooding the zone with warm bodies to bill hours at the taxpayer's expense, but we choose not to because it would represent the end of Palantir. The best builders don't want to log their hours and overtime. They want to work until they've built a great product. Our engineers are crusaders who deliver outsized value for customers; they're not drones for the government. This isn't just a matter of pride for us. Our commercial customers insist on this because they want a good deal. The government, apparently, does not.

A unique virtue of the VC model is that it gives employees ownership of their companies, which creates a strong incentive for rocket ship growth. It does this by giving equity to each employee; equity makes up most of the engineering compensation at technology companies. The primes, hindered by cost-plus contracts that treat engineers as fungible and depress valuations in capital markets, are unable to attract the country's top talent because they cannot award competitive equity packages. For engineers, this is about a principle even more than a paycheck. Equity compensation means ownership over outcomes. The Founders Fund manifesto explains why no great company was ever founded solely to make money:

> If the entrepreneur seeks an impact beyond his own payday and can convince employees of the same, the project is much more likely to get done. The engineers at SpaceX are passionate about commercializing and colonizing space; profit is a significant byproduct of their extraordinary effort to achieve that goal but not enough to get them to pull the thousandth all-nighter. The same is true of Jobs at Apple, or the programmers at Palantir, or the researchers at new drug companies.

When employees don't have ownership and are just collecting a check, they relinquish initiative and autonomy. Great things don't come from faceless factories, but from the heroic efforts of the individuals in the factories. When engineers sign up to work at a cost-plus company, they join the faceless factory. So the best don't—and our national security suffers.

Life, Liberty, and (Intellectual) Property

In addition to avoiding cost-plus contracts and giving the best talent a meaningful stake in the company, creating and retaining IP is high on the list of essential qualities for a venture-backed company. Commercial firms want to retain IP rights for their self-financed R&D because commercializing IP is critical to achieving VC-level returns. Venture-backed companies invest in a portfolio of IP that they hope to commercialize and amortize across customers. This is how a company achieves scale and remains competitive in a commercial market, something that Colonel Cukor understood very well while running Project Maven. Conversely, as we saw in Chapter 4 with airplanes and drones, companies that turn over IP to the government forgo the opportunity to achieve massive success in the (typically) much larger commercial market. They either die on the vine or commit to a lifetime of selling only to the Department of War.

Because IP is so important for commercial viability, the secretary of war is required to "define the legitimate interest of the U.S. government" when asking companies to give up their IP. Yet too often, the government asks for unnecessary and overreaching IP rights. In Palantir's experience, there have been situations where simply asserting basic IP protections has disqualified us from competition. This prevented good-faith negotiations where a path forward was almost certainly possible.

The government should aim to impose the fundamental national security protections it needs while enabling industry to develop IP, commercialize its technology, and reach a broader market. When it fails to do this, American prosperity takes a hit. In the late 1980s, the Pentagon and the Department of Commerce blocked Lockheed from commercializing the technology from its reconnaissance satellites, citing national security reasons. Lockheed was thus unable to take its one-meter resolution imagery to the broader market—which could have turned into a successful commercial business, unlike the primes' other misadventures in diversification. For decades, reconnaissance satellites, or "Earth observation" (EO) satellites, as they are now called, were dominated by the Intelligence Community and a small number of defense contractors. The government was so possessive over certain sensing modalities, like synthetic aperture radar, that it refused to allow American commercial companies to pursue the technology, even as companies in Canada and Europe ran laps around us. Venture money has since poured into EO companies across diverse sensor modalities that were once highly classified. Even still, the bulk of EO companies' business is with the government because of numerous policies that limit the commercial potential of satellites.

In all but the rarest of cases, the country would be better off if government encouraged companies to keep their IP, commercialize it, and create new sources of prosperity for themselves and the country.

Venture Capital as a Natural Resource

The preferences of venture capitalists—for firm-fixed-price contracts, for companies that can award competitive equity, for proper IP protections—matter because venture-backed firms are the engine of technological innovation in America. There would be no SpaceX, Palantir, or Anduril without VC and with cost-plus contracts.

Economists say there's no such thing as a free lunch, but from the perspective of the government, VC might as well be free money. Private capital is willing to show up and accept a huge amount of risk to back companies that may or may not succeed in commercializing their product. In exchange, founders and funders are not asking for handouts or special treatment from the government. They are asking for the government to wield its procurement power fairly and expeditiously, something very much in the government's best interest. (Besides, it's the law.)

In the previous chapter, we mentioned the travails of getting access to SCIFs and classified networks. This is one of many problems that could be solved without any money from the government or the taxpayer. Private industry—backed by VC—would happily pay its own way for this key enabler. It just needs permission. If the Department of War viewed VC as the asset it is, it would enable American capital to purchase network, SCIF access, classified compute, and more—all backed by investor confidence that the company can credibly turn that investment into value.

Venture capital means more to the country than "free" money, though. There's a far more profound reason why the VC model matters: it is carrying the torch of a fundamentally American form of collaboration, work, and innovation.

The Pentagon not using venture-backed technology companies for defense is like Saudi Arabia not drilling for oil. In 2024, 86 percent of the top fifty technology companies in the world by market cap were American. Our dominance is not explained by luck or IQ. There are smart people everywhere. It's about culture. And the culture of Silicon Valley is uniquely American. Bob Noyce, co-inventor of the integrated circuit and co-founder of Intel, is the best embodiment of Silicon Valley. He was from Iowa (Silicon Valley, truly, has always been welcoming to outsiders). Noyce helped to evangelize and codify the ethos of America—strong work ethic, visionary leadership, and an innovative spirit—which in turn produced the hallmarks of Silicon Valley culture: openness, meritocracy, and the willingness to take risks and learn from failure. Noyce's management style—an open-door policy, lack of hierarchy, and encouragement of teamwork and innovation—reflected these values.

Tom Wolfe's iconic profile, "The Tinkerings of Robert Noyce," gives a thorough treatment. We'll summarize, but you should really read it in full. At Fairchild, there was no reserved parking. Noyce would tell employees, junior and senior alike, that "if you come late, you just have to park in the back forty." Hierarchy was mostly nonexistent.

> There was no "staff," no "top management" other than the eight partners themselves. Major decisions were not bucked up a chain of command. Noyce held weekly meetings of people from all parts of the operation, and whatever had to be worked out was worked out right there in the room. Noyce wanted them all to keep internalizing the company's goals and to provide their own motivations, just as they had during the startup phase.

When Noyce left Fairchild to found Intel with Gordon Moore, he had greater creativity to shape his ideal Silicon Valley culture. According to Wolfe:

> [Noyce] had never liked the business of the office cubicles at Fairchild. As miserable as they were, the mere possession of one symbolized superior rank. At Intel executives would not be walled off in of-

> fices. Everybody would be in one big room. There would be nothing but low partitions to separate Noyce or anyone else from the lowliest stock boys trundling in the accordion printout paper.

In short, Noyce created the founder blueprint.

Other countries have tried and failed to copy and paste Silicon Valley. They visit startups and set up accelerators with Ping Pong tables, but it amounts to nothing more than a cargo cult. In the case of China, it's no mystery why our adversary can't build a venture ecosystem. Failed founders in China are put on a national debtor blacklist until they pay back investors. There is no personal bankruptcy law in China, leaving some founders with millions of dollars in debt and banned from activities like air travel and hotel stays. Chinese venture firms seem to have forgotten that the "venture" in venture capital means accepting risk of failure—for founders *and* investors, which in China's case often means government entities. There's a reason why China has created zero global enterprise software companies.

Perhaps what's most striking about China's punitive debt-collector approach is the way dealmaking is treated as a one-time, zero-sum game. You essentially have one shot to make it big or you're ruined. Silicon Valley, by contrast, is defined by the possibility of infinite games among founders, investors, and employees. Blacklisting a founder early on can deprive you of their later successes. Many successful founders have a long string of failures and false starts on their résumés.

Silicon Valley embraces forgiveness in ways that may seem astonishing to outsiders. In 2019, WeWork prepared to go public, but disclosures of massive losses and scandals involving its CEO, Adam Neumann, caused the valuation to plummet from $47 billion to $10 billion, less than the $12.8 billion it had raised in private capital. Neumann was forced to step down. Just three years later, Neumann went on to raise $350 million from Andreesen Horowitz, a top VC firm, for a new residential real-estate company, Flow. You may disagree with Andreesen Horowitz's choice to invest in Neumann. You might question his peculiar style and vision. And you may well be right. But the investment epitomizes venture capitalists' belief in the centrality of founders and the possibility of second chances. That belief is fundamentally American and it helps to explain why technology companies are this country's secret weapons—if we learn from them and use them.

Make the Primes Great Again

While we're talking about second chances, we should talk about what government needs to do to ensure that once founder-driven, once-great companies like the primes can have redemption arcs of their own.

The good news is, there's a clear path to transforming the primes into technology companies and making them more valuable in the process. It involves changing their business model in a way that, while painful at first, ultimately will be healthier for the primes and the nation. Primes must rotate their business model away from cost-plus and toward privately funded (that is, non-government reimbursed) R&D. This will enable them to build IP and product portfolios that have commercial pricing, just like venture-backed companies. In doing so, their revenue may shrink as they focus on higher margins and product-driven work, but their valuations will increase as the stocks are rerated, meaning they will have higher price-to-sales multiples. For example, a prime whose revenue shrinks by 30 percent but is valued at six times revenue versus 2.5 times revenue would be worth 108 percent *more* than it is today.

Making Primes More Valuable with Less Revenue

● WHERE PRIMES CURRENTLY SIT --- EFFICIENT FRONTIER

TEV / NTM REVENUE \ REVENUE SCENARIOS (% OF NTM REVENUE)	$363B (100%)	$327B (90%)	$290B (80%)	$254B (70%)	$218B (60%)	$181B (50%)	$145B (40%)	$108B (30%)	$73B (20%)
2X	-1%	-9%	-19%	-29%	-39%	-49%	-60%	-70%	-80%
3X	49%	34%	19%	4%	-11%	-26%	-41%	-55%	-70%
4X	98%	78%	59%	39%	19%	-1%	-21%	-41%	-60%
5X	148%	123%	98%	73%	49%	24%	-1%	-26%	-50%
6X	197%	168%	138%	108%	78%	49%	19%	-11%	-41%
7X	247%	212%	177%	143%	108%	73%	39%	4%	-31%
8X	296%	257%	217%	177%	138%	98%	59%	19%	-21%
9X	346%	301%	257%	212%	168%	123%	78%	34%	-11%
10X	395%	346%	296%	247%	197%	148%	98%	49%	-1%
11X	445%	390%	336%	281%	227%	172%	118%	63%	9%
12X	494%	435%	376%	316%	257%	197%	138%	78%	19%

Primes:
Boeing / General Dynamics / L3Harris / Lockheed Martin / Northrop Gruman / RTX

NTM Revenue:
Aggregate next-twelve-month revenue estimate for the Primes

TEV / NTM Revenue:
Total Enterprise Value divided by NTM Revenue

Percentages in table represent increase / decrease to valuation of the Primes on a Total Enterprise Value basis

Market data as of April 30, 2025

Figure 10

What we propose the primes do—move away from cost-plus contracts and invest their own R&D dollars—must be mirrored by similarly strong actions from the government: stop cost-plus contracts, stop reimbursing R&D, and start incentivizing primes to build up compelling IP portfolios. These policies must be done in tandem. They are self-reinforcing and mutually dependent. And it will be hard.

Firm-fixed-price contracts are not magic. It's true there are many examples of firm-fixed-price contracts leading to bad procurement outcomes. For example, the KC-46 refueling tanker, a modified version of Boeing's commercial 767, suffered cost overruns of $5.4 billion, *exceeding* the contract value of $4.9 billion.

This is just another way of saying that failure is possible with firm-fixed-price contracts—just like it is in a competitive marketplace. When a company addicted to cost-plus contacts fails to perform well on a firm-fixed-price contract, it says more about the company than the contract vehicle. With a firm-fixed-price contract, there is nowhere to hide. For commercial firms, this is usually a good thing—the possibility of failure is a strong motivator. For the primes, it's way outside of their comfort zone. In 2023, Boeing's then-CEO, Dave Calhoun, remarked, "We have a couple of fixed-price development programs we have to just finish and never do them again. That fixed-price development world has to stop. It just doesn't work. It doesn't work for us, and it doesn't work for our customers in my not-so-humble opinion." In our not-so-humble opinion, the primes are capable of firm-fixed-price contracts, just not in their current state. They will have to become more like innovative commercial technology companies. In so doing, they'll also become more like the innovative, founder-driven companies they were at their inception. And that will be good for them and for America.

America's deep, broad capital markets are a great strength. VC investors bet big on the next heretical entrepreneur, and that bet is structured to reward scale. A working system requires big, new players to be created. Every successful industrial mobilization in our country's history is a story of scaled companies delivering results. Why would we think this time will be any different?

In this chapter, we've talked about how defense innovation needs customers, not capital. Crucial to winning customers is winning competitions in the marketplace that prove that your company's product is the best. But when competitions aren't based on merit, there's no hope that our most promising companies will achieve scale. The next chapter looks at the long and ugly history of companies fighting for a fair shake in their dealings with the Pentagon.

CHAPTER 9

When Underdogs Go on Offense

What do *WWE SmackDown* and government procurement have in common? They both engage in "kayfabe," holding elaborate, staged performances with predetermined outcomes that nonetheless keep the audience in suspense. The Undertaker and Stone Cold Steve Austin were the masters of kayfabe in the ring, but the government exhibits great proficiency in this specialized art form.

The government sets the stage with elaborate industry days, builds tension with market research and complex solicitations, evaluates bids in a free for all, and announces the winner for the grand finale. But often, the monopsonist has decided well in advance what the solution will be and who will get paid to build it. Unlike in WWE, sometimes the "wrestlers" competing for the contract are the only ones not in on the act.

The irony of government kayfabe is that the Department of War pays ample lip service to the virtue of competition. Officials often blame a lack of competition for our anemic industrial base and sole-source dependencies for critical products.

But competition as kayfabe is worse than no competition at all. If a government agency has bad requirements or a bad selection process, it doesn't matter how many companies compete for a contract—the result will be bad. Similarly, if an agency's incentives lead it to build its own technology in-house instead of buying from the most innovative company, it makes no difference how many new and innovative companies exist in the wild—the agency will build in-house.

What this means in practice is that the government has to be dragged kicking and screaming to real competition, without artificial limitations and requirements. Some of the biggest breakthroughs in defense technology happened because companies fought for the right to compete on truly fair terms (imagine that—in the Land of the Free!).

This chapter covers two seemingly different stories that illustrate this fundamental truth. First, we'll look at Southern boatbuilder Andrew Higgins' battle with the Navy for the right to build innovative landing craft in the run-up to World War II. Then, closer to home, we'll explore Palantir's battle with the Army intelligence bureaucracy to provide superior technology to our troops during the Global War on Terror.

Both emerged victorious, after bitter and bloody battles. Higgins had to enlist the help of Senator Harry Truman, arguably the country's most powerful senator at the time; Palantir had to sue the government for violating FASA, the commercial-item preference that William Perry championed in the '90s (which we discussed in Chapter 6).

There was competition, all right, but it was the government competing against industry in a rigged game. This is a problem that has persisted for roughly a century, transcending generations and technological eras. Both Higgins and Palantir invested substantial sums of their own money to create innovative products. Both had products that were competitive in the commercial market. And both had strong partnerships with heretics inside the military who helped them to beat the odds. Higgins was the heartland hero fighting against the East Coast shipbuilding elite; Palantir was the high-tech upstart pitted against the Swamp and its preferred Beltway contractors. These stories show that if you want real competition—not kayfabe—you have to be prepared for a grudge match with the government.

The New Noah

In March 1943, Dwight Eisenhower was consumed with worry about getting his men onto the beaches of Europe. The general told an aide that when he died, "his coffin should be in the shape of a landing craft."

Fast-forward to Thanksgiving of 1944, and Ike's fears had turned into relief. Allied troops had stormed the beaches of Sicily, Salerno, and—in far greater numbers—Normandy. "Let us thank God for Higgins Industries, management, and labor which has given us the landing boats to conduct this campaign," he said in a Thanksgiving address. Hitler had a different name for these landing craft. He bitterly called them the "Alligator Ark[s]" produced by "the New Noah": Andrew Jackson Higgins.

Neither man was exaggerating much. Higgins' biographer, Jerry Strahan, reports that by September 1943, 12,964 of the Navy's 14,072 vessels—92 percent of the fleet—had been designed by Higgins Industries of New Orleans.

Andrew Higgins built the US Navy. Every step of the way, he had to fight the Navy bureaucracy for the right to compete.

Today, Higgins is a hero of New Orleans to rival his namesake, Andrew Jackson. He was actually a transplant, born near Omaha, Nebraska. Higgins was a risk taker and a builder from the start. As a young man, he built a sail-powered ice boat in his basement that could hit sixty miles per hour on a frozen lake. He later moved to the coastal South and entered the import-export business for lumber, a trade that gave him working knowledge of shipbuilding. The company began designing its own, shallow-draft boats to access flooded timber where other boats couldn't go.

By the mid-1920s, Higgins pivoted to shipbuilding as his main focus. His company filled a valuable niche. The trappers, loggers, and oilmen in the area needed boats that could navigate the bayou. Those boats needed to run in water at times less than a foot deep without damaging the propellor. And they needed to land on the beach under power, without damaging the hull. Higgins mastered the art of boatbuilding for his local market, making speedy, shallow-draft boats with recessed propellors and strong wooden bows shaped like a duck's bill.

Higgins' most successful commercial boat was the Eureka, which got its name from the way his company discovered its innovative hull design. Boats with recessed propellors suffered from "cavitation," or air bubbles that formed around the propellor, reducing the boats' power and speed. One day, a Higgins foreman made a mistake while assembling one of the boats, so that the hull aft formed a concave "V." Higgins ordered the boat finished anyway—and employees were astonished when it zipped down the canal upon completion. The foreman's mistake had solved the problem of cavitation, directing unaerated water from the sides of the boat into the propellers' path. Higgins and his employees were learning by doing. A little luck didn't hurt, either.

By the 1930s, Higgins had built a successful but small shipbuilding company. He had stress-tested his products in the commercial market. He had even broken into government contracting by selling motorboats to the Coast Guard, which used them to chase bootleggers. (Higgins sold the same boats to the bootleggers—he was known to enjoy a stiff drink.) As the clouds of war gathered over Europe, Higgins also began selling Eurekas as landing craft to the British, who were only too grateful for the help.

Higgins' own country proved a tougher nut to crack. The US military was in dire need of ships of all kinds, but especially small vessels to traverse the last mile from ship to shore. The Marine Corps alone wanted 120 landing craft (itself a gross underestimate of the actual need). In 1939, the entire Navy had nineteen.

Still, Higgins couldn't get a foot in the door. The Navy's Bureau of Construction and Repairs (BCR, later merged into a new entity, the Bureau of Ships) thought it could design its own boats and viciously defended its turf. The Navy also assumed, wrongly, that landing craft would be unnecessary in the coming war—that it could just use French ports, as it had in World War I. That assumption was destroyed by the collapse of the French army and the evacuation at Dunkirk. Finally, Navy construction, then as now, was clubby and dominated by the Eastern shipbuilding giants. Higgins, a foul-mouthed Irishman from the swamp, was very much not in the club. Rival lobbyists and snobby officers boxed him out.

Higgins had to force his way in over four frustrating years. He hoped his bona fides with the Coast Guard would sufficiently interest the Navy when he visited Quantico in 1934, but the Navy easily rebuffed the outsider with no hired lobbyist. When the Navy finally announced a competitive contract for landing craft in 1935, it conveniently did not notify Higgins. When he found out, he implored the Navy to let him enter his boat in the trials. In a letter to the BCR, he confidently wrote, "We *know* that we have designed, perfected, and are building the very type of boat best fitted for this purpose." The Navy didn't respond.

During trials in 1936, both the Navy's BCR and the Eastern shipyards tested their designs. The boats were, for the most part, minimally modified Atlantic fishing boats—and they performed abysmally. That didn't stop the BCR from taking an agglomeration of the most promising features and designing a new, experimental boat to be constructed by the Philadelphia Navy Yard. As the bad acquisition strategy unfolded, the naval architect for the Coast Guard tried to help out Higgins—and America. He'd tested a Eureka and found it to be "satisfactory and successful under all operating conditions," according to a review he sent to the Navy in 1937. Unmoved, the Navy proceeded with tests of its in-house design. When it, too, performed poorly, the Navy authorized the construction of five more.

After much browbeating, in 1938 Higgins was awarded his first Navy contract for a single, experimental thirty-foot landing boat, which was included in the next round of testing. Compared to his rivals' boats, the Eureka was an ugly duck, with a bulbous bow and strange hull. But it blew the others out of the water. The head of the board conducting the trials reported that "the Higgins boat is considered generally the best of the Experimental Landing Boats thus far tested." Merit didn't much matter. The Navy stole some of the Eureka's design features—although Higgins found that the BCR couldn't even steal properly, as the underwater sections were inferior to his landing craft. The failed design was contracted out to three different Northeastern companies.

Over the next two years, there would be more uncompetitive contests, more piecemeal contracts, and more Navy favoritism for its own designs. Then the Marines rode to the rescue. Marine Corps Brigadier General Holland Smith recognized that Higgins had built something special. Pressured by Smith, in 1940 the chief of naval operations ordered a competition between Higgins, Michigan-based leisure boat company Chris Craft, and the BCR. Almost immediately, a problem arose. Higgins had ignored the official requirement for a thirty-foot boat and—at his own expense—built an improved, thirty-six-foot boat. The Navy didn't want to test it, but the Marines insisted. Higgins' boat "exceeded in performance any other landing boat that members of the board had ever seen." Meanwhile, the chief of naval operations found the BCR boat to be the worst of the bunch.

Even the BCR could no longer ignore the superiority of the Higgins boat. It continued to award contracts for its dramatically inferior design, but on November 18, 1940, it also gave Higgins a contract for 335 of his thirty-six-foot boats. Smith recaps the farcical events well: "Through the unfathomable process whereby the official mind finally emerges from darkness into light, the Navy eventually decided to standardize on the 36-foot Higgins boat."

Despite the Eureka's success in trials, it was not yet the legendary but awkwardly named "Landing Craft, Vehicle, Personnel" (LCVP) that would ferry troops ashore during the war. That required further innovation when Higgins was approached by a Marine Corps officer named Victor Krulak.

Krulak had been a military observer during Imperial Japan's invasion of China in 1937. He had taken a photo of a Japanese landing craft with a ramp in place of the bow, which allowed troops to disembark without clambering over the sides and exposing themselves to enemy gunners. Krulak sent the photo back to the States. The Navy initially dismissed it as the work of "some nut out in China."

Krulak found a more receptive audience in Higgins, who immediately built prototypes. The usefulness of the ramp bow was so obvious that his contract with the Navy was amended to add it to all the remaining boats. Many GIs owe their lives to the fact that a couple of nuts were willing to learn from experience on the battlefield.

A shallow-body LCVP, popularly known as a "Higgins boat," in the South Pacific (1945).

Higgins had an even more dramatic run-in with the Navy to win a contract for tank lighters (the Landing Craft, Vehicle, Mechanized, or LCVM), boats that would carry tanks ashore from their transports. In May 1941, less than three days after hearing of the Navy's interest, Higgins designed and built the forty-five-foot boat, a feat the Navy deemed impossible. During tests, it performed spectacularly, and the Navy and Marines immediately ordered fifty. Higgins thought this order marked an end to his acrimonious relationship with the Navy (by this point, the BCR had been subsumed by the newly created Bureau of Ships). He was wrong.

The Bureau of Ships (Higgins called it the Bureau of Shit), like the BCR, relished its role as judge, jury, and executioner. It evaluated ships, designed ships, and awarded contracts. With these incentives, it would always be locked in competition with industry. The Navy viewed superior performance from the civilian sector as a threat to its technical staff, which engendered a terrible zero-sum mindset.

The Bureau of Ships, stung by its earlier defeat against the Eureka, tried to do an end-run around Higgins by designing a tank lighter on its own. As with the Eureka, it purposefully excluded Higgins from bidding on the production of the 131 Bureau-designed tank lighters. When Higgins caught wind of the plot, he insisted on the right to compete, cursing Annapolis grads who knew more about "fancy dancing" (in his words) than building small ships. The exclusion was more egregious because Higgins was by now a well-known shipbuilder with extensive past performance with the Navy. Further, per Higgins, "we were properly registered with the Bureau of S&A [Supplied and Accounts], and specifications and invitations to bid on anything in that line should automatically be sent to us, as taxpayers, and as Americans, with an opportunity to bid." Higgins concluded that the Navy was motivated by "bias and prejudice with willful intent to disregard our talents." It was treating him, once again, like a backwoods bumpkin instead of America's best hope of out-floating the Axis.

Higgins wasn't looking for special treatment. He was angry that the "Navy had consistently refused to give me the opportunity to cooperate or serve." So, in typical fashion, Higgins forced his way into the office of the admiral in charge of naval procurement and laid into him and his staff. Cowed, the admiral rescinded the old solicitation and released a modified one.

Higgins was sick of the Navy not understanding what it meant to run a business:

> I pointed out to them that if they had any interest in our country, and in the Navy, at that, that they should be aware of the fact…that we were people who knew what it meant to meet a payroll; that we are a commercial firm that had to be efficient because we weren't subsidized by the government, or otherwise suckled by the tax-payers.

It boiled Higgins' blood to see the Navy heaping generous subsidies on its preferred contractors—or worse, favoring Navy designs with no accountability.

In April 1942, President Roosevelt ordered the construction of 600 tank lighters ahead of the Allied invasion of North Africa. Instead of holding an open competition, the Bureau selected its own (inferior) design and then upped the order to 1,100 lighters. Higgins hit the roof. He couldn't sue the government (the laws that would allow him to do so wouldn't exist for another half century), but he could enlist the help of Senator Harry Truman, whose special committee was ferreting out fraud, waste, and abuse in wartime contracting. The Truman Committee was sometimes overzealous, but it did go after industry and the government in equal measure—and Higgins desperately needed congressional support.

At Truman's direction, the Navy ordered a head-to-head competition between the Bureau-designed tank lighter and Higgins's barge-like entry. The competition, held in choppy waters off Norfolk with Higgins and representatives of the Navy in attendance, was no contest. As a Bureau officer admitted, "Higgins's tank lighter came through fine, upside in and made the beach and the poor old Bureau tank lighter was out there wallowing around." Higgins had won again. The 1,100 tank lighters were built to his specification.

He was not magnanimous in victory. When Truman's committee investigated the tank lighter contract, Higgins held nothing back. "The Bureau of Ships has grown like a mushroom," he told an investigator. "No industrial concern with the proper management would ever have such a cumbersome, outlandish, and inoperative octopus as has the present Bureau of Ships." Higgins also offered personnel recommendations: "Nothing could be healthier for the Navy as a whole, and the country that they really desire to serve, than that there be a 'house cleaning' in the Bureau of Ships. It would be preferable that quite a number of officers and civilians therein go to other duties." Truman put the criticism somewhat more artfully, remarking that the Allied war effort had been spared "irreparable damage" by Higgins' "repeated criticisms of the shortcomings of the designs prepared by the bureau of ships...without fear of the results which such criticisms might incur with the agency."

It took years, but Higgins had proven indispensable—and he had proven the doubters wrong. Higgins Industries expanded rapidly in scope and scale as a result. At its peak, Higgins employed 20,000 people manufacturing landing craft, torpedo boats, life rafts, and even components for the Manhattan Project. But it didn't last. The evaporation of military contracts at the end of the war, paired with bitter labor disputes, forced an almost immediate consolidation of the business. The company was scrapped for parts and Higgins was dead before the 1950s were through.

Higgins' vindication was on distant beaches far from Washington or New Orleans, in places with now-immortal names: Normandy. Iwo Jima. Okinawa. Allied forces stormed these beaches in thousands of landing craft that he had fought to design and build for his country. In the ultimate tribute, servicemen didn't call the landing craft by their clunky official designations. They called them "Higgins boats."

Andrew Higgins attends a celebration in his honor in New Orleans. Higgins Industries had just completed its 10,000th boat for the Navy (1944).

Suing the Customer

Swap out boats for software and Palantir's early trials with the Department of Defense look remarkably similar to Higgins' (though admittedly on a much smaller scale). The main difference is that Palantir had the law on its side. In 1994, fifty years after World War II, Congress passed FASA, which would have made the Navy's shabby treatment of Higgins illegal—at least in theory. It would be up to Palantir to ensure that the law was enforced.

In 2016, Palantir sued the Army after it excluded commercial companies—in violation of FASA—from bidding on a contract for an intelligence program called the Distributed Common Ground System (DCGS). (You may remember this ill-starred intelligence system from Colonel Cukor's encounter with it in Chapter 2.) As a reminder: FASA imposes strict requirements on the government to buy commercial products if they meet the government's needs, could be modified to meet the government's needs, or if the government could reasonably modify *its* needs to use commercial products. It's commonsense legislation to save taxpayers money, get superior commercial products into the hands of our troops, and reward American companies for their ingenuity.

The lawsuit was an epic battle and, ultimately, an epic victory. The verdict didn't mean that Palantir automatically won the DCGS contract; it won the right to *compete* for the contract. But that was the point. We sued because we knew a fair competition would allow the best technology to triumph. And that would be good for us, the Army, and the country.

The events that follow are dramatic and contentious. They also occurred ten years ago. Since then, I (Shyam) became a reservist in the US Army, commissioning as a lieutenant colonel. And Palantir's partnership with the Army has improved and grown. The relationship between twenty-first-century technology companies and the Pentagon has changed, and mostly for the better. But there is still room for the relationship to grow. We're telling this story as a reminder that hard-fought change requires vigilance. The work is far from over.

During the wars in Iraq and Afghanistan, improvised explosive devices killed and wounded American troops in astonishing numbers. The root of the problem was boring: the many military and intelligence databases operated by the United States and its allies didn't talk to one another, which prevented useful intelligence analysis. Signals intelligence, geospatial data, weather data, open-source data, and more were all fragmented. As a result, there was no single, integrated software platform a soldier could access that would show the likely positions of enemy combatants and improvised explosive devices. The problem was compounded by the limited bandwidth and intermittent connectivity that soldiers faced while deployed in third-world deserts.

DCGS was supposed to solve this. The US Army Intelligence Directorate had been leading the custom development software project since the late 1990s, yet almost $6 billion and more than fifteen years later, it still didn't work. The Beltway's best were on it: Lockheed Martin, Northrop Grumman, and Raytheon all had cost-plus contracts for the project. Despite the serious engineering challenges involved in deploying such a sophisticated piece of software, the Army wasn't interested in procuring a commercial software platform. The insularity of the Army intel establishment would give the Navy's Bureau of Ships a run for its money.

Everything DCGS was supposed to do, it didn't do. DCGS servers in Afghanistan didn't share data with one another, which made tracking enemy combatants impossible. The product was borderline unusable: it required extensive training, analysis took upwards of ten hours, and system failures frequently deleted work, so analysts used PowerPoint instead. In the eloquent words of one Marine captain who served as an intelligence officer in Afghanistan, the Army's existing solution was "a piece of shit, totally hopeless."

While DCGS was failing, soldiers were dying. Michael Flynn is now well-known for his stint as President Trump's national security advisor in 2017, but he previously served with distinction as an Army intelligence officer. In 2010, then-Major General Flynn rocked the boat by submitting a Joint Urgent Operational Needs Statement (JUONS) for better intelligence tools. A JUONS signals that the normal acquisition process is even more broken than usual and drastic action is needed immediately. Flynn's bluntly worded request left no room for doubt about what was wrong (emphasis ours):

> Intelligence analysts in theater do not have the tools required to fully analyze the tremendous amount of information currently available in theater.... The impact of this shortfall is felt in almost every activity that intelligence supports. Analysts cannot provide their commanders with a full understanding of the operational environment. Without the full understanding of the enemy and human terrain, our

> operations are not as successful as they could be. *This shortfall translates into operational opportunities missed and lives lost.*

Flynn requested "a theater-wide web-based advanced analytical platform to store, organize, access, retrieve and enable full understanding of intelligence and information from multiple large disparate data sets." Unfortunately for Flynn, he was describing DCGS—as it existed on paper, at least. In response, the Army insisted that DCGS was meeting his needs. Then, in a move straight from the Bureau of Ships playbook, it announced a new and improved version of the platform, complete with a fancier-sounding name: DCGS *Cloud*. The architect of this version was Dr. Russell Richardson, a Pentagon consultant and the chief science advisor to Lieutenant General Mary Legere, who was responsible for DCGS as the Army's deputy chief of staff for intelligence. Richardson's qualifications, like the program he worked on, looked sterling on paper. Yet, in a microcosm of the broader DCGS scandal, it was later revealed that Richardson had faked his PhD. The Army briefed Congress in 2011 that Flynn's JUONS had been fulfilled. But in 2013, DCGS Cloud still didn't work. Soldiers reported the system had been "offline for months."

While DCGS foundered, Palantir was saving lives by performing the exact function DCGS was supposed to perform. Palantir's platform integrated all types of data from a variety of sources, providing commanders and soldiers, whether at home or in the field, with a unified view of what was happening. When connections were spotty, Palantir's platform saved analysts' work offline and then automatically synced updates as soon as a connection was re-established. In short, Palantir had built a working military intelligence product for tracking enemy combatants and predicting the ways in which they were trying to kill American troops. It had been a world-class software problem, and it had required a world-class software company to solve it. Our troops got a massive quality of life improvement. And yes, the product undoubtedly saved lives.

By the end of 2010, there was a groundswell of support for Palantir among the elite forces using our product in Afghanistan and Iraq. More than three dozen Special Forces and Marine units used it—and hailed it as a success. Soon, Marine General James "Mad Dog" Mattis extended it to all the troops under his command. A Marine Corps Special Operations Command colonel said, "Marines are alive today because of the capability of this system." Indeed, the whole reason Flynn had filed his JUONS was because he'd learned of Palantir's capabilities.

Flynn was not the only soldier calling for change from inside the Army. The 82nd Airborne Division's request for Palantir is particularly memorable in large part because of how the Army reacted. The 82nd Airborne had requested funding for Palantir via the now-discontinued Rapid Equipping Forces (REF) process, which served a similar function as a JUONS. The officer in charge of the 82nd Airborne's Counter-IED cell wrote in 2012:

> All the bullet points [the Army] can list on a slide sitting back in the Pentagon don't change the reality on the ground that their system doesn't do what they say it does, and is more of a frustration to deal with than a capability to leverage. We aren't going to sit here and struggle with an ineffective intel sys-

> tem while we're in the middle of a heavy fight taking casualties. Palantir actually works.

In response, the Army sent more DCGS equipment and tried to block the REF funding. Ultimately, the Army's chief of staff, General Ray Odierno—who was hardly a Palantir booster, as we will see—had to intervene to approve the REF request.

With controversy over DCGS and Palantir at a boiling point, Odierno ordered the Army Test and Evaluation Command (ATEC) to evaluate the capabilities of both systems. ATEC's report found that 96 percent of personnel surveyed agreed that Palantir was effective in supporting their mission, followed by a recommendation that the Army install more Palantir servers in Afghanistan. The Army had essentially ruled against itself.

But the truth did not set it free. In a display right out of Orwell's *1984*, Legere pushed ATEC to revoke the report and issue a new one that deleted the positive parts about Palantir and the recommendation to purchase its software. (Legere later claimed during a deposition that her "suggestion was a minor one in the context of the report and I was comfortable that it could either be accepted as a constructive suggestion or ignored as immaterial.")

"Suggestion" or not, nobody wanted to go against the boss. In 2012, ATEC promptly emailed recipients of the report to "ensure that any and all copies of the 25 April report are destroyed and not distributed" and to confirm "that all copies of the original report dated 25 April has [sic] been destroyed."

Meanwhile, American troops were still suffering heavy casualties. A Palantir legal filing describes the real-world stakes of this paper war: "Colonel Stock's May 2012 request for the

Palantir Gotham Platform was denied. He requested the Palantir Gotham Platform again. The request was again denied. In September 2012, his unit returned home with 200 casualties."

The Army misrepresented the capabilities of both Palantir and DCGS. In 2013, Odierno forcefully asserted that DCGS "works pretty damn good and has about a hundred apps that work very, very well, so I'm not going to throw that away because of one app, and that one app, by the way, is not interoperable with the other apps, so that's the problem." The "app" to which Odierno was referring was Palantir, which was not, in fact, an app, but an entire substitute platform. Moreover, our product was perfectly interoperable with other military intelligence systems, as determined by yet another report commissioned by the Department of Defense. Another bombshell, followed by another coverup: funding to finalize and publish a report with these findings was cut off.

Like the Bureau of Ships, Army intel was preoccupied with protecting its turf. In the Pentagon's words, systems purchased "outside of the normal acquisition process" were a "sensitive issue" for Army intel. It didn't like outsiders using workarounds like REFs and urgent funding to win over users when Army intel hadn't blessed the contracts via the "normal acquisition process." This was about control, and Army intel increasingly did not have it. By 2015, nearly half the Army's brigades had managed to get access to Palantir and were using it instead of DCGS. They had done so by circumventing the normal, broken acquisitions system.

Finally, after years of dismal reports by the Government Accountability Office (GAO) and heat from both the House and Senate Armed Services Committees, the Army terminated Increment 1 of DCGS in December 2014. The new phase of the program should have been a moment of reckoning for Army intel, but little changed: DCGS Increment 2 doubled down on fifteen years of failure. The "new" phase of the program was a custom, developmental, and entirely service-based software effort built with cost-plus contracts, just like its predecessors. The Army was planning to spend four to five years on development for Increment 2—wasting more time our soldiers didn't have. Commercial companies were excluded from eligibility. During market research for this proposal, the Army didn't even consider whether commercial products could meet its needs, despite the plain text of FASA and despite the Army's obvious awareness of Palantir's existence.

Ironically, right around the time the Army was issuing its new, illegal DCGS solicitation, Secretary of Defense Ash Carter was crusading to bring Silicon Valley back into the fold. Carter was the first secretary of defense to visit Silicon Valley in two decades. He started the Defense Innovation Unit-Experimental (now just DIU) to reforge the ties between the Pentagon and innovative commercial technology companies. In a 2016 speech, he stated, "we're reaching out to America's wonderful innovative ecosystems, which are another great and unrivaled source of national strength, to build bridges to, partner with, and inspire those innovators who want to make a difference in our world." Carter's rhetoric and the Army's actions couldn't have been more different.

When Palantir saw that the Army was proceeding with business as usual, we protested the bid to GAO in early 2016. Thousands of protests are filed each year. For legacy defense contractors, protesting a contract outcome is almost reflexive, a tactic used to delay awards on the slim chance that a decision is reversed. For example, Boeing and Lockheed protested the

Air Force's award of the B-21 bomber to Northrop Grumman, while Northrop Grumman protested the Navy's award of its Next Generation Jammer to L3Harris. What Palantir did was slightly different. We filed a *pre*-award protest. We weren't complaining that we hadn't won—we were arguing that the solicitation itself was wrong and illegal. GAO denied the protest, as it does in 97 percent of cases.

Our protest denied, Palantir was at a crossroads. We could take the L or pursue the nuclear option: suing the government, which is another way of saying suing our biggest customer. Since Palantir ended up winning the lawsuit, it's tempting to look back and view it as inevitable and low stakes. But it was a real "bet the farm" moment. Suing your biggest customer is acrimonious, expensive, and unlikely to succeed. We risked torching relationships we had built over more than a decade. Plus, such a lawsuit was unprecedented: the government had never had to defend itself for violating FASA. Privately, we figured our odds of winning were 1 percent, a number reinforced by the big DC law firms who warned us this was a suicide mission. (In any event, many were conflicted out of working with us because they were already engaged by the defense primes.)

Many hardworking Palantirians made the lawsuit possible; chief among them was Global Defense Lead Doug Philippone, a former Army Ranger who has since gone on to found a VC firm, Snowpoint Ventures. When Philippone approached our CEO, Alex Karp, about pursuing the lawsuit, Karp approved. More than approved, even: in true Palantir fashion, Karp gave Philippone carte blanche. Then as now, the culture was one of total empowerment and total accountability. Working with the legendary lawyer Hamish Hume, who successfully represented SpaceX in its 2014 lawsuit against the Air Force, Palantir escalated by filing a bid protest in the Court of Federal Claims. Philippone's mindset at the time was, "we don't have a business if we don't win this thing." He decided to go for it all.

Like so many things at Palantir, the way we approached litigation wasn't standard. For a couple of years, Philippone and his colleagues moonlighted as "forward deployed lawyers" of a sort. They embedded with Hume's law firm, Boies Schiller Flexner, not because they didn't trust the lawyers, but because of our deeply held conviction that the most critical things should never be completely outsourced to a third party. Palantir's lawsuit centered on an arcane and technical issue, which was made more complicated by our many years of history with the Army. Our argument would be most compelling if it reflected a true mind-meld of the legal and technological issues at hand. The forward-deployed model enabled us to put forth the strongest possible case, which in turn resulted in the deposition of key Army actors—a notable and rare occurrence in procurement lawsuits.

We'll spare the technical details and skip to the result: Army intel did not succeed in skirting the law or getting a FASA exemption. Palantir won the precedent-setting lawsuit. In November 2016, Judge Marian Blank Horn ruled that,

> the Army acted arbitrarily and capriciously when the Army failed to determine, in accordance with the requirements of 10 U.S.C. § 2377 [FASA], whether there were commercially available items suitable to meet the Army's procurement requirements prior to issuing the solicitation at issue.

Judge Horn ordered the Army to go back and see if there were commercial products that could meet its needs. She concluded by concurring with us—and Andrew Higgins before us—on the value of competition: "As Palantir argues, there is a public interest 'in preserving the integrity of the competitive process.'" That was, after all, all we'd ever asked for: a chance to compete.

The Army didn't go down without a fight; it appealed the court's decision. Cost-plus was how the Department of Defense preferred to structure contracts, and the ruling had wide-ranging implications for how the Pentagon would need to do business going forward. But the Army's FASA violation was black and white, and Palantir won on appeal.

Steven Brill, a journalist who closely covered the case, wrote: "In years of writing about legal disputes, I cannot remember one that was this one-sided. And one that so vividly tells a tale of long-running, systemic dysfunction when it comes to how the government spends money." This legal battle was an epic showdown between a commercial company and the entrenched forces of the monopsony. Thankfully, the good guys won.

Then the real work began. Our product was put to the test throughout the—now legal and decidedly non-kayfabe—DCGS procurement process. In March 2019, Palantir won the contract after a competition against Raytheon. The evaluation process had played to our company's strengths with a live, year-long bakeoff where the Army evaluated the performance of the product, not claims made in a white paper. In victory, Palantir proved definitively what the Army had denied for so long: the private sector was ready and willing to meet the Army's needs, if given the chance.

In fighting the Navy, Higgins didn't have the law on his side. All he had to work with was patriotism, conviction, and some really excellent boats. We did have the law on our side, but our offensive wasn't much easier than Higgins' was. Even today, FASA remains the most violated law on the books. Despite Palantir winning the lawsuit and the appeal, and despite the clear language of FASA, agencies across the government willfully violate the law. Commercial companies still have to fight tooth and nail to get a fair shake. What this demonstrates is that true, meaningful competition is a problem of incentives and culture, not legislation alone.

Historically, there have been too many ways to exclude commercial companies, and too few senior leaders who care. Classification is wrongfully used to gatekeep programs of all stripes. The primes plead ignorance of FASA to dominate contracts for generational platforms, then they proceed to build inferior, expensive solutions instead of incorporating proven technology. "National security" is still accepted at face value as a reason why a given program can't possibly use commercial solutions.

We hope this chapter has shown that competition for contracts and commercial buying aren't just niche procurement issues that only affect government contractors. They affect all of us as taxpayers and citizens who rely on our Armed Forces for protection. They can even determine whether the men and women who volunteered to fight on our behalf make it home safe, or not.

Competition and commercial buying also test our foundational concepts of liberty. If we believe in capitalism, we will embrace its fruits. If we don't, we will accept centralized planning, de facto state-owned enterprises, and cost-plus contracting. The changes we're seeing in how wars are fought—cheap drones taking out bomber fleets, AI changing the behavior of weapons—are driven by the dynamism of the commercial economy. Capitalism is undefeated. Americans deserve for every dollar spent on defense to not just keep us safe but also make us more prosperous. That doesn't happen in a world where contracts are distributed based on cronyism and regulatory capture, instead of competition.

It's not scalable for commercial companies to sue the government over each FASA violation. We need the Undertaker instead: someone willing to root out these violations and bury them deep in the ground, where they can never be resurrected. We may have found such a character in President Trump. Recent executive orders signed by the president promise to enforce FASA and finally bring commercial innovation back into government. We'll look at those in more detail in our concluding chapter, but now it's time to turn our attention to another important tool for obliterating kayfabe and introducing real competition to the government. We have to break the monopsony.

CHAPTER 10

Break the Monopsony

By now, we've seen how the Department of War's monopsony is upstream of almost every problem related to building and buying the best weapons. Smart people have tried to reform the Pentagon for decades. For the most part, they've failed. Their recommendations are mostly sound ("define the outcome you want, not the requirements," "fly before you buy," and so on). But the impact of these reforms will be limited if the Pentagon doesn't address the root cause. Behavior will only change when the bureaucracy is forced to compete against itself. There is only one way to cut the Gordian knot of acquisition reform: break the monopsony.

That means creating competition among the buyers of defense technology, not just the sellers. While this approach may seem outlandish—people are used to thinking of the government as a monolith—it doesn't mean we have to build a second Department of War. And in fact, there's good precedent within living memory. Many of the most successful defense acquisitions in history happened because a program broke the monopsony, pitting services and agencies against each other in competitions to procure the best possible technology.

As we've seen, the Allies had enough boats to land troops in Europe and countless remote islands in the Pacific because the Navy wasn't the only buyer of boats. Andrew Higgins, the titan of small boatbuilding during World War II, found his first government buyer in the Coast Guard, and later earned the strong advocacy of the Marine Corps; both understood the value of Higgins' shallow-draft, backwoods boats, while the Navy was too prideful and clubby to buy them. Likewise, while the Air Force eventually learned to love the Predator drone, it was the CIA that made sure the technology (created by Israeli innovator Abraham Karem) got off the ground. The list goes on.

A common misconception is that multiple agencies buying similar technologies or performing similar missions is necessarily more expensive and wasteful; "duplication" is a four-letter word in government. But in the right doses, competition is a powerful hedge against conformity, unearned monopolies, and well-intentioned efforts that simply go wrong. Military scholar Stephen Rosen points out that "we afforded redundant Air Forces and a redundant Marine Corps during the 1930s when defense spending as a whole was, at most, 1.5 percent of GNP." Without the Marine Corps, we likely wouldn't have invented amphibious assault until World War II was well under way, a late discovery that would have been far more expensive in lives lost than paying for a duplicate ground force.

In this chapter, we'll share an inside story from Palantir that demonstrates the power of competition inside institutions, even—or perhaps especially—when it's not welcomed by incumbents. We'll show how America built the first nuclear missiles not only because it was racing against the Soviet Union, but also because the services were racing against each other. And we'll offer a few practical ideas for breaking the monopsony and spurring healthy competition inside government. Let's dive in.

Monocle

Palantir's culture of building embraces chaos and so-called waste. It's a hard-earned, hard-won culture that runs counter to how most institutions operate. At any given time, at least two of our products—and often many more—could be considered in competition with one another. The people running those product teams are empowered to act autonomously, but they are granted neither a monopoly nor an endless stream of resources. Every day, those product leaders must prove that the projects they are building and the code they are shipping are superior.

Monocle, a pillar of the Palantir Foundry platform, emerged from this fierce competition. Monocle enables users to figure out the provenance of data, which is a fancy way of saying where it came from, how it has changed over time, who has access to it, and so on. Monocle is such an integral part of Palantir's products that it's hard to imagine Palantir ever existed without it. But like most great innovations, Monocle started as a disruptive endeavor hated by the "establishment," such as it exists at our company. It was the brainchild of two exceptionally talented individuals, product founder Parvathy Menon and her engineer co-founder Joey Rafidi.

At the time, Parvathy had transitioned from forward-deployed engineering into a founder-esque role within Palantir, where for several years she focused on turning field observations into novel products. While embedded at a leading financial institution, she observed a recurring problem: every Friday, the

CEO received a report hundreds of pages long, filled with insights and recommendations from analysts in the then-current version of Foundry. But when he tried to understand the provenance of a given assertion—such as whether a figure on Chinese shipping flows was hardcoded or derived from satellite imagery, port reports, and vessel traffic—he hit a wall. There was no way to trace it. The inability to distinguish between speculation and well-sourced analysis posed a critical risk to the business.

The problem that Parvathy identified was quite literally a million-dollar question. With virtually zero resources, she and Joey hacked together an early prototype of a lineage-tracing interface, which they named Monocle. They weren't thanked for their exertions, at least not at first. The high priests of Foundry—the product managers most responsible for managing the platform—hated Monocle because it was a competitor to Foundry's existing (and inferior) provenance capability. Just like the Army bureaucrats from our lawsuit, the establishment tried to ignore the insurgent capability. When that didn't work, they tried to break it. Then they tried to copy Monocle. It was a poor imitation of the real thing. At a different company, Parvathy's effort might have been seen as duplicative and certainly insubordinate; the whole effort might have been killed. At Palantir, I (Shyam) intervened to force the product team to turn on Parvathy's Monocle at customer sites. Once it was released, market forces did the rest. People loved it.

This story teaches us that territorial behavior is human. The Department of War isn't uniquely screwed up. Rather, it's a bureaucracy on a scale many orders of magnitudes larger than most companies, with countless little fiefs and monopolies—and it's shielded from market forces, to boot.

At the time of the Monocle showdown, Palantir was a small company of around 1,500 people, yet already we had developed some of the same issues as any large, entrenched bureaucracy. Engineers want monopolies because it avoids the appearance of inefficiency and wasted work, which engineers inherently despise. Managers want monopolies out of a desire for predictability and control—not to mention because it's a personal offense when organizational boundaries are violated. These impulses may be human, but they must be resisted to maintain a dynamic organization. You overcome controlling behavior by resisting unearned monopolies and rewarding individuals based on the outcomes they deliver, not the bodies they manage.

The Race to an ICBM

The Department of Defense's development of ballistic missiles during the Cold War is perhaps the canonical example of duplication done *right.* During this epic, five-year sprint, the Army, Navy, and Air Force all competed against each other to build the better missile. The Air Force's Minuteman and the Navy's Polaris ultimately emerged as winners, but not before the Jupiter, Thor, Atlas, and Titan took their shots at the title. That's six programs total and two winners.

Was this wasteful? Harvey Sapolsky, who wrote the authoritative work on Polaris, summarizes the outcome: "centralizing decision making and eliminating competition would only have decreased the probability of obtaining the best system within any given time period." In other words, the proliferation of programs made it more likely that at least one would be successful. In this case, we got two, both of which seemed impossibly "science fiction" at first.

With Minuteman, we gained hundreds of hardened, underground siloes dispersed across the heartland housing relatively low-cost, solid-fueled ICBMs. With Polaris, we gained dozens of nuclear-powered ballistic missile submarines that constantly roam the ocean, where they can creep up an enemy coast undetected to fire their nuclear-tipped missiles from underwater. Two of the three legs of the US nuclear triad (the third is the bomber fleet) exist because of interservice rivalry. Proliferation of programs didn't cause timelines to extend interminably. The opposite happened. Both the successful and "failed" efforts developed briskly, all moving from contract to operational capability within five years (even faster in some cases). That's unimaginable today. It's time to start imagining how to do it again.

More than any other individual, it was Air Force Lieutenant General Bernard Schriever—whom we met delivering the mail for the Army Air Corps in Chapter 4—who ensured that ICBMs got off the ground and that there was any race at all. Along the way, he would risk everything. The defining feature of a race is that there are winners and losers. Schriever had no guarantee that his name would end up on an Air Force (now Space Force) base and that he'd be christened as the father of the ICBM. He was just as likely to blow up his career on the launch pad alongside the ultimate weapon he was trying to build.

Months before the US declared war on Germany in 1917, a young Bennie Schriever immigrated to America from Germany with his family, where they eventually settled in Texas. He received a frigid welcome in the Southwest heat. Classmates mocked his accent and teased him with the nickname "Kaiser

Wilhelm." But these small hardships paled in comparison to the tragedy that soon struck the Schriever family. Bennie's father, Adolph, died in a horrific industrial accident. Widowed and penniless, Bennie's mother was forced to place her two sons in an orphanage for a year until she could find stable work. Amidst such hardship, Bennie retained nothing but gratitude for America, even from an early age. He would say the Pledge of Allegiance louder than any of his classmates. And when he went to college at Texas A&M, he and the rest of his all-male class were automatically enrolled in ROTC. Upon graduation he joined the Army Air Corps and spent the interwar years in a combination of active-duty, reservist, and commercial pilot jobs. The German accent was long gone.

Schriever was at Stanford getting his masters in aeronautical engineering when World War II broke out. He was itching to fight and finally got the chance when he was shipped out to Australia in 1942 to fly B-17 bomber missions against the Japanese. He proved his bravery and earned some medals on a number of daring combat missions, but he was most valuable in less flashy roles of maintenance and supply. From mass engine failures to cement shortages, there was no problem Schriever couldn't solve. In twenty months, he rocketed through the ranks from captain to full colonel—talent was recognized and elevated in the crucible of war. After the war, Schriever took on an analytical role at the Pentagon, where he was involved in the development of next-generation aircraft.

But Schriever wasn't just a nerdy engineer. Standing six feet three inches with angular features and bright blue eyes, he was tall, dark, and handsome. Schriever would later be compared to movie stars as his own star rose in the public eye. His biographer called him "without a doubt the handsomest general in the

United States Air Force." In addition to having a formidable engineering mind, Schriever possessed people skills and a reserved but personable demeanor that would prove valuable for the bureaucratic maneuvering and large-scale management required to make the ICBMs successful.

America's rapid development of ballistic missiles seems inevitable in hindsight. After all, Americans were obsessed with missiles for much of the Cold War; the "missile gap" entered the American lexicon during JFK's successful bid for the presidency in 1960. But in fact, anxiety about a missile gap with the Soviets was the contrarian view just a few years earlier as Schriever was coming into his own. In Curtis LeMay's Strategic Air Command, the Air Force had a powerful bomber lobby. This lobby held the consensus view of the time that bombers were a reliable, operationally-proven method of delivering nuclear weapons. Therefore, the United States should invest in them as the primary means of deterrence. While the United States pursued various missile development efforts after World War II, none were serious. Regarding the feasibility of a nuclear-armed ICBM in 1945, Vannevar Bush said, "I don't think anybody in the world knows how to do such a thing and I feel confident it will not be done for a long period of time to come." Bush advocated consolidating (cancelling) ongoing missile efforts. Almost ten years later, Eisenhower's secretary of defense, Charles Wilson, echoed this call to cull missile projects.

Although Schriever had been a bomber pilot, he didn't have the bomber blinders on like LeMay and others in the Air Force. As the Eisenhower administration geared up to cancel missile programs, Schriever's gears were turning as to how he could make an ICBM a reality. He faced two challenges: first, the defense establishment doubted that the technology was viable.

Second, he didn't have the organizational autonomy needed to develop such an unorthodox weapon.

To address the first problem, Schriever paid a visit to John von Neumann, America's leading nuclear expert and greatest scientific mind after Einstein. During a 1953 meeting that lasted several hours, von Neumann provided Schriever the scientific validation the eager colonel sought: by the end of the decade, a hydrogen bomb weighing less than a ton would have a yield of one megaton. This miniaturization was essential to fit a nuke on the tip of a missile. (The bombs dropped on Hiroshima and Nagasaki weighed approximately five tons apiece, with explosive yields of about 20 kilotons.) Schriever shared the unofficial findings with an ally working for the secretary of the Air Force, who helped to translate them into the official studies the defense bureaucracy demanded. Von Neumann enthusiastically wrote a report in 1954 recommending that ballistic missile technology be accelerated given the technical feasibility of producing the weapon as early as 1960 or 1961 (as was so often the case, the genius mathematician was right on the money).

After checking the box on technical feasibility, Schriever managed to convince the Air Force to designate ICBMs as its top priority. In that time, he gained a brigadier general's star and assumed command of the newly formed Western Development Division, responsible for Air Force ballistic missiles. Even with this special status, Schriever still had to obtain forty-two approvals across OSD and the Air Force for any missile development plans. Schriever was convinced that the United States would never beat the Soviets to an ICBM unless it got rid of "interference from those nitpicking sons of bitches in the Pentagon." Organizational autonomy—streamlined budgets, less reporting and approvals—were table stakes for success.

Only one man could move these bureaucratic mountains: the president. Schriever would need to convert Eisenhower into a true believer. It was clear that the secretary of defense would not go to bat for the technology, so Schriever had to do an end-run around the Pentagon. He enlisted a political operative to secretly brief key senators who would in turn influence Ike. Schriever provided his shadow agent with the key exhibits and discussion points needed to convince the president. If it had been discovered that he was repeatedly breaking the sacrosanct chain of command, Schriever would have lost his job. But the secret lobbying worked.

By 1955, President Eisenhower had designated ballistic missiles "a research and development program of the highest priority above all others." He authorized four concurrent programs of equal priority, two each of IRBMs and ICBMs. The IRBMs had a distance requirement of just over 1,500 nautical miles, while ICBMs had a far greater requirement of at least 5,000 nautical miles. The shorter-range missiles were thought to be an important hedge against the ICBM's risky development timeline. The Army's Jupiter and the Air Force's Thor IRBMs were to compete against each other, while the Air Force would internally compete its Atlas and Titan ICBMs. The Navy was initially boxed out, but as we'll see it emerged later as a dark horse. Bennie got his missile programs, all right, but he was not given a monopoly on the funding, development, or priority. That turned out to be a blessing for the country.

It's notable that even the economical Eisenhower, who was trying his hardest to rein in defense spending, still thought the best approach to building an effective ICBM faster than the Soviets was to purposefully fund duplicative projects. He was willing to host the bakeoff because the overriding constraint was time. (Plus, Eisenhower had no intention of funding all the efforts in perpetuity. Any competition worth its salt has losers.) The mission was clear: deploy a suitable ICBM as fast as humanly possible—and at all costs—before the communists. The race was on.

While the Army only had one missile program to the Air Force's three (all under Schriever's direction), it had an advantage the Air Force lacked: Wernher von Braun and the Germans. As we saw in Chapter 8, the former Peenemünde rocket engineers at the Redstone Arsenal in Huntsville were among the world's foremost technical experts, from the private or public sector. Overseeing them was the ambitious Major General John Medaris, commander of the Army Ballistic Missile Agency and Schriever's biggest rival after the Soviets. The Army laid claim to the missile mission with the justification that it was responsible for ground targets—and after all, missiles were really a form of guided artillery. Beginning in 1954, it started to build Jupiter, a sixty-foot-tall missile that could travel 1,500 nautical miles.

In Schriever, Medaris found a dedicated but struggling competitor. Schriever's Thor was more or less a duplicate of Medaris' Jupiter—it was even designed by the same engineer. The main difference was the team building them. Schriever's biographer, Neil Sheehan, describes the Air Force engineers as "a pack of amateurs up against professionals." By May 1957, Thor had three disastrous test flights under its belt. In one, the liquid oxygen tank exploded, ruining the missile and the launch pad. In another, the range safety officer misread the tracking console and thought the missile was heading inland, so he terminated the flight—a polite way of saying he blew up a functional missile.

Jupiter's three flights were successes by comparison. The third flew nearly 1,400 nautical miles, almost the entire distance required for an IRBM. Medaris' Germans had more mature testing and remediation procedures, facilitated by the extensive telemetry data that Jupiter collected. Thor had one-third of the sensors.

Schriever did, however, have a doctrinal advantage over Medaris. In 1956, Secretary of Defense Wilson assigned the operational responsibility for IRBMs to the Air Force. Even if the Army's Jupiter proved more successful than Thor, it would still get turned over to the Air Force to operate. Yet these bureaucratic red lines provided Schriever little comfort. Medaris was not willing to concede defeat so easily. He believed if the Army could develop a successful IRBM faster than the Air Force, it could make the argument that the Air Force had no business operating IRBMs, much less developing the more sophisticated ICBMs. By stealing a march, the Army could steal the entire mission and funding right out from under the Air Force. Schriever took the Army's challenge seriously and was terrified that the underperforming Thor would jeopardize his shot at the ICBM. Smelling blood in the water, Medaris advocated that Thor be "cancelled as expeditiously as possible."

While Schriever and Medaris wrestled, they ignored the surprise threat that would kill both generals' IRBMs: the Navy's Polaris. Schriever and Medaris can be forgiven for discounting the Navy. Internal disunity among the Navy's bureaus had prevented it from lobbying the Department of Defense for a piece of the ballistic missile mission until it was too late. Many Navy officers were also bruised from losing their last skirmish with the Air Force over strategic bombing, when a Navy aircraft carrier was canceled in favor of B-36 Peacemaker bombers.

Eventually, the Navy decided that the only way for it to have a role in strategic missiles was to partner with the Army on Jupiter. The joint Army–Navy effort would provide an alternative to the Air Force's Thor while also providing a ship-based ballistic missile capability. The Army agreed to this arrangement because the Navy brought significant funding to modify the Jupiter to be launched from a ship. Also, the Army thought the joint development effort would help bolster its claims to operational control of ballistic missiles. The opposite happened.

The reason was partly technological. Today, it's taken for granted that solid-fueled missiles are superior to liquid-fueled missiles, but this was not at all obvious in 1955. From the beginning, the Army and (to a lesser extent) the Air Force discounted the viability of solid-fueled missiles. Prominent figures, up to and including von Braun, brushed them off as toys: "the farthest east the Navy could hope to reach with a solid-fueled missile fired from the Atlantic coast of Europe would be...Switzerland"—that is to say, well short of the Soviet Union.

Thor and Jupiter, as well as the ICBMs in development, Atlas and Titan, were all liquid fueled. But Navy sailors weren't thrilled with the prospect of filling missiles with explosive liquid propellant on the high seas. Unauthorized, the Navy contracted Aerojet and Lockheed for technical assistance to prove the viability of solid-fueled missiles. The initial results were promising, and the Navy managed to twist the arm of the ballistic missile committee to provide limited funding of $850,000 for a solid-fueled, ship-based Jupiter, called Jupiter-S.

The Navy compromised on key things to get Jupiter-S: it would be launched from a ship, not a submarine, and at forty-four feet tall and 160,000 pounds, it would be huge. Lacking leverage, the Navy could only hope that the second generation of development would yield a smaller missile more aligned with its operational vision. Then came a turning point in 1956 with a Navy-sponsored scientific study on antisubmarine warfare. The most important insight came from Edward Teller, the theoretical physicist known as the father of the hydrogen bomb. Teller corroborated von Neumann's findings: powerful, lightweight missiles were no longer a figment of the imagination. The weight-to-yield ratio of warheads would be good enough by the 1960s. From this insight flowed the conclusion that submarine-launched ballistic missiles were viable after all, and that they were a heck of a lot more compelling than any ship-based variant. That was enough for the Navy to take a big bet on what became Polaris.

Schriever's newest competitor would be Rear Admiral William Raborn, the man selected as director of Polaris. Raborn was an untraditional choice. He had been a naval aviator but had neither a technical background nor prior experience running a significant R&D project. What he did have was charisma and management chops: a unique ability to bring people together despite their differences and to evangelize Polaris across government. Raborn convinced everybody: "Our religion is to build Polaris." He may not have had Schriever's engineering mind, but he did share his single-minded focus on winning.

When the Navy informed the Army that it would be terminating its co-development of Jupiter, the Army was blindsided. The Navy even voted with the Air Force at the Joint Chiefs of Staff meeting to assign land-based IRBMs to the Air Force rather than the Army. Reeling from this betrayal, the Army tried to argue that the Navy's newly announced Polaris would take ten years to develop—much too long. But it was too little, too late. Schriever and Medaris would have to compete with yet another missile effort. The Eisenhower administration was now funding no fewer than five simultaneous efforts (soon to be six, with the addition of Minuteman in 1957) across the three services.

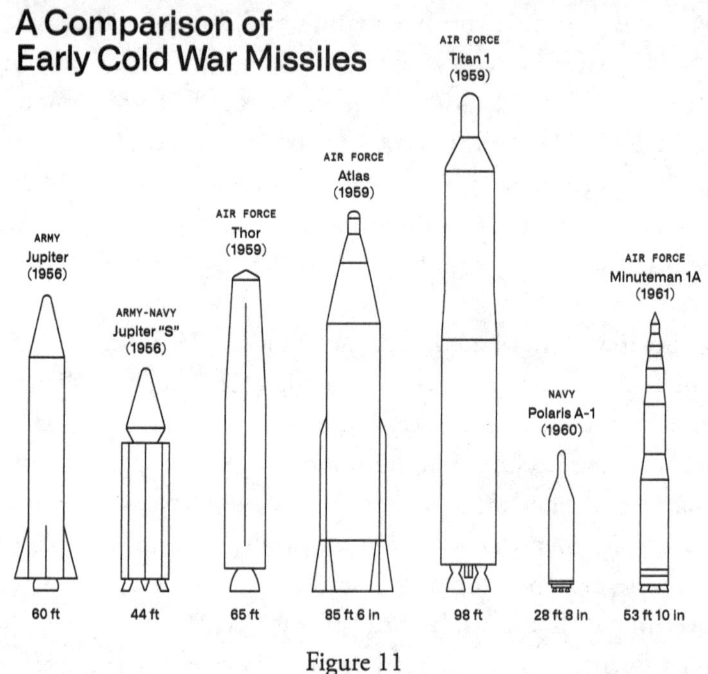

Figure 11

Eisenhower wasn't playing fast and loose with funding and new starts, granting an expensive missile project to anyone who wanted one. He put the squeeze on every ongoing effort to separate the sheep from the goats. Unlike today, Schriever, Raborn, and Medaris couldn't relax, thinking their programs had guaranteed funding for decades. The missile budget had already undergone multiple cuts. Schriever and his team were suffering from low morale as a result, since they were "nearly forced to eliminate overtime costs at the factories, to delay payments, and to slow down production." While the president was willing to fund experimentation, he wasn't willing to fund it indefinitely.

The advent of Sputnik loosened purse strings. Time, however, was more pressing than ever. To meet aggressive deadlines, Schriever introduced into his organization the same competitive dynamics he was experiencing with Raborn and Medaris. He had at least two contractors for each of the major subsystems for the Atlas and Titan ICBMs: airframe, computer, guidance, nose cone, and propulsion. No contractor on Schriever's ICBMs had a guaranteed monopoly on their subsystem. Contractors constantly had to prove that their approach was better than a competitor on contract to build the same thing. Raborn pursued a similar approach on Polaris, where APL and RCA competed to build the best navigation satellite system, and where "eleven different methods of ejecting a missile from a submerged submarine were said to have been simultaneously considered." With constant competition among contractors, Schriever and Raborn could freely explore alternatives and double down on what worked. What looked like duplication was in fact the cheapest and fastest way to build a functional ICBM. Maybe this horseracing sounds familiar; Cukor employed it during Maven to similar success. Deliberate duplication was perhaps most famous on the Manhattan Project, where scientists pursued five different methods of extracting fissionable material for an atomic bomb simultaneously. When speed is the overriding constraint, there is no such thing as wasted work—only wasted time.

Reducing risk and increasing competitive pressure with multiple contractors helped Schriever to pull off the superhuman feat of simultaneously running three—soon to be four—ballistic missile programs. Besides Thor, he was also responsible for Atlas and Titan. Both ICBMs were awarded contracts in 1955 and were operational just four years later, in 1959. While Schriever had a slow start with Thor, he more than made up for it with the rapid deployment of not one, but two ICBMs. That Schriever pulled off such an unlikely feat did not bode well for Medaris and Jupiter.

But it wasn't until Minuteman that Schriever proved beyond doubt that the Air Force had built the second leg of the nuclear triad. The liquid-fueled Atlas and Titan had a major flaw: they had to be fueled right before launch—above ground, no less—wasting precious minutes and making them vulnerable to a first strike. To address these vulnerabilities, Schriever authorized a *third* ICBM, Minuteman, to be led by a volatile colonel named Edward Hall.

Hall's passion for rockets was exceeded only by his recklessness. He once faked an intelligence report of a Soviet super rocket to rescue funding for the early versions of the rocket engines that would eventually go into Schriever's ICBMs. Later, Hall was the program manager of Thor when it suffered its early launch failures, all of which resulted from the testing process rather than failures in the missile itself. Hall was arrogant and competitive even by the standards of the day—he cheered for the Army's Jupiter to "Blow! Blow! Blow!" during its launches. Schriever ultimately fired Hall from Thor, but he didn't banish him from his organization. Schriever knew the immensely talented engineer had more to offer. He was right. Hall's contributions were vital in building the Minuteman.

Where Atlas and Titan had been huge, expensive, and liquid fueled, Minuteman would be smaller, cheaper, and solid fueled. Initially, the Air Force hadn't planned to incorporate solid-fueled technology as part of the initial push to build ballistic missiles, but the Navy's aggressive pursuit of the technology for Polaris provided a strong incentive to start sooner. Plus, Hall had long wanted to build a solid-fueled rocket. He would soon disprove the consensus view that solid-fueled missiles couldn't go the distance. Hall developed a composite propellant that combined a rubbery binder with oxidizers and metallic fuels, which improved the energy density and burn rate of the propellant. The innovative decision to cast a star-shaped cutout through the solid fuel—as opposed to a single, undifferentiated cylinder—further enabled a controlled, sustained burn.

Thanks to Hall, Minuteman missiles overcame the instantaneous launch challenge. They could be pre-loaded and stored indefinitely in hardened, underground siloes. When they were needed, the missiles could launch immediately en masse because they didn't need to be filled with liquid fuel. Minuteman emphasized affordability at the expense of some accuracy. Hall wanted to generate a numerical advantage that would overwhelm the Soviets. When Schriever first heard Hall's pitch, he knew he'd found a winner. Hall's briefing on Minuteman was so compelling that what would become the Air Force's biggest rocket program won approval from top military brass in days, converting the intractably bomber-biased LeMay from a nay to yay on a missile program for the first time. Minuteman development proceeded at a rapid clip, and deployment peaked at 1,000 missiles.

Schriever's Minuteman and Raborn's Polaris won the day, with blazing speed. Polaris started development in 1956 and launched its first missile from an underwater submarine in July 1960, four and a half years ahead of schedule. Minuteman started development in 1957, had its first successful flight test in February 1961, and was operational by 1962.

What should we make of the Army's loss? We're used to headlines announcing failed weapons projects because they're over budget, behind schedule, and terribly underperforming. Medaris' Jupiter was none of these things. It did what it was supposed to do, when it was supposed to do it. It saw action in the Cuban Missile Crisis as a key negotiating chip, to boot. Yet the Army lost the interservice ICBM race. Jupiter wasn't bad, but Minuteman and Polaris were clearly better. We can think of a counterfactual where Schriever and his team failed to execute on both Thor and an ICBM, and the Department of Defense turned away from the Air Force and toward Medaris to save the day. But Schriever didn't screw up. The Air Force retained its mission of operating medium- and long-range missiles, while the Navy unexpectedly got a piece of the action, too.

The smart money had lost to two very dark horses. Rear Admiral Raborn became Vice Admiral Raborn and, briefly, director of the CIA. As for Schriever, he pinned on his fourth star in 1961 when he became chief of the newly created Air Force Systems Command. When LeMay retired in 1965 as Air Force chief of staff, Schriever hoped to take his spot as a final crowning achievement. But as Vietnam raged, he was passed over in favor of someone with an operations—not engineering—background. Schriever retired after thirty-three years of service. The father of the ICBM would have to settle for being the first airman to have a base named after him while he was still alive.

THE COMPETITORS

SCHRIEVER

MEDARIS

RABORN

The ICBM story is well known among defense wonks, but many draw the wrong conclusions. They attribute success largely to Eisenhower designating ballistic missiles as the highest national security priority, which came with a geyser of funding. They say Schriever's Western Development Division (later renamed the Air Force Ballistic Missile Division) and Raborn's Special Projects Office had streamlined processes, less oversight, loose purse strings, and the best talent. *Time*, in its cover story on "Missileman Schriever," presented ICBM development as an inevitability, with little resistance from the services: "The history of the missile has little record of military unwillingness to accept it as the weapon that must be developed at top speed."

These conclusions confuse cause and effect. Polaris and Minuteman didn't succeed because someone labeled them the top priority and threw money at them. We can all think of critical programs with plenty of funding and not much to show for it (GPS modernization and *Virigina*-class submarine production spring to mind today). They succeeded because their leaders—Schriever and Raborn—fought every day to prove that their programs were worthy of less oversight and more funding. The two were exceptional in large part because they were breathing down each other's necks. They were both keenly aware Eisenhower *hadn't* granted them some untouchable forever program where they could fail upwards.

To extract the best performance from our leaders and their disciples, we need to foster demanding environments where success isn't guaranteed and complacency will get you put out to pasture. Sometimes the adversary is too far away or too abstract to stir the necessary motivations. As Schriever and Raborn faced off against each other, neither could afford such a mindset. They served as each other's "great power competitor," to the benefit of us all.

Multiple competing missile programs ensured that the United States quickly possessed a range of options to deter the Soviet Union. In hindsight, some of these efforts seem wasteful. Sapolsky writes, "Looking back it is quite possible to select the 'best missile proposals' (or, conversely, to point to obvious mistakes), but this can be done only because the range of alternatives and their limitations are known." Indeed, Polaris and Minuteman were not even among the initial four missiles selected for development in 1955.

Duplicative programs aren't just useful—often they are the most efficient outcome for the government and the taxpayer. Funding multiple programs is surely cheaper and faster than pursuing full-scale production of the wrong weapon. Multiple bets act as insurance, creating optionality as more information about a technology and operational environment is obtained.

But there's an important corollary to competition: eventually, the competition must crown a winner. Programs can't be funded in perpetuity regardless of results. By crowning Polaris and Minuteman the winners, there were real losers. Thor, Jupiter, and Atlas were swiftly terminated. Titan had a second act through the 1980s until it, too, was killed. In losing Jupiter, the Army lost it all: the funding and the mission. Medaris' Army Ballistic Missile Agency was abolished. He had to watch while his 2,100 engineers at Redstone Arsenal—and the nascent Saturn rocket—were transferred to the newly created, civilian-led NASA. He retired and became a priest. America didn't have time for participation trophies during the Cold War. Programs and careers had to go on the chopping block. This simple dynamic spurred excellence.

Look in the Mirror

How can America regain the competitive spirit and time pressure of the ICBM race? We've fallen a long way from a world where six programs competed to deliver a major capability to a world where we're lucky to have competition at all. The F-35 consolidated the buying of fighter jets across the Air Force, Navy, and Marines, when these should have been three separate programs competing to be America's next fifth-generation fighter. But we're not so far from a reality where the Department of War can rediscover competitive pressures. There are simple ways to increase competition while minimizing the likelihood of waste.

First, the military could have *two* competing program managers within a program executive office (PEO). A PEO is responsible for all elements of a program. Today, the single program manager running a PEO has an unearned monopoly. Imagine if that manager suddenly had to compete against a rival manager every day. The experience would be humbling, challenging, and invigorating. There would be a sense of urgency—driven by the hard-coded desire of Americans to *win*—that is impossible to create when program managers are only judged against the uninspiring triad of cost, schedule, and performance.

The two competing program managers would take the requirements, devise their own acquisition strategies, and compete to deliver capability to the warfighter as quickly as possible. A senior leader from the mission would decide the winner, on a continuous basis. It could be decided that 100 percent of the need would be fulfilled by a single competitor, or it could be 50/50, or anything in between. This would be similar to how the Department of Defense ultimately bought both Minuteman and Polaris. This approach is no different from how a commercial airline might decide to be 100 percent Airbus, 100 percent Boeing, or some mix of the two, a decision that's made continuously on each incremental batch of orders. As a powerful knock-on effect, it would radically increase the competition and agile capacity of the industrial base.

Another approach to competition would be to give combatant commands a small share (say, 2 percent to 5 percent) of the defense budget to compete against the services. The combatant commands have traditionally been excluded from acquisition, but they most intimately understand the needs of the warfighters in their corners of the globe. A common refrain for why combatant commands shouldn't have budget is that the capabilities they buy could generate sustainment costs that the services would then have to bear. Such an objection is easily solved by limiting the scope of the spending to consumables (such as munitions) or mature commercial solutions. Software-as-a-service is a validated business model that makes it relatively easy for companies to turn products on and off at will. Some of our favorite thinkers have further proposed that the Department of War adopt the "as-a-service" model for products that would typically be acquired as a static hardware buy, a change that would afford more flexibility for less traditional buyers, such as combatant commands. For example, rather than buying a tanker, combatant commands would contract for aerial refueling operations. Or, it would be industry, rather than the military, that would own and operate a fleet of unmanned undersea vehicles for missions like sea mine detection and neutralization. Such arrangements already exist today. They are just far less common than they should be.

Even a small amount of funding would introduce competitive pressure on the services to deliver better, faster, and cheaper results. Some of the most successful programs in defense history were developed on shoestring budgets (recall that David Packard was able to develop several pivotal technologies of the Cold War with just $12 million in the 1970s). Imagine what our field commanders could do with a couple billion and the license to spend.

Third, acquisition leaders should have greater flexibility to spend money and change their approach as circumstances demand. With "dynamic budgeting," Congress could act more like a limited partner in a VC firm rather than a bureaucratic bean counter. Instead of haggling over every detail in the portfolio, it could invest in offices and leaders who have compelling theses about how to transform the military and defend the nation. These "VCs," in turn, would make bets on a diverse pool of companies and capabilities. Some of these bets would fail. Enough would be smash hits to underwrite our national security and economic prosperity. Rapid reprogramming of money would create more competition within the government because bad programs wouldn't benefit from the artificial protection of slow spending cycles. And the whole process could move a heck of a lot faster.

The Department of War has tried to externalize competition by calling for more contractors on a given procurement (after calling for *fewer* contractors in the 1990s). It should look in the mirror, internalize competition, and compete with itself. That would be the cheapest weapon the military ever purchased.

CHAPTER 11

The Factory Is the Weapon

To this point, we've focused mostly on how the sausage gets made inside the Pentagon—how it buys weapons, why we spend so much in return for so little, and how to fix it. Now it's time to think about how everything gets made across the American industrial base—from sausage to semiconductors—because the fate of defense industry and commercial industry are intimately linked. We need to think about manufacturing.

As we've seen, the United States drew on deep reserves of expertise and brilliance in the commercial manufacturing sector to win World War II and the Cold War. The Pentagon brass was able to field game-changing technology because the United States empowered founders: executives, engineers, skilled tradesmen, and line workers who loved their country, recognized the stakes, and knew how to build. The American industrial base was unquestionably the country's greatest military asset; our national security hinged on the vitality and innovation of commercial companies.

Many of our problems today stem from the brute fact that our industrial base is smaller and slower than it once was. China's rise (and counterproductive policies in Washington) devastated the industrial heartland. Millions of skilled workers aged out of the workforce, taking vast amounts of implicit knowledge to retirement and the grave. Bureaucracy subverted and suppressed the founder spirit.

As a result, America lost deterrence. If we can't back up our red lines with an endless wave of metal and high explosives, our enemies will cross those red lines. We've seen this lesson play out repeatedly, from Eastern Europe to the Middle East. The stockpile is not the deterrent. Mass production is the deterrent.

A smaller industrial base also causes learning loss. America is forgetting how to build—sometimes literally. In the early 2000s, when the National Nuclear Security Administration refurbished the nuclear warheads used on Trident submarine-launched ballistic missiles, the program was delayed by years because no one remembered how to make a complex aerogel, called "Fogbank," crucial to activating the warhead's second stage. The agency had to spend $69 million to reverse engineer the formula, build a new line, and train workers to recover this lost nuclear knowledge.

The United States will need to relearn a great deal to bring back the American industrial base. Even more important than learning from the past, though, is looking to the future—and dragging it into the present through the process of invention. The mass production of tomorrow will not look like the past. Robotics and digitization are transforming the most advanced factories in the world, propelling China into the lead in mass production. Further advances are within reach, ripe for the plucking. To regain the lead, the United States will not only have to recover manufacturing. It needs to exploit areas where it is still in the lead, like software and AI, to revolutionize manufacturing and leapfrog China.

This chapter is for the builders. It explains how America lost its edge in manufacturing and how it can spark a new, digital Industrial Revolution. We'll meet some of the founders who are putting software-defined manufacturing into practice, bending (and printing) metal in America. But first, we'll meet another founder who warned that American manufacturing was in decline, long before most people even knew there was a problem.

Only the Paranoid Survive

Intel co-founder Andy Grove neatly summed up his life philosophy in the title of his 1996 book: *Only the Paranoid Survive.* He would know. Grove—born András István Gróf—was a Hungarian Jew born in 1936, three years before the outbreak of a war that unleashed hell on Eastern Europe and the Jews. When the Nazis occupied Hungary in 1944, he took on an assumed name and went into hiding with his mother at the house of Christian acquaintances. His father had been conscripted into a labor battalion and sent to the Russian front years earlier.

Young András survived Nazi tyranny only to face communist tyranny on the other side. In 1956, seventeen Red Army divisions rolled into Budapest to crush a student uprising against Hungary's Soviet government. Grove, then a second-year chemistry student at the University of Budapest, heard that the Soviets were rounding people up—young men, students, people like him. So, after much agonizing, he decided to leave, traversing back woods and muddy fields to Austria with the help of a hunchback smuggler. He adopted a new, Americanized name when he reached New York to mark the beginning of a new life.

Grove's experience of total war and the total state bred paranoia. It also bred an ice-cold, sometimes shocking pragmatism that stayed with him long after he became the revered leader of a revolutionary technology company. Decades later, a reporter innocently remarked that the family that had hidden him from the Nazis had done the right thing. Grove responded that it was right only because it worked. "If they had got killed over it, it wouldn't have been the right thing."

As discussed in Chapter 8, Grove's business partner, Bob Noyce, left a personal stamp on Intel and the wider tech world. Silicon Valley's open-door policy, democratic ethos, and tent-revival fervor for technology were byproducts of Noyce's upbringing in the American Midwest. By contrast, Andy Grove brought the steel, urgency, and bluntness (which Intel referred to as "constructive confrontation") of his very different upbringing to his roles as Intel's COO and ultimately CEO. He came up with "OKRs," objectives and key results: concrete goals that are used to judge the performance of employees, divisions, and companies. More fundamentally, Grove believed that every company faces periodic "strategic inflection points," or SIPs: existential events caused by shifts in the market that one journalist likened to the "decisive battle" in military theory. Companies that respond boldly to these inflection points might survive. They might even reap incredible rewards. Companies that don't get crushed and disappeared as surely as the victims of the police state that Grove had escaped.

By the year 1997, Grove's tough-minded management and more than a few high-stakes pivots had turned Intel into a leviathan of semiconductor manufacturing. Nearly 90 percent of the world's new personal computers had "Intel Inside." Intel's $114 billion market cap made it the fifth-largest company in the S&P 500, vaulting over IBM.

To ice the cake, *Time* magazine chose Grove as Man of the Year, the first time a technology CEO had been so honored. Walter Isaacson's article on Grove embodied the euphoric spirit of the age. "The Digital Revolution has created a new economy," it stated. "The old economy was geared to mass production"; the new would be "specialized," based less on making things "spewed from assembly lines" and more on knowing things. The United States of 1997, Isaacson stated boldly, probably enjoyed the healthiest economy "of any nation ever." And Grove was the Moses who had led us to this post-industrial Promised Land.

But as America marched into the new millennium, it became clear that at least one man did not fully believe the hype: Andy Grove. Having stepped down as Intel's CEO, he turned his mind to larger matters. And he believed his country wasn't being nearly paranoid enough.

Grove thought the country's leaders were failing to think seriously about challenges—about possible decisive battles—around the corner. As he wrote in 2007, "if the brutal facts are not faced by the leaders, the brutal reality sets in." He believed America's capacity for scientific and technological achievement was seriously degraded. "Could we pull off the Manhattan Project today? With its complexities of planning and execution, under extreme time pressure? I doubt it." America had lost the need for speed to accomplish great feats.

That was startling enough to hear from America's digital Moses. In 2010, amid the wreckage of the Great Recession, Grove committed a far greater blasphemy: he attacked the New Economy he had supposedly created, along with cherished dogmas of Silicon Valley.

In a cover story for *Bloomberg Businessweek* titled "How to Make an American Job," Grove wrote that American elites fetishized startups as engines of growth, but that startups could only serve this function if they scaled into mature companies that made real things in America—companies like Intel at its peak. The problem, Grove wrote, was that the scaling process had broken. Some startups were still becoming hugely valuable, measured by market cap and stock performance, but they weren't engines of American power like the companies of yesteryear. The New Economy had, quite consciously, separated services, or "knowledge work," from production. Under this bifurcated model, a relatively small number of highly educated, highly compensated Americans performed very profitable, specialized services, while outsourcing production to armies of contractors in Asia. The phrase on iPhone boxes reflects this approach: "Designed by Apple in California. Assembled in China."

The root of the problem, Grove wrote, was "a general undervaluing of manufacturing—the idea that as long as 'knowledge work' stays in the U.S., it doesn't matter what happens to factory jobs." Not true, he said. When mass production leaves, it breaks the "chain of experience" that enables subsequent innovation and production. He predicted, with uncanny foresight, that China would dominate the industries of the future, such as EV batteries, because it dominated supposedly low-value, commodity production today. He made this prediction long before Chinese companies like BYD and CATL rose to prominence.

The solution, Grove wrote, was to "rebuild our industrial commons." Business leaders had to acknowledge their "responsibility to maintain the industrial base on which we depend." Washington, for its part, had to "develop a system of financial incentives" to make domestic manufacturing attractive, such as "an extra tax on the product of offshored labor" (otherwise known as a tariff), the proceeds of which could be reinvested in scaling US manufacturing. The pivot needed to happen fast, or America would lose. "If we want to remain a leading economy," Grove concluded, "we change on our own, or change will continue to be forced upon us."

Grove's manifesto prompted much debate, and more than a little bewilderment, in the Valley. "I can't believe what I read this weekend from Andy Grove," one venture capitalist wrote in *The Wall Street Journal*. Tech was booming. Silicon Valley was the beating heart of global innovation. "So what if we have outsourced 100,000s of low-level semiconductor manufacturing jobs to China?"

Grove was warning that the decisive battle was upon us. Most didn't know it was even taking place.

Andy Grove died in 2016, late enough to see that his prophecies, like Cassandra's, had largely gone unheeded. And why should they have been? The United States had shaken off the Great Recession. Silicon Valley continued to mint SaaS unicorns. Stocks were ripping. Money was cheap and consumer imports cheaper. "Chimerica," Niall Ferguson and Moritz Schularick's term for the fusion of American finance and Chinese production, seemed to be working fine—if you lived in Palo Alto or DC.

Around that time, though, cracks were starting to appear in the façade—caused, notably, by a presidential candidate who talked loudly about how America was getting ripped off on trade. There were other signs. Beijing unveiled a stunningly ambitious industrial strategy, called Made in China 2025, that announced China's intention to dominate high-tech sectors, such as electric vehicles and robotics. Closer to home, Intel fell behind TSMC in logic-chip manufacturing. It never caught up, and spent the next few years plowing money into stock buybacks instead of investing in fabs. For the first time since the invention of the transistor, American companies were not at the bleeding edge of semiconductor manufacturing.

That was a decade ago. Subsequent events, like the coronavirus pandemic and Russia's invasion of Ukraine, further vindicated Grove's views about the decline of American manufacturing and its serious consequences for the economy and especially for national security. In 2025, the US government took a nearly $9 billion equity stake in Intel to help the company to catch up.

In the next section, we'll discuss the fundamental reasons why American manufacturing fell behind, and how some of the most innovative founders in the world are bringing it back with futuristic factories.

The Software Is the Platform

Building a competitive manufacturing sector ultimately hinges on the problem of productivity: how can we organize a range of inputs, including human work (labor), technology, and management practices, to make the most valuable possible outputs?

Judged by this standard, American manufacturing is in a troubling, decades-long stall. In 2023, the total factor productivity of US manufacturing was lower than at any point since 2003, which means that today's industrial base is roughly as efficient as it was when George W. Bush was a first-term president and Facebook was a twinkle in Mark Zuckerberg's eye.

This fact is more disturbing when we consider the technological advances that have taken place elsewhere in the economy over the same period. In the past two decades, the iPhone was introduced. Software ate the world. Data shifted to the cloud. Cars started driving themselves. Artificial intelligence put brains in machines. These are productivity-boosting technologies. And indeed, total factor productivity for the whole economy has steadily increased, just as one would expect. Yet this revolution seemingly passed by US manufacturing, one of the most critical sectors to our national security. Why?

Total Factor Productivity in the US Manufacturing Sector

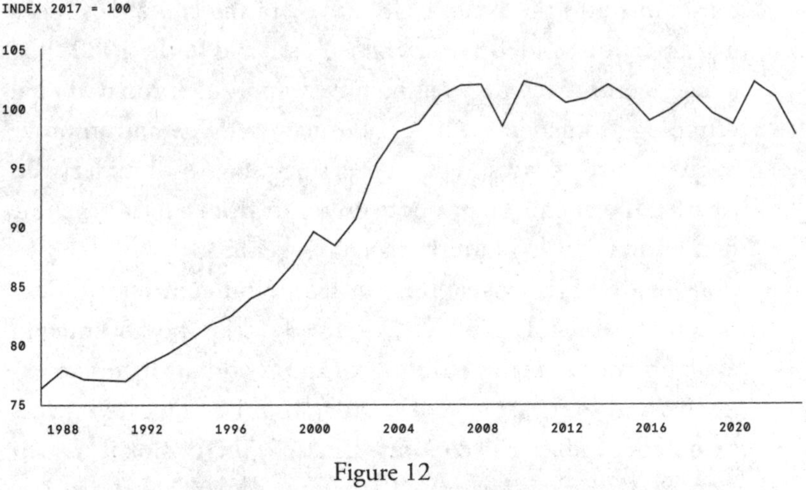

Figure 12

The causes of this productivity puzzle are complex, but several explanations jump out.

The first is underinvestment. Private investment in capital goods like factories and machine tools had been declining for thirty years, roughly since the fall of the Berlin Wall. Declining investment means that US manufacturing companies were competing with older factories and older tools during a global boom in factory building and automation.

We can see this by comparing levels of automation across countries, measured by robot density, or the number of industrial robots relative to a country's manufacturing workforce. South Korea had more than 1,000 industrial robots per 10,000 workers in 2023, according to the International Federation of Robotics. China had 470 robots, but was by far the world's leader in number of robots installed each year. The United States had just 295 robots per 10,000 workers, despite being a much richer country. And the problem extends beyond robots. As Rob Atkinson of the Information Technology and Innovation Foundation points out, the average US factory in the late 2010s was a quarter-century old, up from sixteen years old in the 1980s; the average age of machinery has increased, too. Adoption of digital technology to generate sales, coordinate activity, and improve manufacturing processes has been sluggish. Any builder who has tried to get an instant quote on a part from a local machine shop knows that US industry is falling behind.

A second factor weighing on US manufacturing productivity is overregulation. We've already seen how Pentagon regulations have made building weapons and airplanes an expensive and long struggle. The story could be repeated across the broader industrial economy. In 2023, the National Association of Manufacturers found that the regulatory burden imposed on manufacturers was more than double the burden on non-manufacturing companies, due largely to environmental regulations. This regulatory bill amounted to $29,000 per manufacturing worker. Even worse, regulations greatly increase the time it takes for new factories to be built. Wasted time means that each new factory that comes online becomes obsolete faster and has less time to recoup its costs.

One of the consequences of overregulation was to shift capital, talent, and energy away from industrial projects into relatively less regulated, and therefore more attractive, industries. Peter Thiel has described this as a double standard, "in which bits were unregulated and atoms were regulated." The Digital Revolution was a (positive) side effect of this double standard. Other investment poured into finance, logistics, and high-end services. Growth in these fields masked the relative decline of manufacturing, suppressed by regulation.

Another consequence of overregulation was offshoring, as corporations shifted production overseas to avoid higher labor and regulatory compliance costs at home. This shift explains, in part, why corporations look and sound so different today than they did a generation ago. Modern, multinational industrial companies may be headquartered in America, yet their production is spread across many countries and continents. In many cases, these companies have spun off supposedly non-core functions to third-party suppliers. The wings on your American jet could be from Italy, the landing gear from Czechia, and so on, made by second-tier and third-tier suppliers, with all the parts of this global supply chain coming together at the factory for final assembly. In theory, the multinational model allows companies to focus on the highest-value, core activities of its business, while arbitraging the costs of domestic and in-house production. They become master assemblers and managers of global supply chains. In practice, however, the multinational model has made companies hostages to global events, from pandemics to trade wars, while weakening their understanding of how the parts in their products are made. Globalization may have been good for stock valuations in the short term, but innovation and quality eventually suffer when your production is done far away by other people. You have to be in the room where it happens to learn and grow.

Finally, labor force and skills issues have made manufacturing less competitive. This problem is largely cultural. For decades, American policymakers and tastemakers dismissed manufacturing as a relic of the "old economy" (remember the *Time* article from 1997). Mostly they ignored it, taking for granted that the nation that produced General Electric and Intel would retain its lead in the manufacturing that counted. This cultural devaluation translated to underinvestment in technical and STEM education and, ultimately, brain drain in the manufacturing workforce. Elite university graduates who in past generations might have gone to work for GM or Bell Labs (or started their own company) went to work in finance or at Facebook instead. Less educated workers were shunted into lower-paying service jobs instead of factory jobs offering better pay and higher satisfaction.

The combination of underinvestment, overregulation, and brain drain explains why America's industrial base has lost so much ground. It also helps to explain the rift that opened between "software" and "hardware," between Silicon Valley startups and legacy defense companies. Bending metal and writing code are seen as unrelated and perhaps oppositional activities. In this view, you can either be a producer for the Old Economy or a disruptor for the New Economy. Andy Grove knew that was a false choice: hardware and software reinforce one another. Software breathes life into inert metal; hardware gives ephemeral code the ability to reach out and touch you. Combining the two is a superpower. We saw what that superpower could achieve during the Cold War, when Silicon Valley technologists wrote code, forged chips, and used them to manufacture some of the most advanced machines ever made. Tech and manufacturing need each other. It's time to reunite the houses.

Reversing America's industrial decline will require changes in attitude, policy, and priorities. It will require us to come to terms with mistakes made in the past and with the current state of play in global manufacturing, where the United States is distant second to a rising China. Above all, it will require government and industry to adopt new approaches to revitalize our industrial commons, as Grove counseled two decades ago.

Refocusing on manufacturing doesn't mean we have to "become like China" as some fear (although we should be humble enough to admit that its economic model has proven more dynamic than many Western observers predicted). Nor does it mean we should abandon the New Economy of technology and high-skilled services, which has produced many incredible advances. Instead, we should harness the country's asymmetric advantages in technology to leapfrog China and fuel a genuine revival of domestic manufacturing.

Creating this system will require ruthlessly eliminating regulations and red tape that stand in the way of industrial projects and infrastructure development. The Trump administration's deregulatory actions are a start, but Congress can and should follow up with a serious effort to slash red tape and expedite projects. No doubt deregulation will have critics and externalities, but a bipartisan coalition for reform exists, from the "Tech Right" and traditional business interests to a center-left increasingly concerned with rebuilding state capacity.

Revitalization will also require changes from businesses, which have spent decades building global supply chains that are now in peril, and which in many cases are hostages to a hostile communist country. We don't think it's too much to ask that these companies rediscover a sense of patriotism, but if they don't rebuild at home out of principle, they should do so out of self-interest. The world has reached a strategic inflection point, as Grove would say, with rising trade barriers and the emergence of economic blocs. Companies will have to pick sides and relentlessly innovate, or else they will be caught in the crossfire and left for dead in no man's land.

More important to reindustrialization than any single policy change is a culture change—a shift in perspective. We need to give manufacturing its due as an activity intimately linked to our security and worthy of our time, attention, and concern. We also need to reject the false choice between "bits" and "atoms" or "software" and "hardware," which contributed to the stagnation and brain drain of America's industrial sector. The truth is that their fates are linked. Our response should be to link them in practice, using our aptitude in software and services to level up and revolutionize the way we build. We should use digital power to boost production power.

Technology is the key to surviving the strategic inflection point and reviving production, and that fact should give us hope. Cutting-edge factories are built on a digital foundation, and the United States still has a considerable lead in digital technology. China has a deep industrial base with impressive levels of automation, but it has zero globally competitive enterprise software companies to serve as the native nervous center of its factories. By contrast, this is an area where the United States excels. And while DeepSeek demonstrated that China has a serious AI contender, the United States and its allies have many outstanding AI companies and a sizeable lead. With the right investment, policy support, industry buy-in, and spirit of heretical optimism we can build modern, highly automated factories and warehouses with digital nerves.

Achieving this goal means inverting the way we think about manufacturing. We tend to think about products in terms of their finished, material form. A smartphone is the slim yet substantial black mirror we hold in our hands. An F-35 is thirty tons of metal, composites, jet fuel, and explosives sitting in a hanger. The conventional way to think about factories is similar: the factory is the metal forest of structures, raw materials, machine tools, forklifts, and workers that make the product. We understand that there's a digital layer, making the factory hum and the screen dance on our phone. But for most users (and even many producers), software is an afterthought rather than the main event.

What if we flipped that on its head? What if factories and products were built around software, not the other way around? In this paradigm, the material world is designed for maximum manipulability by software—and therefore, by human beings. Factories would be laid out so every machine and component is legible and changeable from a digital command center. Hardware would be designed with a unified software OS capable of touching and tweaking its every component in real time. Managers and line workers would be able to see into the system, reach into its guts, and make near-instantaneous changes to improve efficiency and clear bottlenecks. Recall that US manufacturing is in the middle of a productivity slump. The way to end the slump and supercharge productivity is to unleash technology in the factory, with software at the center.

"Software-defined manufacturing," as this paradigm is called, isn't new or untested. It's already used to build some of the most impressive products in the world, commercial and military.

Tesla's Model S was the first-ever "software-defined vehicle"—and this fact was critical to building the first successful new car company of the twenty-first century. Auto analysts famously dismissed Musk's chances. Many still do. The auto sector is notoriously expensive and competitive; it has dashed plenty of egos and fortunes. (Henry Kaiser, one of America's greatest builders, tried and failed to build a car company after World War II; when he told a group of Detroit executives that he was prepared to invest $1 billion in the enterprise, the chairman of General Motors reportedly said, "Congratulations. Give that man one chip.")

But Elon had a couple things these analysts—and existing automakers—did not: an outsider's perspective and an abundance of world-class Silicon Valley software engineers. Legacy automakers were stuck with a "hardware first" mentality. They didn't understand software, it wasn't their core business, and consequently they were happy to outsource it to suppliers and contractors. The result was a patchwork quilt of electronics and software systems, many of which weren't interoperable. In increasingly complex cars, boasting dozens of sensors, chips, and electronic control units, this was a recipe for clunky, frustrating, and bug-ridden vehicles.

Tesla flipped the industry trend on its head: instead of focusing solely on the car, it would be a full-stack company. Software would be core to every Tesla, rather than an afterthought. And instead of relying on third parties to manufacture auto parts like electrical components, cables, and fuses, Tesla would do as much of the production in-house as possible, producing and iterating parts on pilot assembly lines and only contracting out when it needed to achieve volume. Tesla's vertical integration allowed its engineers, designers, and assembly workers to operate under one roof, gaining implicit knowledge and coordination benefits along the way. "We didn't leverage the way other people built cars," recalled Craig Carlson, Tesla's vice president of software and electrical integration during the company's early years. "But we were also kind of ignorant about how they'd been developed in the past." What he calls ignorance was in fact a competitive advantage in an industry set in its ways. Tesla vehicles would have a unified software architecture and cutting-edge electronics throughout, including constant Wi-Fi connectivity, creating an excellent and fully customizable driver experience. Because it controlled its software stack, Tesla could also push instantaneous, "over-the-air" updates to every vehicle in its fleet. The company's software-first approach means that it can fine-tune vehicles years after they drive off the lot. Japanese manufacturers have a concept, *kaizen*, that means "continuous improvement." Tesla's software-defined approach extended *kaizen* from the factory floor to the product itself—even as it was charging overnight in its owner's garage.

Tesla's interconnected fleet and vertical integration have also enabled continuous improvements in its manufacturing process. The typical product development cycle in the auto industry is measured in years. Predictability and consistency are viewed as synonyms for quality, so factory assembly lines are "locked" for long periods, producing a single, consistent type of vehicle. Minor improvements are bundled into packages and rolled out every couple of years. Tesla turned this practice on its head, too. Taking a page from software development, Tesla engineered its factories so that changes to work instructions can be implemented on active assembly lines. As early as 2017, the company's former head of production, Greg Reichow, could report that Tesla was implementing up to fifty such changes every week. What this means, practically speaking, is that a Tesla that drives itself off the assembly line of a Gigafactory in the afternoon might be subtly different from one that drove off the line that morning. As Reichow wrote, "We often joked that if you wanted to know the 'model year' of your Tesla, you needed to look at the individual car's VIN number." This is yet another radical application of *kaizen*.

Tesla was the prime mover in software-defined manufacturing, but now it has company. At Palantir, we've experienced a surge of interest from industrial companies seeking to level up their digital operations. Palantir's industrial customers use our software platform—including our manufacturing-specific OS, Warp Speed—to improve resource management and quality control and boost output of some of the most complex products known to man. Airbus, for instance, used Palantir Foundry to scale production of the A350, a wide-body, dual-aisle passenger jet with millions of components and a global supply chain. It was able to increase production by a third by fusing data on parts, deliveries, defects, and more into a single platform that could be operated by its line workers. Similarly, Panasonic uses our software to train workers for its EV battery factory in Nevada by pairing them with an AI copilot that can visually flag parts that need to be manipulated or repaired. The company is able to take workers with a high school education and no prior experience in manufacturing and bring them up to the level of Japanese career technicians in months, not years.

Perhaps the best example of software-first manufacturing in defense is Anduril, the innovative company we first met in Chapter 8. The company's head of manufacturing, Keith Flynn, is a twenty-year veteran of mass production who got his start at Toyota, one of the world's strongest legacy automakers, and then went to Tesla, which opened his eyes to the possibilities of a software-first approach.

The decline in defense manufacturing, Anduril says, ultimately was caused by the customer (or as we call it, the monopsony). Weak demand signals and small buys dribbled out over long periods of time hollowed out industrial capacity. Mass production is like a muscle: if you don't use it, it atrophies. Mass production also requires huge amounts of capital upfront. As Anduril's chief business officer (and former Palantirian) Matt Steckman notes, "you're mid-eight figures before anything interesting starts to happen." Most companies recoil from those kinds of investments to upgrade facilities and keep manufacturing lines warm when the only customer won't commit to buying the products on the other end; it would be betting the company on the whims of appropriators and bureaucrats.

The result is an industrial base that's small, undercapitalized, and wholly divorced from what it takes to succeed in the punishing world of mass production. "You don't have to be really good at low volume production," Keith says. Only when the numbers ramp up are world-class manufacturers separated from mediocrities. Just as bad, a small-volume industrial base makes the military even more risk-averse in what it chooses to buy. If the United States can only make a few dozen fighter jets a year, naturally the military will put all its chips on "proven" designs that are as exquisite as possible. It won't be getting any more.

Anduril was founded to turn these dynamics on their head, and it's putting serious money behind this effort. In early 2025, the company announced Arsenal-1, a "hyperscale manufacturing facility" in Columbus, Ohio, which will be built with $1 billion in private capital. Production is expected to start in 2026, with an eventual aim to replicate the Arsenal model in other states and allied countries.

Anduril's factories and weapons start with software. The company's operating system, Lattice, serves as the common foundation of its offerings, from intelligence, surveillance, and reconnaissance capabilities on the Southern border to unmanned fighter jets like Fury, which the Air Force is testing for its Collaborative Combat Aircraft program. The unified software layer means these disparate systems and sensors can talk to each other, trade intelligence, and choreograph movements. The military talks a big game about jointness; software is how you achieve it, not requirements documents or drawn-out bureaucratic processes. A software-first approach means that every part of the product lifecycle—from design, to production, to service and sustainment—can be tweaked and improved over time.

Anduril designs its products for manufacturability. Taking a page from the Tesla playbook, the company focuses ruthlessly on simplification. Legacy defense products are gold-plated, with sprawling supply chains, production in all fifty states (and many foreign countries), and materials and manufacturing processes so exotic that some are classified. Anduril takes the opposite approach, searching for commercial substitutes that are widely available and cost competitive. The company boasts that the fuselage of its Barracuda cruise missile is made with the same manufacturing process used to make bathtubs. Anduril also consolidates production geographically, to liberate itself from vulnerable, international supply chains and unlock the process synergies that come from comingling talent and technology. Such unorthodox methods would never fly in the world of bespoke defense contracting, but they're the recipe for production at speed and scale. Anduril can flood the zone with super-fast, software-powered "bathtubs" in a crisis—and that's central to its appeal for a military in desperate need of mass. As the company states in its manifesto, "Rebuilding the Arsenal," using technology for mass production means "manufacturing becomes a product unto itself." The faster producer wins on the battlefield.

4D Chess

We hope that these examples have shown that software-defined manufacturing is the future—and the key to leapfrogging China. To understand more deeply what it looks like in practice, we need to travel to Los Angeles, where another company is proving that revolutionary products can still be Made in America.

Kevin Czinger is the founder (along with his son, Lukas) of Divergent Technologies, a digital manufacturing company that reached unicorn status in 2023. Born and raised in Cleveland, Czinger saw the American industrial base in its heyday. Evidence of manufacturing's centrality to the American way of life was all around. He remembers the North American X-15 rocket plane booming overhead while he sat at the library, poring over the works of John von Neumann, the twentieth-century polymath (and, like Andy Grove, a Hungarian Jewish émigré) who theorized about a "Universal Constructor," or a machine capable of replicating itself. Closer to home, Czinger and his older brothers tinkered with cars, motorcycles, and anything else with an engine. His brothers went to trade school and the Army; Kevin was the first in his family to go to college, attending Yale on a football scholarship. Today, at age sixty-six, Kevin has the wiry frame and California tan of an athlete.

After stints in the Marine Corps Reserve, law, and finance, Czinger returned to manufacturing in middle age. It was a very different world than the one in which he had grown up. Cleveland, previously one of the richest cities in the United States, was now among its poorest. Decades of overregulation and outsourcing had strip-mined the country of manufacturing. Then, in the early to mid-2000s, the China Shock had ripped through the industrial heartland, dealing a fatal blow to countless manufacturing towns.

Czinger's first startup, CODA Automotive, was a lesson in the new, global landscape of manufacturing—and in the school of hard knocks. The company was ahead of its time in many respects, producing a fully electric mass-market sedan before Elon Musk's Roadster hit the pavement. But the car didn't find a receptive audience. The public wasn't ready for EVs, and wouldn't be for many years. The Detroit automakers were dismissive and "short-termist," in Czinger's words, confident of their long-term superiority and blind to threats on the horizon. The Obama administration dangled but ultimately failed to deliver advanced-manufacturing funds, which Czinger planned to use to build a battery factory in Ohio. In a sign of the times, practically the only enthusiastic business partner was the Chinese government, which pledged hundreds of millions of dollars for a joint venture between CODA and a Chinese battery maker. The Chinese battery factory got built; the Ohio factory didn't.

And in 2013, CODA filed for bankruptcy, bringing the experiment to a bitter end.

The idea for Divergent sprang from CODA's ashes.

Czinger's experience convinced him of two key facts. First, auto manufacturing was stuck in the past. Even relatively modern methods, like the lean manufacturing pioneered by Toyota, were variations on the mass production model introduced by Henry Ford more than a century ago. It was all incredibly wasteful, in money, time, materials, and environmental impact. Second, and perhaps more significant, China was the world heavyweight champion of this type of manufacturing. It had the workforce, the supply chains, and strong support at the highest levels of government. Over the course of the decade, these advantages would compound as China employed vast numbers of industrial robots in true "lights out" factories. It was a bitter pill to swallow, but necessary: China had won this round. "We're [still] talking about Industry 4.0," Czinger told us. "China has already done it." He concluded that if America wanted to win, it would have to leap ahead to an entirely new production paradigm. Like any good founder, he decided to build it himself.

Divergent's Los Angeles factory is like none other in the world because it is modeled on a three-step, proprietary manufacturing method used nowhere else in the world: the Divergent Adaptive Production System (DAPS).

The first step is design. The design process starts like all modern manufacturing, with an idea of the product that's going to be built and the constraints defining that product, in the form of digital engineering files. These inputs are fed into Divergent's AI-powered design software, which digitally optimizes the design to reduce the number of parts and the amount of material used, within specified performance tolerances. For larger designs, like cruise missiles or car bodies, the optimization software also breaks the design into modules for ease of assembly.

The second step is additive manufacturing. Divergent's digitally optimized designs are sent to a massive 3D printer, which uses lasers to sculpt blocks of application-specific metal alloys into modules. We use the word "sculpt" intentionally. The final products of Divergent's additive manufacturing are intricate and beautiful, with Antoni Gaudí–like undulating curves and lattice interiors dreamt up by an AI brain to save weight without sacrificing performance. The shapes are organic, like the interior of a cave or a beehive. A Divergent 3D printer can produce a module two feet across by two feet high in less than a day. It can start on the next module immediately, with minimal downtime. The company's ability to scale is limited only by its fleet of printers and the availability of raw materials.

The third and final step is assembly. In normal factories—even cutting-edge factories with minimal human intervention—assembly is done linearly, in a series of steps on a line that is unique to the good being produced. A factory line for smartphones produces smartphones and nothing else. To change the product, the line would have to be retooled, a process that can take months.

Divergent's method of assembly is as revolutionary as its design and production. 3D printed modules are joined by a forest of industrial robots and machines capable of assembling any product that can be made with the company's 3D printers, with zero custom tools or reconfiguration required. This assembly line can make trucks, performance super cars, cruise missile airframes, or practically anything made of metal. Czinger boasts that his system can even build new DAPS factories, thus bringing humanity one step closer to von Neumann's dream of the Universal Constructor—or perhaps, a *Star Trek* replicator. Only science-fiction metaphors seem appropriate to describe advances of this magnitude.

The Czinger production process is built around what he calls the "Four Ds": digitize, dematerialize, distribute, and democratize. Together, these attributes illustrate the revolutionary potential of software-defined manufacturing.

Digitize: Custom-developed software powers production, from design through assembly. The same software binds all aspects of production into a seamless, end-to-end process, coordinating robots and giving humans unprecedented control.

Dematerialize: AI-powered design reduces the number of parts and wasted material, creating simpler, cheaper, and environmentally friendly products without sacrificing performance.

Distribute: Because the Divergent process is end to end, with a small footprint, eventually the company's omni-factories could be spread across the country and the world, supplying military bases and commercial customers one door over. This would dramatically simplify supply chains and logistics, while strengthening resilience. In a major war, industrial parks will be at the top of the target list for bombardment and sabotage. If every military base, airstrip, and arsenal has a built-in factory, the enemy's job is many times harder.

Democratize: Perhaps the most revolutionary aspect of Divergent's work is how it could transform *who* qualifies as a manufacturer. Divergent promises to unleash the creative potential of everyone with an idea. Separating design from production has already transformed many parts of the economy. For example, today "fabless" chip companies like NVIDIA and AMD design chips that are manufactured on contract by foundries like TSMC. A similar division exists in other segments of manufacturing (Hon Hai Precision Industry Co., better known as Foxconn, is the supreme example of an electronics contract manufacturer). Divergent could take it to the next level. In the future, Czinger envisions, original equipment manufacturers like Boeing and Ford won't be the only players capable of making planes or cars. Anyone with a CAD file and a dream could hire Divergent as an omni-contractor to refine, produce, and assemble hardware on demand. Think cars by Gucci, or missiles designed by an officer on the back of an Army and Navy Club cocktail napkin.

If Divergent succeeds in this game of 4D chess, it will be a technological leap for manufacturing as large as the leap from the mainframe to the PC. Previously, computers were massive, expensive, and accessible only to an elite in academia and government who had the resources and training to use them. Andy Grove and Steve Jobs changed that, putting a computer in every household and ultimately every pocket. Kevin Czinger and Divergent want to take the same leap with factories, vaulting China and putting the United States back on top.

We can't say whether Divergent will succeed in sparking this new industrial revolution. But we can say that any revolution that brings America back from the brink will depend on founders as bold as Kevin Czinger. A manufacturing revival depends on technology that's battle tested and validated in the crucible of the commercial market. That's where the rubber meets the road, taking technology from the world of sci-fi pipe dreams and lab experiments to real-life revolutions. Early signs are promising for Divergent, which has a mix of commercial and defense customers.

On the defense side, Divergent's production process has manufactured spare parts and entire weapons systems. Czinger boasts that Divergent produced a flight-critical part for the C-130 Hercules whose original supplier had long since gone out of business. The time it took Divergent to make the part, from order to delivery, was three days—and AI-powered optimization reduced the part's weight by half. Divergent also partnered with General Atomics, maker of the Predator drone, on an unmanned aerial system. It reduced the number of parts in the airframe from 184 to four, boosted the rate of production, halved the cost, and saved 5 percent on weight, to boot. Those are SpaceX-sized performance improvements. They show, if there was ever any doubt, the transformative effects that technology can have—when the military chooses to use it.

Like many of the founders profiled in this book, Czinger didn't get his start selling to the Department of War. If you get him talking, it's clear that his passion is cars—fast cars. One of the company's earliest products was a hypercar, the Czinger 21C, created by subsidiary Czinger Vehicles. And Divergent has found rapid success as a tier-one supplier to luxury automakers like Bugatti, Aston Martin, and Mercedes Benz. The company's alien-like, 3D-printed hardware is now inside some of the most exclusive and expensive sports cars on the planet.

The Czinger 21C—a $2.1 million, 1,250-horsepower hypercar with a top speed of 219 miles per hour—is the pinnacle of Divergent's manufacturing applied to a performance-driven, consumer product. The car's lean, wicked chassis was designed, printed, and assembled in house. And it competes with the best. Czinger has been dogfighting for lap records at fabled racecourses like the Circuit of the Americas and Laguna Seca since 2021, neck and neck with storied carmakers like McLaren and Koenigsegg.

The Czinger 21C has a small production run now: eighty cars, all priced well beyond the reach of the ordinary driver. But Czinger sees a future where Divergent's methods are employed even in mass-production vehicles. DAPS has already been validated in the marketplace and on the unforgiving pavement of the track. All it needs is scale. Then, we would truly be in an uncharted world of software-defined manufacturing. China, Detroit, and countless legacy manufacturers would be playing checkers, while Kevin Czinger plays 4D chess.

Kevin and Lukas Czinger stand next to the Czinger 21C.

These examples show that a different future is possible for American manufacturing. We have the technology, the skills, the capital, and the motive to rebuild. What's needed is willpower, plus cultural and political changes to place mass production back at the center of our economy and military.

In the twentieth century, great technologists like Andy Grove served as the human bridge between the New Economy of technology and the supposedly Old Economy of manufacturing. A new crop of heroes is emerging today to do the same, from Palmer Luckey at Anduril to Kevin Czinger at Divergent to the dozens of young guns in El Segundo, California, building hard-tech startups in fields like aerospace and nuclear engineering. The story of American manufacturing for most of the twenty-first century has been of sadly avoidable decline. We're confident that's not the end of the story.

The future of American mass production is Anduril's Arsenals pumping out sleek, software-powered drones by the thousands. It's hundreds of Divergent factories printing and robotically assembling vehicle chasses, airframes, and parts, on demand and on the same day. It's dozens of startups whose founders and names are still obscure, but that will forge a New Industrial Revolution.

In the next chapter, we'll talk about the leadership, grit, and vision it takes for companies just like these to succeed.

CHAPTER 12

Anti-Playbook for Founders

All happy organizations are alike; each unhappy organization is unhappy in its own way. Happy organizations are laser-focused on winning. By creating a culture around the primacy of winning, they provide every member with an easy-to-use compass: are my actions moving the organization toward its ultimate goal (winning), or away from it? Management treatises and theories of organizational optimization often pontificate at length about the purpose of the corporation while missing this fundamental point. Key metrics, stock prices, and product roadmaps may be leading or lagging indicators of winning, but they should never be confused with the thing itself. Winning is about fulfilling your mission, delivering outcomes, and going faster, higher, and further than anyone thought possible. If you accomplish that, then the numbers will take care of themselves.

I (Shyam) developed the "primacy of winning" to inspire and build Palantir's engineering team, but the concept is as old as business and warfare. For soldiers, winning is a matter of freedom or servitude, life or death for themselves, their homeland, their families, and their friends. It is the most important thing. Existential risks are excellent motivators.

Despite its importance, the primacy of winning does not lend itself to a prescribed set of rules. For that reason, what follows is an anti-playbook for building (or reforming) a winning organization, which our country will need to revitalize its military and defense sector. We share pitfalls to avoid and mindsets to cultivate, but winning is inherently messy and complicated. Learning to win is as much a matter of repetition and reflex as conscious strategy. As champion cyclist Greg LeMond said, "it doesn't get easier, you just get faster."

A government agency and a seed-stage startup that are both winning will look remarkably similar, in large part because they are composed of people. Those people will be fired up, empowered by their leaders, and driving relentlessly to achieve the ultimate goal. The conditions (and scale) may differ, but human tendencies are consistent. The right culture amplifies the best while suppressing the worst.

The Person Is the Program

In the beginning of every revolutionary endeavor, there was a founder. The first lesson to learn about the primacy of winning is the primacy of people.

A founder is someone who forges something from nothing—who has the inspiration to move humanity from zero to one. That's why we often think of founders in the context of startups: Steve Jobs or Bill Gates founding legendary companies in their garages, or the Traitorous Eight abandoning Shockley Semiconductor to found Fairchild, or Gordon Moore and Bob Noyce defecting from Fairchild, in turn, to found Intel. That's also why founders are so closely associated with the formation of nation-states: we call George Washington, Alexander Hamilton, and Thomas Jefferson "Founding Fathers" for a reason. However, the act of founding can also take place within an existing organization, usually when a founder figure creates a new unit within the organization or hijacks an old one and shepherds it to greatness over the course of many years. This is typically how revolutionary feats of invention occur within government and the defense industry, as borne out by the careers of so many heretical heroes we have profiled in this book. Kelly Johnson's Skunk Works, for instance, started as a secret division within Lockheed, noted for its thick culture and virtually boundless freedom of action. Similarly, America wouldn't have launched its first nuclear-powered submarine in fewer than seven years without Hyman Rickover and the singular culture he created within Naval Reactors. The person is the program.

There's a reason that Rickover was the director of naval reactors for more than thirty years: he had an almost uncanny ability to see into the future and realize what his organization would need to succeed. Rickover understood that nuclear power was a unique technology that required a unique organization and culture. Well before the nuclear incidents at Three Mile Island and Chernobyl, he realized that nuclear power's reputation and viability hinged on its safety record; the public would not be willing to fund, much less send its sons to operate, technology they thought fundamentally unsafe. So, he insisted on stringently high safety standards, for the crew and the environment. This included reactor shielding well beyond what most scientists at the time deemed necessary to protect the crew.

The Soviet navy used far less shielding, which made its boats lighter and faster—but exposed the crews to dangerous levels of radiation. Soviet submariners had mandated rest periods between deployments so their bone marrow could regenerate. There were so many deaths from accidents that the Soviet navy built common graves at submarine bases. Meanwhile, Rickover's legacy lives on with a continued safety record of zero fatal submarine reactor accidents (the United States has lost nuclear submarines due to mechanical failures, but none due to reactor issues).

Similarly, Rickover didn't bet the farm on his own genius. He knew he needed the best talent, at every level, to ensure that the standards he set were followed—and to freelance, when circumstances demanded. So, Rickover hand-selected a team of all stars, personally grilling every applicant for the large and growing organization. He picked submariners with sharp minds and, more important, with excellent leadership potential and the demonstrated ability to act in the face of adversity. Once admitted, he guided his flock in their careers with the personal and hands-on devotion of a father. Critically, though, he gave his employees the agency to make high-stakes decisions in the field when lives were on the line. Rickover often ended phone calls with an impatient, "Do what is right!" His disciples almost always did.

What winning lesson can we take from Rickover's example? We learn that talent is not fungible. Talent–problem fit is rare and hard and determinative. When the right person is attached to the right problem, he should be protected and encouraged at all costs.

Unfortunately, this is the opposite of how the military manages talent today. The Defense Officer Personnel Management Act (DOPMA) of 1980 governs the careers and promotions of military officers. DOPMA makes it almost impossible to create a founder-led organization. Officers are rotated to new assignments every two to three years, on average, just long enough to ensure that they haven't had time to build anything of consequence. Under today's DOPMA constraints, Drew Cukor's five-year tenure at Maven is considered exceptionally lengthy. It shouldn't be. Knowledge and know-how compound. We need to care more about winning than about forcing officers to fill out a bingo card for promotion.

This is where congressional oversight can be a boon rather than a burden. Congress should protect heretical founders that the services would prefer to rotate or eject as a matter of convenience. Rickover made plenty of enemies in the Navy. Elmo Zumwalt, a former chief of naval operations, said, "the US Navy's enemies were first, the Soviet Union and second, Hyman Rickover." Yet Congress intervened when Rickover was wrongly passed over for promotion to rear admiral, and intervened again—and again—when he needed exceptions to the mandatory retirement age of sixty-two (Rickover, who retired at eighty-two, got many such extensions). Congress didn't offer the same protection to Drew Cukor—but it should have.

Founders are outlier talent. They most closely resemble the best artists: creative, difficult, and capable of prodigious output. You can't manage artists. You can only create artist colonies with the conditions for their talent to flourish. If you want to win, you need to unleash these outliers on big problems, and give them the space and time to come up with a masterpiece.

Taking the Quantum Leap

Humans are status-seeking creatures. Since the days of the cave and the tribe, we crave legibility, a clear sense of where we sit on the totem pole, and the material rewards we associate with status (such as a larger budget or expense account or a company car). Consequently, the rigid and well-defined organization chart is like a siren song to strivers: alluring but sure to lead to disaster. At Palantir, there are very few job titles. Whether you've been at the company for one year or ten, you are likely a deployment strategist, a forward deployed engineer, or a product development engineer.

We call this the "quantum organization structure," and it is a quantum leap in getting things done. The quantum organization structure isn't quite the same thing as the mythical "flat organization." It is both flat and hierarchical, functional and horizontal. At any given point in time it manifests in an observed state by organizing around the problem that needs to be solved right now. Then it reorganizes around the next problem with a different structure more appropriate to the new challenge. Because humans are status-seekers, we will find a way to either assert dominance or submit to others. The trick is to give all employees opportunities to inhabit these roles at various points in their career, and to decrease the legibility of the hierarchy so that people aren't automatically cowed into submission—or worse, sycophancy. The artist colony has leaders, but they often emerge in unpredictable ways at unpredictable times.

We consciously cultivate this mindset in employees. New hires at Palantir get to "Ask Me Anything" at an open Q&A, a common practice at technology companies. I (Shyam) do something very uncommon at these sessions: I make all the hires tell me, in unison, to "fuck off." This is step one of establishing a culture that values winning over dogma.

Former Palantirian Nabeel Qureshi writes about how this culture works in practice: "one person showed me an email chain where an entry-level software engineer was having an open, contentious argument with a Director of the company with the entire company (around a thousand people) cc'd." Public interactions like this signal to employees that others can and should be challenged when they're wrong. Palantir employee Dan Cervelli, a prodigy at building user interfaces, was a new hire in 2008 and a former volcanologist—with a volcano's explosive energy. He was arguing with Bob McGrew, former vice president of research at OpenAI, about building a new map in Gotham, our battlefield intelligence product at that time. Bob, who was head of the project, didn't believe it was feasible. Dan did, and what he built during one of our hack weeks was so eye-wateringly impressive that we reorganized violently around it (much to Bob's credit). It changed the trajectory of our business, not only because his product was so good, but because it encouraged us to allow Dan to continuously throw himself off the deep end in pursuit of his convictions and intuitions.

Maybe you're thinking, well, it's nice that Palantir has managed to create a culture that rejects standard organizational charts, but those practices don't apply to a military that has a legislated hierarchy, the chain of command. Such thinking ignores the history of innovation within the Pentagon, where heretical individuals fought for the best ideas to win. Cukor purposefully cultivated an environment within Project Maven that minimized rank to the greatest extent practical. John Boyd, the legendary fighter pilot and strategist, was known to spew all manner of four-letter words at his superiors when they promoted status over truth (Boyd's behavior is perhaps not a model to emulate, but it's proof that radical truth-seeking is possible). We tell the stories of these heretics because they show that things can be different. But it requires subordinates who are free to speak and superiors who aren't overly convinced of their own superiority.

Former Air Force Commander Tony Carr diagnosed the military's culture problem in a viral article, titled "We Need Different Generals." Modern commanders, Carr wrote, "struggle to hear and act on feedback from the field, partially because they surround themselves with hyper-loyalist horse holders who create an insular distortion field preventing the intrusion of unsettling truth." What's more, these leaders are "padlocked on budgets rather than people." They mistake the size of their budget, rather than the brilliance of their team, as the criterion of success.

Companies, including technology companies, are not immune to this dynamic. In fact, it's the default. It's more exaggerated in the military, deeply rooted in centuries of tradition and without mechanisms for course correction short of defeat in war, but not by much. Most companies treat career progression as linear. You start as software engineer I, then you advance to software engineer II, and so on until you reach the zenith of status and hierarchy as head of engineering.

But the career progression of the most exceptionally talented people is not linear. It zigs and zags. Some years it will seem like a rocket. Others might be punctuated by catastrophic failure. Churchill led the disastrous Gallipoli campaign during World War I and was expelled from the government before he helped to save the world as prime minister. In 1942, General Brehon Somervell was simultaneously finishing up construction of the Pentagon while also beginning the boondoggle Canol Project, an expensive, failed effort to establish an oil pipeline in Alaska for energy independence in the event of a Japanese attack on the West Coast. The most successful organizations roll with the punches allowing the best talent to rise to the level of their abilities in their own way. Doing so comes with plenty of false starts, dead ends, and spectacular blowups—but they are worth it for the spectacular achievements and organization-saving "fuck you's." If you lop off the left tail of outcomes, you foreclose the possibility of right-tail outcomes, too.

One way to achieve the quantum organization structure and counteract the rigidity of a linear career path is to decouple position from portfolio.

The traditional model says that you should combine a defined position with a defined portfolio. So, for example, the vice president of digital transformation oversees digital transformation. The promised virtues of this approach are predictability and legibility. But in reality, linking position and portfolio explains why conventional organizations are so often ruthless and dysfunctional. Because things change, and monopolies prevent organizations from responding swiftly and flexibly to change outside of the scope of the monopoly. It simply isn't possible that the leader you appoint for "digital transformation" will always be right about matters in his portfolio, or even have the knowledge to do so. And as we observed in the last section, even the most talented artists and founders go through ups and downs. Not every work is going to be beautiful. But episodic hits transform your business (or mission), and those hits can come from unexpected corners—if you forgo control. That was certainly the case when Schriever kept Colonel Hall close after the Thor failure. Sure enough, the Minuteman missile sprang forth from Hall's brain.

In the military, it's more challenging to decouple position from portfolio, but not impossible. The Naval Ordnance Test Center at China Lake, California designed three-quarters of the air-launched ordnance used in Vietnam. Bill McLean built a legendary engineering organization as the technical director of China Lake for thirteen years. He shared a similar philosophy on how to build a team. McLean's approach, according to author Ron Westrum, was that "Projects should determine the organization, not the reverse. If a key person was needed, McLean tried to recruit that person. He tried to create whatever structure was necessary to build ideas." It was an unpopular approach because it generated chaos: "Functional departments resisted these personnel forays fiercely and fought back as they could." When McLean finally retired in 1967, China Lake shelved his wild ways in favor of predictability. Engineering suffered accordingly.

Reorganizing around artists and their ideas is not a panacea of any kind—it requires constant engagement and examination. But for humble leaders with an appetite for risk and a shrewd eye for talent, it can be an unfair advantage they can use to win.

A Little Rebellion Is a Good Thing

Founders also understand that winning sometimes requires breaking the rules. We're not advocating breaking the law, but there is a case to be made for raging against rules that inhibit progress and the overall mission of an organization. Joseph Heller's *Catch-22* and Franz Kafka's *The Trial* resonate deeply because they skewer and satirize bureaucratic procedures that are often illogical and contradictory. To follow each rule would be to chart a course toward stagnation—or madness. An aversion to arbitrary and absurd authority is nothing if not American. Thomas Jefferson put it best: "A little rebellion every now and then is a good thing."

And a little rebellion is often a condition for survival when your nation is under existential threat. There's a shared understanding that the rule book goes out the window when the nation is at war. The trope of the "wartime general" who bucks the system but gets results exists for this reason. It's a tacit admission that there are circumstances when it is right to break the rules. General Somervell dramatically overspent on the construction of the Pentagon (and even added an additional floor to the design without approval), reasoning that it was easier to ask forgiveness than permission. He was correct: when he delivered the Pentagon ahead of schedule in the middle of World War II, he was met with gratitude; the intense furor and congressional howls over the financials melted away in the face of success.

The IDF's Danny Gold had a similar experience. He rapidly developed the missile defense system Iron Dome without the formal authorities or funding to do so. In early 2009, the State Comptroller of Israel released a report condemning Gold for breaking the rules and "overriding the exclusive jurisdiction of the IDF chief of staff, the minister of defense, and the Israeli government as a whole." The report alleged that billions of shekels and countless man hours had been wasted on a technology that still hadn't been proven. The charges are laughable in retrospect—and they didn't stand up long at the time, either. Within months of the report's publication, Iron Dome intercepted multiple targets in tests. Within two years, the first battery was deployed near Gaza. Iron Dome intercepted its first enemy rocket in April 2011, just five years after Gold announced the project's start. As with Somervell's Pentagon, complaints over funding for Iron Dome quietly became a non-issue.

This last example illustrates another point: waiting to rebel until wartime is often too late. Complacency in peacetime can lead to war. When the United States was mobilizing before its entrance into World War II, Bill Knudsen ignored a Pentagon directive that prohibited locating defense plants within 250 miles of a foreign nation. Following the directive would have prevented him from building in Detroit (bordering Canada), which ultimately accounted for more output than anywhere else during the war.

Similarly, in the early 1960s, John Boyd decided he wasn't happy with the make-work jobs he was assigned at Eglin Air Force Base, so he gave himself a new mission—systemizing his knowledge of flying to determine the performance characteristics of any airplane, at any point in the flight envelope. This was an ambitious and compute-heavy task, in an era when computers filled rooms and computing time was more precious than flight time. Boyd's eccentric project didn't qualify—so he stole the time, running his calculations under the guise of a different, approved project. When this came to light, he was threatened with court martial.

Boyd not only admitted the crime but explained to investigators how he had pulled it off. He was saved by the fact that his findings, which he codified as the energy-maneuverability (E-M) theory, proved immediately useful in predicting how American planes would fare against their Soviet counterparts. Boyd got an award instead of a court martial. E-M would be foundational to the designs of the F-15 Eagle and F-16 Fighting Falcon.

Ultimately, the rule breakers must be convinced of their own righteousness, and must choose their battles carefully. The best defense is being right, as Somervell, Gold, Knudsen, and Boyd demonstrated. Even that might not save you. But a righteous crusade is worth a little rebellion, and a little risk.

Requirements Only Work in Reverse

Winning can't be reverse engineered, although that fact has never stopped the Pentagon from trying with lengthy requirements documents. Technology companies are guilty of this, too. The product manager (PM) role is one of the most desired jobs in the industry for the authority and status it tends to confer. PMs manage an engineering team, create product specifications (requirements), and decide what gets built, when. They are the officers, and their job is to reverse engineer victory with a unit of unruly, generally unmanageable software engineers—the corporate equivalent of *The Dirty Dozen*.

Palantir has PMs, but we reject the standard PM role. We don't hire PMs from outside Palantir (you won't get hired here by grinding on the Ultimate PM Interview Study Plan). In fact, the only way to become a PM at Palantir is to have first worked as a forward deployed engineer or a deployment strategist—our version of combat experience. In other words, you must have a proven record of being in the field with customers and understanding firsthand how Palantir's product is—or is not—solving their problem. If an engineer never felt a customer's pain up close, there's little chance he will relieve it from far away, fancy title or not.

Even with these precautions against divorcing requirements from reality, the temptation to perfect a roadmap in the quietude of an office is always present. For that reason, PMs are expected to regularly travel to customer sites to see with their own eyes how their decisions affect outcomes. Palantir has product roadmaps, but they are neither sacred nor overly prescriptive. For every product breakthrough we've had, the requirements for that breakthrough could only be written down on paper after the fact—something that heretics in the Department of War understand well.

One of the military's most successful joint programs didn't have requirements at all. McLean, of China Lake fame, was the father of the AIM-9 Sidewinder, a heat-seeking air-to-air missile first deployed in 1956. Upgraded versions are still widely used by the US Navy, US Air Force, and more than thirty allied nations.

In developing Sidewinder, McLean faced two big obstacles: first, the Navy didn't have a requirement for a heat-seeking missile. Second, McLean's division at China Lake was explicitly told *not* to develop an air-to-air missile (McLean would continue the tradition of great founders breaking the rules). Both the Navy and the Air Force were fixated on a requirement for an "all weather missile," which, given the technology of the day, meant a radar-guided missile. Heat-seeking, infrared missiles were considered inferior because of their degraded performance in cloudy weather.

Further complicating matters was the ongoing turf war within the Navy over which bureau had the privilege of building guided missiles. The Navy's Bureau of Ordnance competed with the Navy's Bureau of Aeronautics. After bureaucratic trench warfare, the battle lines settled on Ordnance building missiles for ships, while Aeronautics built missiles for airplanes. China Lake was nowhere in that division of labor. It was only authorized to test missiles, not build them.

The Air Force was also investing in guided missiles. It backed the Falcon, built by Hughes Aircraft. The Navy backed the Sparrow III, a medium-range fleet defense missile. In 1950, 600 Raytheon engineers were toiling away on it. Both radar-guided missiles were well funded, well staffed, and had the blessings of their respective services. Infrared missiles had none of those things.

But radar had its own, serious drawback. In the early days of radar-guided missile development, systems like the Falcon and Sparrow III required the launching aircraft to maintain a continuous radar lock on the target until the missile reached it and blew up—a difficult and dangerous feat for the operator. This drawback was largely due to the size and complexity of the radar systems, which, in the era of radio-tube electronics, could not be miniaturized to fit within the missile itself. They were also extremely expensive and difficult to operate.

Starting in 1946, McLean became absorbed in the problem of improving fire-control systems, which was a legitimate function of his division. He decided the way forward was to make a new missile, specifically, a smart missile with fire control inside it. He thought infrared could be the solution to building a true fire-and-forget capability. With no money for his mission, McLean scrounged for funding from his proximity fuze group. This creative accounting enabled Sidewinder to operate in stealth mode on a shoestring budget as a "fuze" project. McLean gave the effort inconspicuous names like "Local Fuze Project 602" and "Feasibility Study 567." In Skunk Works–style, the early team had just a couple dozen employees.

The key challenge was creating a reliable infrared homing system capable of accurately locking onto the heat signatures of enemy aircraft, even under adverse conditions. Isolated in the Mojave Desert, McLean's staff lived and breathed Sidewinder. They all lived on campus, so there was nothing better for them to do. Happy hours and Saturday nights were fair game for resolving issues with the missile. It was not a nine-to-five gig, even though it paid like one.

Sidewinder escaped the executioner's blade many times before succeeding. Each time, McLean and his team found stop-gap measures, kept a low profile, or won over an influential figure so that their baby could live another day. In 1951,

Rear Admiral William Sterling "Deak" Parsons of the Bureau of Ordnance gave the effort $3.5 million, a small but real development budget. Parsons had confidence in McLean, but he was likely spurred to action by rivalry with the Bureau of Aeronautics, the official party authorized to build air-to-air missiles. A year later, KT Keller, Eisenhower's missile czar, gave the order to ax Sidewinder. But by then, its performance had won influential admirers who refused to let that happen. Even the skeptical Guided Missiles Committee of the Research and Development Board couldn't help but be impressed. One member stated, "It [Sidewinder] got authorized because it *had* to be. It worked! That was rather unusual back then. There were gobs of missiles [but they didn't work well]."

By 1956, McLean and his ragtag team had done it. With no operational requirement for a heat-seeking missile, the Navy decided to buy a heat-seeking missile. But China Lake's ambition didn't stop there. It wanted a reluctant Air Force to buy it, too. A Sidewinder engineer recounts the conversation he had when he pitched one of the Air Force's top planning officers on the missile:

> I found that he had no interest whatsoever. He explained to me that the Air Force had its own all weather Falcon...I found the colonel quite deaf to all my arguments. The Air Force requirements document specified "All weather capability" and the Sidewinder did not boast "all weather capability" so that was that.

An internal champion intervened to force the issue. Trevor Gardner, the assistant secretary of the Air Force for research and development, ordered a shoot-off between the Sidewinder and the Falcon. The Navy test pilot summed up Sidewinder's performance: "It was a turkey shoot—nothing to it."

In 1957, the Air Force finally bought Sidewinder, beginning the missile's storied career as a joint program that emerged from a decidedly non-joint process. The Air Force initially bought both Falcons and Sidewinders. However, Falcons flew so poorly in Vietnam they were phased out in favor of Sidewinders. The Navy's Sparrow was retained, but Navy planes were modified to accommodate the better-performing Sidewinder. As always, the best way to settle an argument is a head-to-head competition. You have to prove it to win.

Developed at one-tenth the cost of the Sparrow or Falcon, the Sidewinder has been a mainstay of air combat arsenals worldwide—allied and enemy. Early on, the Soviets created a high-fidelity dupe of the Sidewinder to great effect. Sidewinder's first significant combat success occurred during the 1958 Taiwan Strait Crisis, where it achieved multiple kills against Chinese MiGs. Sidewinder became the missile of choice for US pilots during the Vietnam War. It also shone during the Falklands War. British pilots, outnumbered ten to one by the Argentines but armed with Sidewinders, shot down twenty-three enemy aircraft and didn't lose any of their own in air to air combat. The Sidewinder's hit rate was 87 percent.

McLean believed, and proved, that requirements only work in reverse. Westrum writes: "He [McLean] hated formal requirements in advance of development. What was going to work, McLean thought, could seldom be known in advance. Requirements were appropriate when, and only when, a system had already been proved…"

Despite working for a government lab, McLean rejected many of the features we associate with government outfits: rigid organizational charts, extensive pre-determined requirements, bloated teams, and isolation from the operating environment. McLean cared about winning, and because of that fact, he gave our pilots the tools to dominate the skies.

Dr. Bill McLean poses with the Sidewinder missile (1963).

Empower talent. Organize (and reorganize) around the problem. Recognize that rules exist to be broken. Focus on the problem, not the process.

These insights propel the most innovative individuals and organizations. But they aren't part of a playbook. Their application isn't obvious in every instance. They can't merely be written down and codified in a handbook—at least, not without plenty of caveats and debate. Their successful application depends on context, taste, and intuition. It takes idiosyncratic and courageous leaders to apply them even in best-case scenarios. And the work of winning is always hard.

It would be an understatement to say that our government and military haven't excelled at implementing these insights. This book is littered with examples of the bureaucracy squashing talent, inflexibly responding to problems, punishing heretics, and elevating process above outcomes. Bureaucratic dysfunction may always be with us, but improvement and mission success are possible, too. We point to heroes within government like Cukor, Rickover, McLean, and countless others to prove the point: incredible things are possible when talented, mission-focused patriots rage against the machine. They shouldn't have to rage. With the right reforms, we can overcome the worst of the dysfunction and replicate the daring feats of past generations.

This belief is based on more than hope. As we'll see in the concluding chapter, brush fires of liberty are being set across the country even now. A Defense Reformation is afoot, from the Pentagon, to industry, to Congress, to the White House. These reforms show that, whatever our faults, America can't be counted out yet. Mobilization is possible. We can build on these changes to restore our position in the world, awe our enemies, and stop World War III before it begins.

CHAPTER 13

Mobilize

The year is 2030. Three years before, China's military, the PLA, completed preparations to "reunify" Taiwan by force, meeting the 2027 deadline set by General Secretary Xi Jinping. Chinese shipyards have produced hundreds of dual-use landing craft, barges, and other vessels suitable for ferrying an invasion force across the strait. The PLA Rocket Force has massed thousands of missiles along China's coast, ready to strike Taiwanese targets and American military bases in Japan, the Philippines, Guam, and elsewhere. The pace and scale of military exercises in the South China Sea have intensified, along with the frequency of intrusions into Taiwan's airspace.

The "exercises" are dress rehearsals for invasion, preparing PLA servicemembers to conquer and die and accustoming the Taiwanese to the invasion force right off their shore. They are meant not only as training, but as camouflage to hide the real invasion when the time is right. Intelligence agencies around the world hunt for clues to discern Xi's intentions. There are worrying signs this time could be different.

The stridency and nationalism of Chinese state media have grown, with frequent denunciations of Taiwan's "separatist" government and its "collusion" with foreign powers. National reunification, China's propagandists declare, is a historical necessity that cannot be delayed.

It's not just talk. Satellite imagery indicates that China's defense plants are working around the clock, forging munitions into the dark of night. Across China, hospitals hold blood drives. Field hospitals pop up near supply depots on the coast. The Ministry of State Security clamps down inside China, detaining political enemies and other "subversive" elements. Markets tremor as Beijing announces dramatic economic interventions, including strict capital controls. Taiwan reports an alarming barrage of cyberattacks, industrial espionage, and propaganda aimed at undermining the island's critical infrastructure and the public's will to resist.

What many dismissed as paranoid fantasy only a few years before, now appears inevitable. The peace of the world hangs by a thread. World War III could commence at a single word from Xi.

But it doesn't. The seasonal invasion windows come—and go. Exercises conclude. PLA assets disperse to their bases. The volume of state media falls. An anxious world breathes a sigh of relief.

Officially, nothing has changed. According to the party line, Taiwan remains a province of China. And the CCP reserves the right to bring it back into the fold, by any means necessary.

Unofficially, however, a significant—indeed world-historic—event has taken place: the CCP decided not to take the world to war. In 2031, the cycle repeats: tensions rise, then fall. Then it happens again in 2032.

By 2033, a more lasting change takes place. Xi and the CCP settle—internally—on a long-term strategy to reunify Taiwan through diplomatic isolation and economic coercion. They decide not to gamble it all on an invasion. Why? Because the math changed, and not in China's favor.

In war, the enemy gets a vote—and China's most powerful adversary, the United States, finally voted to mobilize. Each year we bought another year by imposing new and higher prospective costs on an already risky operation. PLA war planners informed Xi of new American and allied assets in theater, dispersed and dug in on islands scattered across the Pacific. Hundreds of NMESIS mobile anti-ship missile launchers were tucked away in remote locations like the Philippines' mountainous Batan Island, ready to remotely fire their high-precision missiles from unmanned trucks. Large autonomous underwater vehicles roamed the South China Sea, each carrying dozens of ship-killing munitions. Counter-unmanned aircraft systems were on standby to take down coordinated swarms of Chinese drones. More American and allied assets were surely out there, lurking in the depths, undiscovered and with unknown capabilities. Projections of the invasion's casualties and cost climbed. Previously confident admirals and generals started to qualify and hedge their reports, unsettling the political leadership.

In short, we made it too risky for the PLA to invade Taiwan. We achieved deterrence: a devastating world war was averted without firing a shot.

A mobile Navy Marine Expeditionary Ship Interdiction System (NMESIS) launcher at Pacific Missile Range Facility Barking Sands, Hawaii (2021).

China's changed calculus had cascading effects around the world. Our adversaries in other theaters took note of our military strength and strategic resolve and acted accordingly. Doubts crept in about China's strength and reliability as a partner. If the United States could so ably turn the tables on a peer competitor, what could it do to less powerful foes? And so, after years of war with Ukraine, Russia was finally cowed into a negotiated settlement. Moscow quietly tabled its expansionist ambitions, for the time being, focusing instead on licking its wounds and shoring up support at home. Iran, already crippled by America's damage to its hardened nuclear sites, pulled back on its support for terror groups in the region. Hamas, in turn, lost a critical source of funding and weapons. American mobilization exposed how tenuous the bonds between our enemies really were.

Bill Gates said, "most people overestimate what they can do in one year and underestimate what they can do in ten years."

But Gates has it exactly backwards. Once the Department of War and the industrial base stop believing the comforting fiction of their ten-year plans and start taking radical and immediate action, the progress they could make in a year would astonish. Not everything would be accomplished at once—but it wouldn't have to be. What we need to do is buy a year.

That goal requires a commitment to painful change, every morning when we roll out of bed.

People, Ideas, Hardware (and Software)

Beyond commitment, what do we need to buy that extra year—and then the second, and then the third? What do we need to re-establish deterrence and prevent World War III? As John Boyd said, we need "people, ideas, hardware—in that order" (although we would update his aphorism to include software).

Mobilization must begin, necessarily, with people—not policy or process. The single most important shakeup that the Department of War could initiate is installing high-agency heretics into its most critical positions. Some of those individuals would be elevated from obscurity within the Pentagon, where they'd been sidelined for refusing to pretend everything was fine while the ship sank. Others would come from outside the military and its establishment. The Department of War must recruit the top engineers from dynamic technology companies—with a special focus on veterans who left the services because a military career meant bureaucratic politics and stagnation. We need to track down the individuals who were forced out as captains or colonels but who should have worn four stars; the Cukors of the world must be invited back into the fold—and their relentless focus on outcomes and winning must be encouraged rather than punished.

The private sector must take on a greater role. The Department of War's longstanding goals of connecting sensors and shooters, integrating AI into weapons and operations, and turning factories into force projection all depend on symbiosis with America's technology sector. We're confident that the nation's business leaders will answer the call, like Bill Knudsen before them—but the military needs to pick up the phone and dial them up. America's most talented should be given the opportunity to join the reserves as officers on an accelerated timeline, waiving irrelevant training and testing. That way, business executives, coders, engineers, and other skilled workers with uniforms and security clearances can start mobilizing the American industrial base before the next crisis. Onboarding talent now is the best way to prevent war later.

Leaders who prove themselves should be encouraged to remain in their role and build something exceptional, instead of rotating to a new program every two years. By granting longer tenures, the military can unlock the full potential of outlier talent and deliver groundbreaking capabilities like hypersonic missiles, drone swarms, and others yet to be imagined.

Secure in their positions, these future Schrievers and Rickovers can empower their subordinates to run through walls to accomplish the mission. Civilian and uniformed personnel would find themselves with more responsibility than they've ever had in their careers. Freed from the Pentagon's culture of compliance and risk aversion, these personnel would be able to focus on outcomes instead of box-checking.

As for ideas, the only ones worth considering are those that save time—whether on the battlefield, on the factory floor, or in the acquisition process. Boyd's OODA loop (short for observe, orient, decide, and act) can and should serve as the model for all military decision making. The OODA loop is the process by which a commander gets inside the mind of the enemy and then acts to confuse, confound, and sow chaos in his ranks. When your OODA loop closes faster than your enemy's, you gain a decision-making advantage that compounds with time.

Boyd's OODA loop has such staying power because it provides a mental model that enables grunts and commanders alike to understand their enemy, situate themselves within a challenging environment, and win. Technology and tactics change; the OODA loop is forever. This time is no different. Between 2026 and 2030, we must harness technology to shorten our OODA loops until we live rent-free inside the heads of China's war planners.

We do this by connecting sensors and shooters, accelerating the time from detection to destruction. In layman's terms, this means getting way faster at putting warheads on foreheads. Commercial satellites, ground radars, RF jammers, undersea mobile sensors, and unmanned surface sensors are just some of the hardware that connect space to mud to sea. These sensors in turn talk to shooters—the submarines, drones, fighter jets, and other weapons platforms—telling them what to target and when to fire. Software serves as the connective tissue between the two, empowering humans with the information needed to make life-and-death decisions while automating lower-level decisions.

For too long, these concepts have existed mostly as buzzwords and boxes on PowerPoint slides. That needs to change through serious investment in technology.

In addition to changes in leadership, tempo, and technology, we also need to change the way our military rehearses for war. Military exercises need to get a whole lot more realistic.

No more kayfabe, no more orchestrated stunts that hand-wave the hard and dangerous parts. Exercises need to increase the number of red assets to accurately represent the forces that our troops will be expected to face. Think orders of magnitude more enemy drones, missiles, and autonomous vessels. We also need to get real about likely attrition rates—meaning we'll lose a lot of stuff, both cheap and expensive. The vulnerabilities of even our exquisite platforms must be ruthlessly laid bare. Electronic warfare—enemy jamming that renders drones useless—must be incorporated into exercises to provide our troops with experience countering this invisible threat. The first realistic exercises could be embarrassing. They could even end contracts and careers. But realistic conditions are necessary to uncover the best and worst ideas. Better to discover that your fancy kit doesn't work during a weekend exercise than when you're on a remote island in the Pacific with Chinese missiles homing in on your electronic signature.

Relatedly, we need to start treating exercises as commercial tryouts. Special exercises should be set up that are open to all comers in a kind of technological battle royale. Real competition should be backed up with real rewards for winners—and real consequences for losers. Companies whose technology accelerates the OODA loop should win significant contracts following the conclusion of an exercise. Significantly, companies should only be rewarded if their products perform *and* if they are employed correctly by the end user. This additional criterion would incentivize close partnership and tight feedback loops between industry and the government. There should be zero tolerance for companies that chuck their product over the wall and hope for the best.

Even the most realistic exercises will never be as valuable as testing in the field. Technology that proves its mettle should be swiftly transitioned to real operations and conflicts around the globe. Rapid deployment of technology, both to our troops and to allies through reforms to arms-control regulations, will help us to discover the capabilities of our systems and refine vulnerabilities. Systems that don't hack it in real-world conditions can be fixed or terminated early—before their failure is exposed in a major conflict, with deadly consequences.

I (Shyam) was in the audience in November 2025 when Secretary of War Pete Hegseth announced sweeping reforms to the Pentagon's bloated and outdated acquisition bureaucracy. I applaud this move, but much work remains to be done to empower the "heretical heroes" both inside the Department of War and in the defense and technology industries. To begin with, the secretary of war must make rapid commercial buying a top priority. Enforcing the law by requiring the military to buy commercial products would not only accelerate the OODA loop—it would liberate our troops from underperforming developmental "solutions," like the Army intelligence platform we described in Chapter 9, that suck so much time and energy from our troops, while making them less lethal and safe. Commercial buying increases upside *and* decreases downside.

Money has a big part to play in mobilization, but not in the way you might think. More important than the topline number is the speed with which dollars are distributed and the flexibility with which they can be spent. Congress and the defense acquisition bureaucracy need to internalize that fiscal agility is a key component of the OODA loop. Program managers should be able to reprogram money in two weeks, not two years. Innovative companies with breakthrough capabilities should glide through the process to receive meaningful contracts with the Department of War. The flip side of the coin is that underperforming and outdated programs should be cancelled to free up fiscal space for new and promising capabilities. The culling should be as rapid and ruthless as on a battlefield.

As we increase competition on the supply side by supporting innovative capabilities and new entrants, we should also increase competition on the demand side. In other words, we should smash the monopsony, just as our military did during the heyday of Cold War competition. No single service, office, program, or person should be able to claim a monopoly on pivotal technologies like autonomous drones or AI. Instead, competing and overlapping programs should be allowed—even encouraged—to proliferate. Combatant commands should be given modest budgets and the authority to use them, spurring healthy competition with the services. The most important programs should have competing program managers within the same office, each pursuing the technologies and approaches they think will lead to victory. Undoubtedly, many will decry such competition as "duplicative" and "wasteful." But as we've seen, healthy competition reduces risk by ensuring that the military isn't stuck with a single point of failure, while encouraging speed and creativity. Acquisition officers are like any other servicemember—they want to win, too. We just need to give them a race to run, and a visible competitor.

Realistic exercises, fast and flexible contracting, commercial buying, and internal competition are the key variables that will ensure that the best ideas are selected and accelerated into the field. With the right people and the right ideas, America will be well positioned to build the right hardware and software.

To achieve that important goal, we need to think about force composition and the "high-low mix"—another concept championed by Boyd and his acolytes. The high-low mix provides a framework for building an effective force while confronting the economic reality of budget constraints. Boyd's solution? Pair a smaller number of more expensive, high-complexity, multi-mission platforms with a larger number of less expensive platforms that are highly capable but that serve narrow roles. The quintessential example of the high-low mix was the F-16 Fighting Falcon (low) to complement the more expensive F-15 Eagle (high). But the high-low mix was never implemented to Boyd's satisfaction. Instead, the Department of War tends to equate expensive weapons with high tech and high performance, and less expensive weapons with inferior tech and low performance—a costly misunderstanding.

We can fulfill Boyd's vision of the high-low mix by embracing software-defined weapons. In such a paradigm, we would still rely on the conventional parts of our "high" mix—think nuclear-powered submarines and stealth bombers—but our "low" mix would assume an outsized role. The low mix would be diverse and heterogeneous, composed of a range of systems at various price points and performance levels, like Anduril's Barracuda (a cruise missile), Saronic's Marauder (a medium unmanned surface vessel), and Epirus's Leonidas (a directed energy weapon that zaps drones out of the sky). These inexpensive, "low-end" systems are software driven, and they can be leveled up further using software based on lessons learned in the field. The adaptability of these weapons would in turn pose greater and costlier dilemmas to the Chinese as they try to plan for different contingencies. Fielding many low-end systems effectively allows us to field many different armies.

Deploying a high-low mix will require software-defined manufacturing to flood the battlefield with mass. This means that factories and engineers must be treated as components of the fighting force itself. The Department of War can help by recognizing the industrial capacity for a given weapon as part of that weapon system, just as much as a radar or a fuselage is part of a fighter jet. Program offices should likewise prefer systems with a demonstrated ability to be built at speed and scale. Gold-plated systems with insecure supply chains and low-volume production are luxuries that a mobilizing society cannot afford. We should build accordingly.

In this new paradigm, the companies that survive will be the ones that embrace software and speed in manufacturing. The ones that move beyond platitudes about digital transformation. Companies that resist investing in their capital plant or updating their decades-old software will fall behind and never catch up.

The Gundo boys (and gals)—patriotic young founders building hard tech companies in storied El Segundo—along with ground-breaking companies like Anduril, Divergent, and Hadrian, prove that reindustrialization is more than a meme. With the right leadership, purposeful deregulation, and a strong and consistent demand signal from Washington, we can unleash a renaissance of American manufacturing. Fusing the unique virtues of the industrial heartland and Silicon Valley will create a manufacturing sector greater than the sum of its parts. These manufacturers will employ cutting-edge techniques like additive manufacturing to print spare parts and entire fleets of drones, sometimes on location from printers embedded with military units. They will bring best practices and supply chains from commercial manufacturing to ruthlessly slash costs and boost production.

There will be plenty of attractive manufacturing jobs in the new American industrial base. The most successful companies will pay manufacturing employees salaries commensurate with those of software engineers—and the two roles will start to blur, as expertise in manipulating bits translates to expertise in manipulating atoms. Manufacturing will start to command the respect and premium it lost decades ago, as digital upgrades and automation increase sectoral productivity. We'll relearn that mass production of chips, ships, and much more isn't just critical to our national security—it can be massively profitable, too.

Our allies have critical roles to play to close the production gap, invest in the American industrial base, and end our dependence on China. For example, South Korea and Japan, the world's number two and three shipbuilders, respectively, can contribute know-how and investment to revitalize the American shipbuilding industry, while their own yards can produce everything from oilers to amphibious assault ships. With help from Australia, Canada, and the UK, we can onshore and friend-shore the supply chains for rare earth elements, semiconductors, and other critical components. Friend-shoring must not become an excuse for failing to get our own house in order. What we can make competitively in America, we should. But our allies can help us to negate China's advantage in sheer size and industrial strength through reciprocal investment and sharing of technology and talent.

If we make these changes, we can reunite commercial innovation with national purpose, just as we did during World War II and the Cold War. Commercial companies can get back in the business of national security, competing for projects previously reserved for a dwindling number of defense specialists. A flood of startups can reignite the American industrial base and reverse the decline of past decades. Innovative companies like Divergent will manufacture critical components for missiles, not just race cars. Ursa Major will make rocket engines, both for hypersonic missiles and commercial space launch. Saronic's autonomous fleet will escort container ships through chokepoints while escorting destroyers in the South China Sea. The flywheel of innovation will spin, and our renewed ability to make products that defend America will translate into renewed ability to make products that enrich America. By mobilizing, we'll show yet again that America's prosperity and national security go hand in hand.

The Defense Reformation

The recommendations above may seem daunting. Perhaps they even seem fanciful on the radically compressed timeline we have described. After all, this is a mobilization scenario where momentous cultural and policy changes occur, repeatedly, for years; a scenario where America's leaders and public recognize that our default course of action is leading us into World War III—and correct course fast. Pulling it off without becoming distracted, without the spilling of American blood, and without capitulation is the strategic equivalent of sticking the landing on a triple axel. But we believe mobilization, deterrence, and peace are possible. More than that: we believe mobilization is happening now. For the first time in a long time, the trendline is positive. A Defense Reformation has started, across party lines, branches of government, and the country.

The reformation started, as it did in the run-up to World War II, with leadership at the very top. A flurry of executive orders from President Trump's White House in April 2025 initiated the most serious effort at military reform since the days of William Perry.

The executive orders enforce the preference for commercial buying first established by FASA, which, as discussed in Chapters 5 and 8, is the most violated law in the land. The orders stress that buyers across government, whether in the Pentagon or elsewhere, must demonstrate a "first preference" for commercial products—and must prove to the Office of Management and Budget that exceptions to this rule are warranted. The orders even change performance review standards for acquisition personnel so that employees are rewarded for taking "measured and calculated risks" that deliver the goods, fast. This alone is a revolutionary culture shift inside the Department of War, elevating patriots in the building who are willing to take chances to deliver for our warfighters.

The orders also encourage the use of alternative acquisition pathways like Other Transaction Authorities, which sidestep the long and winding process for most programs. Such pathways were used during the wars in Iraq and Afghanistan to quickly deliver up-armored Humvees to the troops. Using those pathways more often has the potential to slash the time it takes to deliver new systems.

And that's just the start. The president's orders attack red tape, calling for the elimination or revision of acquisition regulations that are duplicative, wasteful, and slow, spanning the entire federal government. They call for a systematic review of the joint requirements process and all major programs that are overbudget and behind schedule, with the worst offenders slated for cancellation. They kickstart a shipbuilding revival, encouraging domestic and allied investment through the establishment of "maritime prosperity zones" and a shipbuilding financial incentives program. And they streamline the federal permitting process, which has long slowed down construction of critical infrastructure projects.

Buying commercial, raising the bar for personnel and programs, and slashing burdensome regulations and requirements are key levers to reorient the Department of War toward the primacy of winning.

Executed faithfully, these EOs have the potential to transform how the federal government spends your money and interacts with the most innovative parts of our economy. The government can buy better technology, faster. It can waste less money. It can deliver the goods, instead of fueling the pessimistic belief that the United States and the West are destined for a world of scarcity and decline.

And that's just what the White House is doing. The Defense Reformation is happening elsewhere in government, too.

Not long after the president issued these orders, Secretary Hegseth detonated another bombshell, ordering a "comprehensive transformation" of the Army by shifting funding from legacy defense programs to asymmetric upstarts and shaking up the Army's acquisition process and command structure.

The order sets ambitious timelines for new capabilities: field new, long-range missiles capable of striking targets on land and sea by 2027; enable AI-driven command and control by 2027; embed advanced manufacturing capabilities like 3D printers in operational units this year. The order also directs the Army to "end procurement of obsolete systems," singling out manned aircraft, excess ground vehicles like Humvees, and "outdated UAVs." It calls for greater use of rapid acquisition pathways and a "shift from program-centric funding to capability-based funding." And it recognizes the primacy of people by prioritizing merit and skill, making it easier to hire and retain civilian experts, and culling the herd of general officers.

The tight timelines speak to the nature of the threat: this is a sprint to prevent Xi from invading Taiwan. The timelines inject much-needed urgency into the equation, which is essential to action. Time pressure, like hunger, focuses the mind. It approximates competitive market forces in a decidedly non-market environment by spurring leaders to find leeway in the rules to get the job done.

Pulling it off will be no small feat. This is the bureaucratic equivalent of charging a machine-gun nest. The order states that the Army will have to "overcome parochial interests," and that may be the only understated part of the document. Many of the programs in the crosshairs are long-standing and expensive, with real constituencies and special-interest firepower. Change will be painful. But if the Army accomplishes even some of these goals, it will come out the other side with a more fearsome, survivable force.

The Defense Reformation gained even more momentum in the summer of 2025 when Secretary Hegseth ordered the "disestablishment of JCIDS" and a halt to the joint requirement process. In Chapter 5, we covered the history of JCIDS and the bureaucratic cruft it created. By ripping out useless process when others might have taken an extended August vacation, Hegseth demonstrated that change is possible if we're willing to ask the simple question: "What if we actually tried to win?" (We should also note the key intellectual roles that Bill Greenwalt and Dan Patt, featured in Chapter 5, played in this decision. Precious few thought JCIDS could be deleted. It seemed as permanent as the Pentagon, even though it was only a few decades old. Greenwalt and Patt had the courage to argue for its elimination, anyway. The primacy of people strikes again.)

These are just a few of the bold reforms that have been initiated in recent years to shake up the bureaucracy, mobilize the American industrial base, and win the peace. We could list many more, from the Marine Corps' revolutionary Force Design 2030, which is preparing our Marines for island-hopping, amphibious warfare far from home, to congressional reforms like Senator Roger Wicker's Fostering Reform and Government Efficiency in Defense (FORGED) Act, which would make a generational investment in the mass production of vital systems, including new and emerging technologies. There's Senator Joni Ernst's Investing in National Next-Generation Opportunities for Venture Acceleration and Technological Excellence (INNOVATE) Act, which would reform the Small Business Innovation Research program from corporate welfare to critical investments in truly innovative companies that are capable of scaling. And there are efforts to mobilize technologists for national service, like the US Army Reserves' Executive Innovation Corps. I (Shyam) am one of the corps' first recruits.

We could also point to the sea change taking place in industry. After the dark night of the Last Supper comes the dawn of a First Breakfast. Dozens of startups are toiling away to solve the hardest problems facing our nation: they're building modular nuclear reactors, providing advanced manufacturing as a service, and designing revolutionary jets, submarines, and much else. These companies are not only willing to work with the government—they are eager to do so, both from a sense of mission and a sense that this time might be different. The government may finally be ready to work with commercial companies again to reignite the American industrial base. If they're right, then our adversaries should watch out. A very different strategic picture may emerge at startling speed.

In this book, we've tried to glean lessons for the present by telling stories from the past. America's successful mobilizations for World War II and the Cold War show the importance of leadership, individual initiative, competition, and speed. They also show the importance of eccentricity and even rebellion. Revolution is in the American bloodstream, a fact that we (and our enemies) occasionally rediscover when we need it most.

We'll conclude with one more story that illustrates this point nicely. William "Wild Bill" Donovan was one of the United States' most decorated soldiers and the creator of the Office of Strategic Services, the band of spies that eventually became the CIA. In 1940 and 1941, he took a wartime tour of free Europe to assess the Allies' prospects of victory.

He returned impressed by Britain's willingness to fight on against long odds, and by the "guerrillas," or commandos, it was training for asymmetric war against a conventionally superior German army. Britain had absorbed the lessons (and blows) from decades of imperial anti-insurgency campaigns, from Afghanistan to Mandatory Palestine to South Africa. Now Britain had to wage a guerrilla war of its own to survive.

Donovan advised President Roosevelt that the United States, which was in the early stages of rearmament, needed a similarly unconventional approach to take on the Axis. The Germans, he wrote, were "big league professionals," while America was a "bush league club"—albeit one with vast, untapped potential. Until the American industrial base retooled and poured it on, the United States would have to "play a bush league game, stealing the ball and killing the umpire."

The United States is back in the position of having to play a bush league game. For the first time in living memory, we face an adversary that is as powerful as us and that even has significant strategic advantages in some areas: advantages of size, terrain, industrial capacity, perhaps even technology. Simultaneously, we face less powerful but equally determined adversaries in other theaters.

But America has strategic advantages of its own, and now Americans are starting to use them. Perhaps our most significant advantage, we humbly submit, is that we're crazy. As a democratic power, we don't do long-term planning or strategy very well (just look at the Whiz Kids and their legacy). But we do empower crazy innovators. We can pivot on a dime. And if you punch us in the face, there's no telling what we might do.

This is just the start of a rough-and-tumble, bush-league game against the bureaucracy and special interests that are making our military slow, small, and vulnerable. It's the necessary beginning of rebuilding. It's a warning to communist China and other enemies that America is lacing up its cleats—and filing the studs into spikes. Wild Bill would be proud.

When we get the right people in place, focus on speed and the OODA loop, and fire up the American industrial base, there is no limit to the chaos and uncertainty we can impose on our adversaries. And those things buy time: 2027 will turn into 2028, then 2029, then 2030. The peace will hold. And if it doesn't, at least America will be prepared to fight and dominate.

ACKNOWLEDGMENTS

The requirements for a new weapon should be easier to write than a book, but as we've seen, that's rarely the case today. *Mobilize* was a whirlwind project that serves as our humble contribution to helping America win the twenty-first century. As we put pen to paper, the challenge lay in how to make a book about defense procurement more than just a book about defense procurement. The solution started with people, as it so often does. We owe a debt to the patriots, in uniform and out, who have worked tirelessly and even given their lives to forge a stronger America. Some of their stories are told in this book. Others served as quiet inspiration. Thank you.

All writers need editors, but not all writers fully appreciate a talented editor. We do! Thank you to Blake Seitz, Palantirian and editor extraordinaire, without whom this endeavor might not have crossed the finish line. We especially appreciate your steadfast commitment to *Mobilize* following the birth of your second child.

Thank you to Don Fehr, our agent at Trident Media, who immediately understood why *Mobilize* needed to exist. Don helped us to navigate the Wild West of book publishing as two enthusiastic but first-time authors. Thank you to the talented team at Bombardier Books and Post Hill Press. Like Don, David Bernstein from Bombardier Press recognized the potential of *Mobilize* and encouraged us to get our message to the world as quickly as possible. When David left Bombardier for Wicked Son, he left us in the capable hands of Lauren Campbell, our managing editor.

Mobilize would be nothing without the individuals who shared their trials, tribulations, and triumphs working with the Pentagon. Thank you to Drew Cukor for reluctantly agreeing to be the center of attention so we could finally share the unvarnished and incredible story of Project Maven. Thank you to Trae Stephens for providing an insider look at the intersection of VC investing and national security. Thank you to Kevin Czinger of Divergent and Matt Steckman and Keith Flynn of Anduril for taking time away from building incredible companies to talk with us about reindustrializing America. Thank you to Doug Philippone and Bryant Choung for sharing war stories about the Army lawsuit.

Thank you to Bill Greenwalt for reviewing our manuscript in detail. You are a defense insider who has maintained an outsider's skepticism and hunger for change. Your work was critical to the thesis of *Mobilize*.

Thank you to the many Palantirians who contributed their time: Samuel Byers, Scott Hsu, Parag Shah, Sasha Spivak, Sam Feldman, David Worn, Antonin Scalia, Eliano Younes, Ben Radford, and Parvathy Menon, among others. Special thanks to Greg Little for being a co-conspirator on *First Breakfast*, which seeded many of the ideas in this book.

And of course, thank you to Palantir's foremost heretic and hero, Alex Karp. Any wisdom that *Mobilize* offers is based on lessons learned at Palantir.

ART CREDITS

The following images have been created or redrawn based on data from the following sources:

Figure 1: Matthew P. Funaiole, Brian Hart, and Aidan Powers-Riggs, *Ship Wars: Confronting China's Dual-Use Shipbuilding Empire* (Washington, D.C.: Center for Strategic & International Studies, March 2025), 4. Reprinted or redrawn with permission.

Figure 2: The National WW II Museum, "'Out-Producing the Enemy': American Production During World War II"; John Ellis, *The World War II Databook: The Essential Facts and Figures for All the Combatants* (Aurum Press, 1993); Wesley Frank Craven and James Lea Gate, eds., *The Army Air Forces in World War II, Volume Six: Men and Planes* (University of Chicago Press, 1955), 350; and Richard Overy, *The Air War, 1939–1945* (Europa Publications, 1980), 150.

Figure 3: William Greenwalt and Dan Patt, *Competing in Time: Ensuring Capability Advantage and Mission Success through Adaptable Resource Allocation* (Washington, D.C.: The Hudson Institute, February 2021), 24. Reprinted or redrawn with permission.

Figure 4: William Greenwalt and Dan Patt, *Competing in Time: Ensuring Capability Advantage and Mission Success through Adaptable Resource Allocation* (Washington, D.C.: The Hudson Institute, February 2021), 40. Reprinted or redrawn with permission.

Figure 5: Gregory C. Allen and Doug Berenson, "Why Is the U.S. Defense Industrial Base So Isolated from the U.S. Economy?" *CSIS Commentary*, August 20, 2024. Graphic used data from Martin Bollinger as presented in Allen and Berenson. Reprinted or redrawn with permission.

Figure 6: Robert S. Walker, et al., *Final Report of the Commission on the Future of the United States Aerospace Industry*, (Arlington, VA: Aerospace Commission, November 2002), 74.

Figure 7: "The Starship Report" (Payload Research, January 2024), 13; and Thomas G. Roberts, "Space Launch to Low Earth Orbit: How Much Does It Cost?" *Aerospace Security: A Project of the Center for Strategic and International Studies*, September 1, 2022. Reprinted or redrawn with permission.

Figure 8: "Top 100 Defense Companies: Top 100 for 2025," *Defense News*, accessed October 1, 2025, https://people.defensenews.com/top-100/. Reprinted or redrawn with permission.

Figure 9: Market data.

Figure 10: Market data.

Figure 11: Elliott V. Converse, *Rearming for the Cold War, 1945–1960* (Washington, D.C.: Historical Office of the Office of the Secretary of Defense, 2012); Neil Sheehan, *A Fiery Peace in a Cold War: Bernard Schriever and the Ultimate Weapon* (Vintage Books, 2010); Harvey M. Sapolsky, *The Polaris System Development: Bureaucratic and Programmatic Success in Government* (Harvard University Press, 1972); "The Titan Missile," National Park Service, accessed October 14, 2025, https://www.nps.gov/articles/titan-icbm.htm; "Boeing LGM-30A Minuteman IA," National Museum of the United States Air Force, accessed October 14, 2025, https://www.nationalmuseum.af.mil/Visit/Museum-Exhibits/Fact-Sheets/Display/Article/196028/boeing-lgm-30a-minuteman-ia/; and "Convair SM-65 Atlas," National Museum of the United States Air Force, accessed October 14, 2025, https://www.nationalmuseum.af.mil/Visit/Museum-Exhibits/Fact-Sheets/Display/Article/197976/convair-sm-65-atlas/,

Figure 12: "U.S. Bureau of Labor Statistics, Manufacturing Sector: Total Factor Productivity [MFGPROD]," retrieved from FRED, Federal Reserve Bank of St. Louis, October 9, 2025, https://fred.stlouisfed.org/series/MFGPROD.

NOTES

FOREWORD

Venture capitalists have invested: Heather Somerville, "Defense-Tech Startups Need a New Supplier: Anyone but China," *The Wall Street Journal,* September 30, 2024.

CHAPTER 1: THE PRECIPICE

They spared his life: Stephen Kalin, Isabel Coles, and Ievgeniia Sivorka, "The Russian Solider Who Surrendered to a Ukrainian Drone," *The Wall Street Journal,* June 14, 2023.

"first AI war": Vera Bergengruen, "The First AI War," *Time,* February 26, 2024.

"first large-scale drone war": Tomas Milasauskasa and Liudvikas Jaškūnas, "FPV Drones in Ukraine are Changing Modern Warfare," *Atlantic Council,* June 20, 2024.

Billions of dollars of hardware: Kateryna Bondar, "How Ukraine's Operation 'Spider's Web' Redefines Asymmetric Warfare," *CSIS Critical Questions,* June 2, 2025.

Russia's invasion of Ukraine: Sunny Nagpaul, "Russia's War on Ukraine Enters Its Fourth Year," *PBS,* February 24, 2025.

Dead bodies pile up: Nataliya Gumenyuk, "Ukraine's New Way of War," *The Atlantic,* May 27, 2025.

"dumping ground": Brandon J. Weichert, "NATO Isn't Exactly Sending its Best Weapons to Ukraine to Fight Russia," *The National Interest,* March 15, 2024.

France has provided: David Axe, "Ukraine's French Recon Vehicles Are Too Flimsy for Frontal Assaults, So the Marines Are Using Them as Artillery," *Forbes,* September 17, 2023.

After much prodding, Germany provided: David Axe, "As Ukraine Loses More and More of Its Best Leopard 2 Tanks, It's Turning Back to Old T-72s," *Forbes,* October 29, 2023.

The United States shipped: Ellen Mitchell, "US Will Send Ukraine More Modern Version of Abrams Tank," *The Hill,* January 26, 2023.

The Russians offer a blunter assessment: Nick Paton Walsh, et al., "Soldiers in Ukraine say US-supplied tanks have made them targets for Russian strikes," *CNN,* May 29, 2024.

well above 100,000 per month: Nataliya Gumenyuk, "Ukraine's New Way of War," *The Atlantic,* May 27, 2025.

fewer than 5,000 per month: Sam Skove, "Wartime need for drones would outstrip US production. There's a way to fix that," *Defense One,* August 7, 2024.

"on track to build a stockpile": *The posture of United States European Command and United States Africa Command in review of the Defense Authorization Request for Fiscal Year 2026 and the Future Years Defense Program: Testimony before the Senate Committee on Armed Services,* 119th Cong. (2025) (testimony of Christopher G. Cavoli. Commander U.S. European Command and Supreme Allied Commander Europe).

But we can't give Ukraine: "Russia is raining hellfire on Ukraine," *The Economist,* May 25, 2025.

"Russia and China are united": Nectar Gan and Ben Westcott, "US and allies are pushing China and Russia closer together, but will their 'unbreakable friendship' last?" *CNN,* June 16, 2021.

In return, China: Kylie Atwood, "China is giving Russia significant support to expand weapons manufacturing as Ukraine war continues, US officials say," *CNN,* April 12, 2024.

"there are changes": Mark Leonard, "China Is Ready for a World of Disorder," *Foreign Affairs,* June 20, 2023.

For many years: Paul Rahe, "Defending Taiwan," *Strategika,* June 6, 2022.

In 2014, China began: Rupert Wingfield-Hayes, "China's Island Factory," *BBC,* September 9, 2014.

China transformed what was previously: Ankit Panda, "It's Official: Xi Jinping Breaks His Non-Militarization Pledge in the Spratlys," *The Diplomat,* December 16, 2016.

It has doubled: Noah Robertson, "China leading 'rapid expansion' of nuclear arsenal, Pentagon says," *Defense News,* October 24, 2024.

Its navy already has: Alexander Palmer, Henry H. Carroll, and Nicholas Velazquez, "Unpacking China's Naval Buildup," *CSIS Commentary,* June 5, 2024.

And it's going all-in: Department of Defense, *Military and Security Developments Involving the People's Republic of China, 2024, Annual Report to Congress* (Washington, D.C.: Department of Defense, 2024).

Xi's goal: Carol Shiue and Wolfgang Keller, "Modernisation and China's 'century of humiliation,'" *Centre for Economic Policy Research,* December 5, 2021, https://cepr.org/voxeu/columns/modernisation-and-chinas-century-humiliation.

The deadline for accomplishing this: "Great Rejuvenation of the Chinese Nation," The Center for Strategic Translation, accessed October 6, 2025, https://chinaopensourceobservatory.org/glossary/great-rejuvenation-of-the-chinese-nation.

Xi has instructed: Noah Robertson, "How DC Became Obsessed with a Potential 2027 Invasion of Taiwan," *Defense News,* May 7, 2024.

China's rocket stockpiles: Christopher Bodeen and Johnson Lai, "China Conducts Military Drills Focusing on Taiwan Strait," *AP News,* April 2, 2025.

Its military is practicing: H.I. Sutton, "China Builds Missile Targets Shaped Like U.S. Aircraft Carrier, Destroyers in Remote Desert," *USNI News,* November 7, 2021.

And as China's "no limits" partnership: Antoni Slodkowski and Laurie Chen, "China's Xi affirms 'no limits' partnership with Putin in call on Ukraine war anniversary," *Reuters,* February 25, 2025.

Its vertically integrated stack: Lindsay Maizland, "China's Repression of Uyghurs in Xinjiang," Council on Foreign Relations, accessed October 6, 2025, https://www.cfr.org/backgrounder/china-xinjiang-uyghurs-muslims-repression-genocide-human-rights.

The Ukraine war has only accelerated: Andrea Kendall-Taylor and Richard Fontaine, *The Axis of Upheaval: Gauging the Growing Military Cooperation Among Russia, China, Iran, and North Korea* (Washington, D.C.: Center for a New American Security, July 2024).

"comprehensive strategic partnership": Dzirhan Mahadzir, "Russia, North Korea Sign Strategic Partnership Treaty, 6 ROK P-8A Poseidons Arrive in South Korea," *USNI News,* June 20, 2024.

Iran, for its part: Ryan Brobst, Bradley Bowman, and Mike Daum, "Hamas used Iranian-produced weapons in October 7 terror attack in Israel," *FDD Long War Journal,* October 19, 2023.

Increasingly, it's getting into the fight directly: Gerry Doyle, et al., "Israel's Iron Dome: How layers of air defences protected the country against the biggest onslaught of missiles and drones in its history," *Reuters,* April 18, 2024.

Using a novel combination: Benjamin Jensen, "Ungentlemanly Robots: Israel's Operation Rising Lion and the New Way of War," *CSIS Commentary,* June 13, 2025.

Stealthy B-2s dropped: Ashley Roque, "Operation Midnight Hammer: How the US conducted surprise strikes on Iran," *Breaking Defense,* June 22, 2025.

The United States reached deep: "U.S. Used Up 15-20 Percent of its Global THAAD Anti-Missile Arsenal in Just 11 Days of Mid-Intensity Combat: Cost Over $800 Million," *Military Watch Magazine,* June 25, 2025.

Admiral James Kilby remarked: Stephen Sorace, "Navy using munitions at 'alarming' speed to defend Israel," *Fox News,* June 24, 2025.

Both interceptors cost: Lauren C. Williams, "Mideast missile duels have cost US Navy nearly $1B, secretary says," *Defense One,* April 16, 2024; Amira El-Fekki, "US Missile Defenses Heavily Depleted in Shielding Israel: Report," *Newsweek,* June 27, 2025.

Chinese-made fighters shot down: Saeed Shah and Idrees Ali, "Exclusive: Pakistan's Chinese-made jet brought down two Indian fighter aircraft, US officials say," *Reuters,* May 9, 2025.

World War II had officially begun: Alan Taylor, "World War II: Before the War," *The Atlantic,* June 19, 2011.

"By the time Germany invaded": Andrew F. Krepinevich, Jr., *The Origins of Victory: How Disruptive Military Innovation Determines the Fates of Great Powers* (Yale University Press, 2023), 284.

Part of Germany's punishment: Krepinevich, *The Origins of Victory,* 255.

The lifespan of a radio: *Too Critical to Fail: Getting Software Right in an Age of Rapid Innovation: Testimony before the House of Representative Committee on Armed Services Subcommittee on Cyber, Information Technologies, and Innovation,* 118th Cong. (2024) (testimony of Daniel Patt, Hudson Institute Senior Fellow).

For a drone: John Grady, "Ukraine's Experience in Developing Lethal Drones Should Be Lesson for NATO, Says Panel," *USNI News,* April 18, 2024.

In 1939, when President Roosevelt: Arthur Herman, *Freedom's Forge: How American Business Produced Victory in World War II* (Random House, 2012), 13.

The inventory of fighters and bombers: Herman, *Freedom's Forge,* 7.

But the United States: Herman, *Freedom's Forge,* 336.

Yes, Ford built B-24s: Herman, *Freedom's Forge,* 241.

The United States didn't hit peak: Tyler Hacker, *Arsenal of Democracy: Myth or Model? Lessons for 21st Century Industrial Mobilization Planning* (Washington, D.C.: Center for Strategic and Budgetary Analyses, May 2025), 26.

The delivery is years behind: Stefano D'Urso, "Lockheed Martin Unveils Taiwan's First Newly Built F-16 Block 70," *The Aviationist,* April 1, 2025.

"it's through making things": *Back to the Future: Testimony Before the House of Representatives Committee on Armed Services Subcommittee on Cyber, Information Technologies, and Innovation,* 118th Cong. (2023) (testimony of Arthur Herman, Hudson Institute Senior Fellow).

The United States was the world leader: Hacker, *Arsenal of Democracy: Myth or Model?,* 52.

The US Navy built 151: Shyam Sankar, "Rebooting the American Industrial Base: Software and the Future of Manufacturing," *American Affairs* VIII, *no.3* (Fall 2024): 70–77.

China has the capacity: Cathalijne Adams, "China's Shipbuilding Capacity Is 232 Times Greater Than That of the United States," *Alliance for American Manufacturing,* September 18, 2023.

In 2024, a single Chinese shipbuilder: Matthew P. Funaiole, Brian Hart, and Aidan Powers-Riggs, "Murky Waters: Navigating the Risks of China's Dual-Use Shipyards," Center for Strategic & International Studies, accessed October 14, 2025, https://features.csis.org/hiddenreach/china-shipyard-tiers/.

Meanwhile, the global market: "Connected Commercial Drones Report 2025: Asia-Pacific Leads in Drone Adoption, with DJI Holding a Dominant 70% Global Market Share," *Research and Markets,* April 8, 2025.

China is the world's largest producer: Agnes Chang and Keith Bradsher, "How China Became the World's Largest Car Exporter," *The New York Times,* November 29, 2024.

China also makes: Antonio Varas, et al., *Government Incentives and US Competitiveness in Semiconductor Manufacturing,* Boston Consulting Group and Semiconductor Industry Association, September 2020, 7.

Those contracts support: Sydney J. Freedberg, Jr., "Nearly one in 10 'Tier 1' subcontractors to defense primes are Chinese firms: Report," *Breaking Defense,* June 27, 2025.

But many Americans: Michael Dahm, "China's Desert Storm Education," *U.S. Naval Institute Proceedings* 147, no. 3 (March 2021).

Simulations of war: Seth G. Jones, "The U.S. Defense Industrial Base Is Not Prepared for a Possible Conflict with China," *Center for Strategic and International Studies*, February 22, 2023.

It takes an average: William Greenwalt and Dan Patt, *Competing in Time: Ensuring Capability Advantage and Mission Success through Adaptable Resource Allocation* (Washington, D.C.: The Hudson Institute, February 2021), 46.

The F-35 fifth-generation fighter: Jon Ludwigson, *F-35 Joint Strike Fighter: More Actions Needed to Explain Cost Growth and Support Engine Modernization Decision*, GAO-23-106047 (Washington, D.C.: Government Accountability Office, May 30, 2023).

The program to modernize intercontinental ballistic missiles: Chris Gordon, "Air Force Orders Halt to Some Work on Sentinel ICBM," *Air & Space Forces Magazine,* February 11, 2025.

The new ground stations: Greg Hadley, "Space Force Adds $196 Million More for Its Long-Delayed GPS Control System," *Air & Space Forces Magazine,* December 2, 2024.

their cost has increased: Maddy Saines, "GPS OCX still delayed and lawmakers are not happy," *GPS World,* August 24, 2023.

"Our problems are a function": Michael J. Mazarr, "Beating the Ossification Trap: Why Reform, Not Spending, Will Salvage American Power," *War on the Rocks,* February 15, 2024.

During the Cold War: "Defense Spending as a % of Gross Domestic Product (GDP)," Department of Defense, accessed September 24, 2025, https://www.defense.gov/Multimedia/Photos/igphoto/2002099941/.

"We need more money": Franklin C. Spinney, *Defense Facts of Life* (Washington, D.C.: Office of Secretary of Defense, December 5, 1980 https://apps.dtic.mil/sti/tr/pdf/ADA111544.pdf.

CHAPTER 2: COLONEL CUKOR'S ODYSSEY

Distraught, Khalid promised: Dunya Mikhail, *The Beekeeper: Rescuing the Stolen Women of Iraq* (New Directions: 2018), 77.

Idrees later discovered: Mikhail, *The Beekeeper,* 265-66.

Nazik was left: Mikhail, *The Beekeeper,* 64.

He sent a smuggler: Mikhail, *The Beekeeper,* 12-14.

More than 400,000: Inci Sayki, "Where Are the Yazidis Today, Almost a Decade After ISIS' Genocidal Campaign?" *PBS,* March 13, 2024.

The boys were indoctrinated: Lin Taylor, "Nearly 10,000 Yazidis killed, kidnapped by Islamic State in 2014, study finds," *Reuters,* May 9, 2017.

A small number of US Marines: Jane Arraf, "5 Years After The U.S. Tried To Protect Yazidis In Iraq, The Minority Still Suffers," *NPR,* August 7, 2019.

"the plan was" Jim Michaels, "Marines had prepared for major rescue on Mount Sinjar," *USA Today,* October 7, 2014.

These stories are documented: Margaret Evans, "Beekeeper turned spymaster searches for Iraq's missing Yazidis," *CBC News,* April 16, 2021.

Marine Corps Colonel Drew Cukor: Drew Cukor in discussion with Madeline Hart, January and February 2025. Note: Unless otherwise specified, all information and quotations in this chapter are derived from personal author interviews with Drew Cukor.

When the United States evacuated: Katrina Manson, "AI Warfare Becomes Real for US Military with Project Maven," *Bloomberg,* February 28, 2024.

When Iranian proxies: Katrina Manson, "US Used AI to Help Find Middle East Targets for Airstrikes," *Bloomberg,* February 26, 2024.

"to be or to do": Robert Coram, *Boyd: The Fighter Pilot Who Changed the Art of War* (Back Bay Books, 2002), 183.

"faces a serious dilemma": Drew E. Cukor, "Marine Ground Intelligence Reform: How to Redesign Ground Intelligence for the Threats of the 21st Century" (MS Thesis, Naval Postgraduate School, December 1997), i.

"intellect-centric network organization": Cukor, "Marine Ground Intelligence Reform," 205.

"Therefore a significant challenge": Cukor, "Marine Ground Intelligence Reform," 209.

"Intel, GE, and Silicon Graphics": Cukor, "Marine Ground Intelligence Reform," 209.

"the 10–15 year acquisition cycle": Cukor, "Marine Ground Intelligence Reform," 208-209.

"With a focus on power projection": Cukor, "Marine Ground Intelligence Reform," 75-76.

In 2017, years after: Special Inspector General for Afghanistan Reconstruction, *Afghanistan National Defense and Security Forces: DOD Spent $457.7 Million on Intelligence Capacity-Building Programs, but Impact Cannot Be Fully Assessed Because of a Lack of Performance Metrics* (Washington, D.C.: Special Inspector General for Afghanistan Reconstruction, 2017).

"After immense investment": Drew E. Cukor, "Operate to Know: An Operational and Intelligence Design for the Operational Level of War" (MS Thesis, Joint Forces Staff College, 2014), 81.

"in the minds of operational leadership": Cukor, "Operate to Know," 83.

CHAPTER 3: PROJECT MAVEN

"Can machines think?": Alan Mathison Turing, "Computing Machinery and Intelligence." *Mind* LIX, no. 236 (October 1950): 433-460.

Turing's work on computation: Graham Oppy and David Downe, "The Turing Test," Stanford Encyclopedia of Philosophy, updated October 4, 2021, https://plato.stanford.edu/entries/turing-test/.

Researchers were optimistic: "Artificial Intelligence Coined at Dartmouth," Dartmouth College, accessed October 6, 2025, https://home.dartmouth.edu/about/artificial-intelligence-ai-coined-dartmouth.

Researchers developed programs: Hansen Hu, "AI and Play, Part 1: How Games Have Driven Two Schools of Research," *Computer History Museum,* July 23, 2020.

A classic example: B.J. Copeland, "MYCIN: (artificial intelligence program)," *Encyclopedia Brittannica,* November 21, 2018, https://www.britannica.com/technology/MYCIN.

Progress in AI research slowed: Tom Villani, "AI Hype Cycles: Lessons from the Past to Sustain Progress," *New Jersey Innovation Institute,* May 13, 2024.

In 1997, IBM's Deep Blue: Tim Mucci, "The history of artificial intelligence," IBM, accessed October 6, 2025, https://www.ibm.com/think/topics/history-of-artificial-intelligence.

In 2016, deep learning received: Mucci, "The History of Artificial Intelligence."

Work's Third Offset: Robert Work, "Remarks by Deputy Secretary Work on Third Offset Strategy," Department of Defense, April 28, 2016, https://www.war.gov/News/Speeches/Speech/Article/753482/remarks-by-deputy-secretary-work-on-third-offset-strategy/.

In fact, he saw the job: Drew Cukor in discussion with Madeline Hart, January and February 2025. Note: Unless otherwise specified, all information and quotes in this chapter are derived from personal interviews with Drew Cukor.

The memo clearly laid out: Robert Work, "Establishment of an Algorithmic Warfare Cross-Functional Team (Project Maven)" (official memorandum, Washington, DC: Office of the Deputy Secretary of Defense, April 26, 2017).

An estimated 85 percent: Sydney J. Freedberg, Jr., "'Success begets challenges': NGA struggles to meet rising demand for Maven AI," *Breaking Defense,* September 3, 2024.

Cukor built a team with tech companies: Emelia S. Probasco, *Building the Tech Coalition: How Project Maven and the U.S. 18th Airborne Corps Operationalized Software and Artificial Intelligence for the Department of Defense* (Washington, D.C.: Center for Security and Emerging Technology, August 2024), 10.

Google, famously, pulled out: Daisuke Wakabayashi and Scott Shane, "Google Will Not Renew Pentagon Contract That Upset Employees," *The New York Times,* June 1, 2018.

Google simultaneously was working: Jillian D'Onfro, "Google CEO: We're 'not close' to launching search in China," *CNBC,* August 16, 2018.

Donald Trump had just been elected: "A License to Discriminate: Trump's Muslim & Refugee Ban," Amnesty International UK, April 1, 2025, https://www.amnesty.org.uk/licence-discriminate-trumps-muslim-refugee-ban.

"were not immediately impressed": Richard H. Shultz and Richard D. Clarke, "Big Data at War: Special Operations Forces, Project Maven, and Twenty-First-Century Warfare," *Modern War Institute at West Point,* August 25, 2020.

"Early in Project Maven": Shultz and Clarke, "Big Data at War."

Cukor eventually found traction: Shultz and Clarke, "Big Data at War."

He was partial: Nick Rife and Joshua Brown, "New and Different: 2nd Security Force Assistance Brigade's Digital Strategy," *Army Intelligence Knowledge Network* (July-September 2020): 77-81.

Kurilla kept firing: Michael Yon, "Gates of Fire," *Michael Yon.com,* August 31, 2005, https://michaelyon.com/dispatches/gates-of-fire/.

In 2023, Maven transitioned: Jaspreet Gill, "Now that Maven is a program of record, NGA looks at LLMs, data labeling," *Breaking Defense,* November 16, 2023.

As of this writing, it is used: Courtney Albon, "Palantir wins contract to expand access to Project Maven AI tools," *C4ISRNet,* May 30, 2024.

"Using Maven Smart System": Probasco, *Building the Tech Coalition*, 4.

"have a propaganda machine" Alan Rems, "A Propaganda Machine Like Stalin's," *U.S. Naval Institute Proceedings* 33, no. 3 (June 2019).

"AWCFT did not document": Department of Defense Office of Inspector General, *Evaluation of Contract Monitoring and Management for Project Maven* (Washington, D.C.: Department of Defense, January 2022), i, https://www.dodig.mil/reports.html/Article/2893388/evaluation-of-contract-monitoring-and-management-for-project-maven-dodig-2022-0/.

"are not captured in current procedures": DOD Inspector General, "Evaluation of Contract Monitoring and Management for Project Maven," 7.

"future DoD acquisitions": DOD Inspector General, "Evaluation of Contract Monitoring and Management for Project Maven," i.

CHAPTER 4: AMERICAN PROSPERITY IS NATIONAL SECURITY

It was February 1934: Neil Sheehan, *A Fiery Peace in a Cold War: Bernard Schriever and the Ultimate Weapon* (Vintage Books, 2010), 21.

In just over two months: Sheehan, *A Fiery Peace in a Cold War,* 21.

It didn't matter that smaller airlines: Lyndon Baltazar, "Airmail Comes of Age," Federal Aviation Administration, accessed September 24, 2025, https://www.faa.gov/sites/faa.gov/files/about/history/milestones/Airmail_Comes_of_Age.pdf.

"publicly posing as patriots": "Special Committee to Investigate Air Mail and Ocean Mail Contracts," U.S. Senate, accessed October 7, 2025, https://www.senate.gov/about/powers-procedures/investigations/mail-contracts.htm.

Unlike industry, many of the military's planes: Sheehan, *A Fiery Peace in a Cold War,* 20.

Other pilots crashed: Sheehan, *A Fiery Peace in a Cold War,* 20-21.

We have Schriever to thank: "General Bernard Adolph Schriever," U.S. Air Force, accessed September 24, 2025, https://www.af.mil/About-Us/Biographies/Display/Article/104877/general-bernard-adolph-schriever/.

The early market for Silicon Valley's: Chris Miller, *Chip War: The Fight for the World's Most Critical Technology* (Scribner, 2022), 22, 32.

Eventually, the commercial market: Miller, *Chip War,* 32.

He grilled hundreds of executives: "Merchants of Death," U.S. Senate, accessed October 7, 2025, https://www.senate.gov/about/powers-procedures/investigations/merchants-of-death.htm.

"desirability of creating a government monopoly": *Investigation of Munitions Industry: Hearings before the Senate Special Committee to Investigate the Munitions Industry,* 73rd Cong. 2 (1934).

American giants like General Electric: Herman, *Freedom's Forge,* 6.

At the time of the hearing: Hunter DeRensis, "Merchants of Death," *The American Conservative,* November 8, 2021.

The hearings produced thousands of pages: *Report of the Special Committee on Investigation of the Munitions Industry (The Nye Report): U.S. Senate,* 74th Cong. (1936), 6, https://resources.saylor.org/wwwresources/archived/site/wp-content/uploads/2011/08/HIST312-10.1.3-The-Nye-Report.pdf.

Nye's assistant counsel: "The Alger Hiss Story: Search for Truth," Maryland State Archives, accessed September 24, 2025, https://msa.maryland.gov/megafile/msa/speccol/sc5300/sc5339/000030/000000/000010/restricted/hiss%20nyu/homepages.nyu.edu/_th15/timeline.html.

"The Committee majority recommends": *Investigation of Munitions Industry: Hearings before the Senate Special Committee to Investigate the Munitions Industry,* 74th Cong. (1936), 121, https://archive.org/details/munitionsindustr36unit/page/120/mode/2up.

(Master industrialist Henry Kaiser): Herman, *Freedom's Forge,* 191.

"in the same way": Sen. *Investigation of Munitions Industry,* 121-122.

Americans at the time agreed: DeRensis, "Merchants of Death".

US companies were prohibited: "The Neutrality Acts, 1930s," Department of State Office of the Historian, accessed October 7, 2025, https://history.state.gov/milestones/1921-1936/neutrality-acts.

But the damage was done: Jacob Vander Meulen, *The Politics of Aircraft: Building American Military Industry* (University Press of Kansas, 1991) 144.

His arguments for ending: "How did Public Opinion About Entering World War II Change Between 1939 and 1941?" United States Holocaust Memorial Museum, accessed September 24, 2025, https://exhibitions.ushmm.org/americans-and-the-holocaust/us-public-opinion-world-war-II-1939-1941.

A commercial aviation market: Vander Meulen, *Politics of Aircraft*, 57.

Rather than nurturing: Vander Meulen, *Politics of Aircraft*, 44-45, 57-60.

Firms consistently lost money: Vander Meulen, *Politics of Aircraft*, 44-45, 58-59.

To make matters worse: Vander Meulen, *Politics of Aircraft*, 44-45, 58-59.

Martin was so put off: Vander Meulen, *Politics of Aircraft*, 59.

Meanwhile, the company: Vander Meulen, *Politics of Aircraft*, 59.

"it cannot be expected": Vander Meulen, *Politics of Aircraft*, 45.

"For Moffett the distinction": Vander Meulen, *Politics of Aircraft*, 86.

Moffett pushed for the use: Vander Meulen, *Politics of Aircraft*, 86.

But this influx of private capital: Vander Meulen, *Politics of Aircraft*, 133.

When Congress held a hearing: Vander Meulen, *Politics of Aircraft*, 135.

"contractors always bear the losses": Vander Meulen, *Politics of Aircraft*, 106.

"Without further compensation": Vander Meulen, *Politics of Aircraft*, 136.

No such evidence was uncovered: Vander Meulen, *Politics of Aircraft*, 144-145.

The bill wasn't meant: Charles F. Elliott, "The Genesis of the Modern Navy," *U.S. Naval Institute Proceedings* 92, no. 3 (March 1966).

In particular, the bill required: Vander Meulen, *Politics of Aircraft*, 142.

What's more, profits: Vander Meulen, *Politics of Aircraft*, 142.

"This of course means": Vander Meulen, *Politics of Aircraft*, 143.

"losses on development contracts": Vander Meulen, *Politics of Aircraft,* 195.

Leroy Grumman complained: Vander Meulen, *Politics of Aircraft,* 198.

During a three-year period: Vander Meulen, *Politics of Aircraft,* 194.

Martin consistently lost money: Vander Meulen, *Politics of Aircraft,* 197.

Boeing lost 28 percent: Vander Meulen, *Politics of Aircraft,* 190.

produced the B-17 at a loss: Vander Meulen, *Politics of Aircraft,* 213.

The bombers held up well: Mark Lorell, *The U.S. Combat Aircraft Industry: 1909–2000* (Santa Monica, CA: RAND, 2003), 42.

How did the US aircraft industry transform: Aaron Spray, "Allies vs Axis: What Were the Most Produced War Planes of WW2?" *Simple Flying,* June 2, 2024.

Formerly a shipyard worker: Herman, *Freedom's Forge,* 17.

He worked at Ford: Herman, *Freedom's Forge,* 28-29.

Out of pure patriotism: Norman Beasley, *Knudsen: A Biography* (Papamoa Press, 2017), 269.

At the recommendation of Bernard Baruch: Herman, *Freedom's Forge,* 13.

Third, the amortization period: Beasley, *Knudsen,* 249-250.

Many, including Senator Harry Truman: Herman, *Freedom's Forge,* 198.

After Knudsen's call: Herman, *Freedom's Forge,* 96.

"organizational genius": Harry S. Truman, "Letter to William S. Knudsen on His Retirement From Active Duty," June 7, 1945, The American Presidency Project, "https://www.presidency.ucsb.edu/documents/letter-general-william-s-knudsen-his-retirement-from-active-duty".

In 1942, Knudsen: Herman, *Freedom's Forge,* 164.

The firing came right on the heels: Herman, *Freedom's Forge,* 157.

It was only at the direct intervention: Herman, *Freedom's Forge,* 165-166.

Knudsen approached his new role: Herman, *Freedom's Forge,* 330.

"American production": Herman, *Freedom's Forge,* 336.

If Nye had his way: Herman testimony *Back to the Future.*

a trio of American car companies: Larry P. Vellequette and Automotive News, "A Brief History of Jeep: 75 Years from Willys to Wrangler," *Autoweek,* July 13, 2016.

Kaiser Shipbuilding wouldn't: "The Aircraft Carriers of World War II," Great American Ships.com, accessed October 7, 2025, https://www.greatamericanships.com/ships_of_world_war_two/aircraft_carriers/.

a single Chinese firm: Zeyi Yang, "Why China's Dominance in Commercial Drones Has Become a Global Security Matter," *MIT Technology Review,* June 26, 2024.

It wasn't until 2019: David Shepardson, "US House panel seeks ban on federal purchases of China drones," *Reuters,* November 1, 2023.

It would take another five years: "New drone laws take effect: What public safety agencies need to know," Axon, accessed October 7, 2025, https://www.axon.com/resources/new-drone-laws-take-effect.

The US Air Force deployed: Richard Whittle, *Predator: The Secret Origins of the Drone Revolution* (Picador, 2014), 13.

The first highly capable: Whittle, *Predator,* 76-81.

When the IDF proved a fickle customer: Whittle, *Predator,* 18-19.

Karem's prototype, named Amber: Whittle, *Predator,* 49, 56

The six surviving prototypes: Whittle, *Predator,* 63.

"poor man's cruise missile": Whittle, *Predator,* 40.

Their drone was primitive: Whittle, *Predator*, 66.

Amber was reborn: Whittle, *Predator,* 83.

General Atomics deployed: Whittle, *Predator,* 79-81.

While BVLOS does introduce additional challenges: Jim Magill, "Trump Executive Orders Push FAA to Act on Long-Awaited BVLOS Rule," *Drone Life,* June 17, 2025.

Finally, arms-control laws: Linden Blue, "Reforming Defense Acquisitions to Promote Global Security," General Atomics, January 24, 2025. https://www.ga.com/reforming-defense-acquisitions-to-promote-global-security.

It was France and the United Kingdom: Lorell, *U.S. Combat Aircraft Industry*, 48.

"Within GA-ASI's own export market": Blue, "Reforming Defense Acquisitions."

And so, despite an estimated $29 billion: Zachary Morris, "U.S. Drones: Smaller, Less Capable Drones for the Near Future," *Military Review* 98, no. 3 (May-June 2018): 42.

Civilian Lockheed test pilots died: Ben R. Rich and Leo Janos, *Skunk Works* (Little, Brown, 1994), 266-267; "F-22 crash claims life of Edwards pilot," U.S. Air Force, March 25, 2009, https://www.af.mil/News/Article-Display/Article/120820/f-22-crash-claims-life-of-edwards-pilot/.

The World War II–era arsenal of democracy: "Hazards on the Home Front: Workplace Accidents and Injuries during World War II," National Park Service, accessed October 13, 2025, https://www.nps.gov/articles/000/hazards-on-the-home-front-workplace-accidents-and-injuries-during-world-war-ii.htm.

Arthur Herman reports: Herman, *Freedom's Forge*, x.

"Until the latest of our world conflicts": Dwight D. Eisenhower, "President Dwight D. Eisenhower's Farewell Address," National Archives, January 17, 1961, https://www.archives.gov/milestone-documents/president-dwight-d-eisenhowers-farewell-address.

CHAPTER 5: BREAKING THE PENTAGON

"Competing in Time": Greenwalt and Patt, *Competing in Time*, 24.

Hyman Rickover's first nuclear-powered submarine: Greenwalt and Patt, *Competing in Time*, 18-19.

The list goes on: Patrick Collison, "Fast," *Patrick Collison,* accessed September 29, 2025, https://patrickcollison.com/fast.

On average it, took seventeen years: Greenwalt and Patt, *Competing in Time*, 40.

They went head to head: Elliott V. Converse, *Rearming for the Cold War, 1945–1960* (Washington, D.C.: Historical Office of the Office of the Secretary of Defense, 2012), 41.

That roof was the Pentagon: Steve Vogel, *The Pentagon: A History* (Random House, 2008), 346.

As a senator and then vice presidential candidate: Douglas T. Stuart, *Organizing for National Security* (U.S. Army War College Press, 2000), 10.

"a dreary succession": Converse, *Rearming for the Cold War*, 41.

The debate was resolved: National Security Act of 1947, Public Law. No. 80-253, 61 Stat. 495 (1947).

He was responsible: "James V. Forrestal: Harry Truman Administration," Historical Office of the Office of the Secretary of Defense, accessed October 7, 2025, https://history.defense.gov/Multimedia/Biographies/Article-View/Article/571293/james-v-forrestal/.

It had operated with autonomy: Charles A. Stevenson, "The Story Behind the National Security Act," *Military Review* 88, (May–June 2008): 15-16.

"My chief misgiving": James Michael Roherty, *Decisions of Robert S. McNamara: A Study of the Role of the Secretary of Defense* (University of Miami Press, 1970), 30.

He'd seen many an M&A deal fail: Eric M. Lofgren, *Programmed to Fail: The Rise of Central Planning in Defense Acquisition, 1945-1975* (Acquisition Talk, October 2019), 19, https://acquisitiontalk.com/wp-content/uploads/2023/02/Lofgren_Programmed-to-Fail-DRAFT_2019.10.14.pdf.

The patriot agreed: Vogel, *The Pentagon,* 344-45.

The services independently prepared: Converse, *Rearming for the Cold War*, 37.

"principal assistant to the President": National Security Act of 1947, Public Law No. 80-253, 61 Stat. 495 (1947), as amended by Act of August 10, 1949, Public Law No. 81-216, 63 Stat. 578, Title II, § 202(b).

Then, just two months after his resignation: Townsend Hoopes and Douglas G. Brinkley, *Driven Patriot: The Life and Times of James Forrestal* (U.S. Naval Institute Press, 2000), 451, 466.

Forrestal had eagerly signed up: Herman, *Freedom's Forge*, 347.

"We finally succeeded": Herman S. Wolk, "The Quiet Coup of 1949," *Air Force Magazine*, July 1949, 81.

After Sputnik lit up: Greenwalt and Patt, *Competing in Time*, 9.

"assume with top efficiency": Dwight D. Eisenhower, "State of the Union Address," Eisenhower Presidential Library, January 9, 1958, https://www.eisenhowerlibrary.gov/sites/default/files/file/1958_state_of_the_union.pdf.

And for the first time: Department of Defense Reorganization Act of 1958. Public Law 85-599. U.S. Statutes at Large 72 (1958): 514, enacted August 6, 1958; John T. Correll, "Eisenhower and the Eight Warlords," *Air Force Magazine,* July 2017, 61.

Congress, in particular: Thomas L. McNaugher, *New Weapons Old Politics: America's Military Procurement Muddle* (The Brookings Institution Press, 1989), 40, 49-50.

Secretaries of defense certainly tried: Converse, *Rearming for the Cold War*, 323.

His résumé was impeccable: *The Fog of War: Eleven Lessons from the Life of Robert S. McNamara*, directed by Errol Morris (Sony Pictures Classics, 2003).

McNamara's analysis also found: *The Fog of War*, Morris.

"Whiz Kids": Walter S. Poole, *Adapting to Flexible Response: 1960-1968* (Washington, D.C.: Historical Office of the Office of the Secretary of Defense, 2013), 24.

Most didn't have college degrees: *The Fog of War,* Morris. See: "Of the top thousand executives at Ford Motor Company, I don't believe there were ten college graduates."

Eventually he was elevated: *The Fog of War*, Morris.

McNamara was Ford's president: "Robert S. McNamara: John F. Kennedy / Lyndon Johnson Administration," Historical Office of the Office of the Secretary of Defense, accessed September 30, 2025, https://history.defense.gov/Multimedia/Biographies/Article-View/Article/571271/robert-s-mcnamara/.

The Planning, Programming, and Budgeting System: "Planning, Programming, Budgeting & Execution Process (PPBE)," Defense Acquisition University, accessed September 30, 2025, https://www.dau.edu/acquipedia-article/planning-programming-budgeting-execution-process-ppbe.

"McNamara Fallacy": Johnny Thomson, "The 'McNamara fallacy': When data leads to the worst decision," *Big Think,* October 18, 2014.

"establishes the primacy of technical process": Roherty, *Decisions of Robert McNamara,* 100.

Founded shortly after World War II: Converse, *Rearming for the Cold War*, 214.

A Rhodes Scholar: Poole, *Adapting to Flexible Response,* 24, 25.

In 1960, during the end: Lofgren, *Programmed to Fail,* 69, 77-78.

The total defense budget: Roherty, *Decisions of Robert McNamara,* 75.

"Support Vehicles": Eric Lofgren, Jerry McGinn, and Lloyd Everhart, *Execution Flexibility and Bridging the Valley of Death* (Fairfax, VA: George Mason University, October 2022), 8-9.

Almost 40 percent: Whitney M. McNamara, Peter Modigliani, Matthew MacGregor, and Eric Lofgren, *Report of the Commission on Defense Innovation Adoption* (Washington, D.C.: Atlantic Council, January 2024), 8.

PPBE culminates: Brendan W. McGarry and Heidi M. Peters, *Defense Primer: Future Years Defense Program,* CRS Report No. IF10429 (Washington, D.C.: Congressional Research Service, 2020), https://apps.dtic.mil/sti/pdfs/AD1169604.pdf.

"This ideology and management approach": Bill Greenwalt, "Competing in Time: How DoD Is Losing The Innovation Race To China," *Breaking Defense,* March 9, 2021.

Enthoven was a Whiz Kid: Poole, *Adapting to Flexible Response,* 28.

"pipe-smoking": Poole, *Adapting to Flexible Response,* 28.

OSD acquisition history: Poole, *Adapting to Flexible Response,* 25.

"IBM machine with legs": *The Fog of War,* Morris.

"The social scientists": Peter T. Tarpgaard, "McNamara and the Rise of Analysis in Defense Planning: A Retrospective," *Naval War College Review* 48, No. 4 (Autumn 1995): 67-87.

The firms in turn sent: Poole, *Adapting to Flexible Response,* 204.

The culture of acquisition: Barry D. Watts, *U.S. Defense Industrial Base: Past, Present, and Future* (Washington, D.C.: Center for Strategic and Budgetary Assessments, 2008), 22.

"The essential operational requirements": McNaugher, *New Weapons Old Politics,* 58-59.

The resulting design: Poole, *Adapting to Flexible Response,* 216-18.

The problem was exacerbated: Poole, *Adapting to Flexible Response,* 229.

MOBILIZE

In 1967, two test pilots died: Francis X. Clines, "2 Die in L.I. Crash of F-111B Test Jet; JET Crash on L.I. Kills Two Pilots," *The New York Times,* April 22, 1967.

Any deviation in performance: Poole, *Adapting to Flexible Response,* 232.

None of the promised commonality: Poole, *Adapting to Flexible Response,* 241.

"For the Air Force": McNaugher, *New Weapons Old Politics,* 31.

He then returned: "David Packard: Richard Nixon Administration," Historical Office of the Office of the Secretary of Defense, accessed October 1, 2025, https://history.defense.gov/DOD-History/Deputy-Secretaries-of-Defense/Article-View/Article/585238/david-packard/.

"father of fourth-generation air power": Brian M. Fredrickson, *The Laird-Packard Way: Unpacking Defense Acquisition Policy* (Air University Press, 2020), 7.

His prototyping competitions: Fredrickson, *The Laird-Packard Way*, vii.

He had an innate love: David Packard, *The HP Way: How Bill Hewlett and I Built Our Company* (Harper Business, 1995), 7.

Packard attended Stanford University: Packard, *The HP Way,* 16-17.

One of HP's first major customers: "HP Tech Takes: The History of HP," Hewlett-Packard Company, September 1, 2019, https://www.hp.com/us-en/shop/tech-takes/history-of-hp.

In 1969, he resigned: Packard, *The HP Way,* 174-176.

He wanted to select: Fredrickson, *The Laird-Packard Way*, 75.

"requests for proposals for the development stage": David Packard, "Policy Guidance on Major Weapon System Acquisitions" (official memorandum, Washington, D.C.: Department of Defense, 1970), 94.

"put more capable people into program management": Packard, "Policy Guidance on Major Weapon System Acquisition," 92.

"I am a little concerned": Fredrickson, *The Laird-Packard Way*, 75.

In the end, he received: Fredrickson, *The Laird-Packard Way*, 85.

(The loser did alright, too.): Fredrickson, *The Laird-Packard Way*, 78.

The establishment: Fredrickson, *The Laird-Packard Way*, 82.

"the LWF contracts": Lofgren, *Programmed to Fail,* 128.

When Secretary of Defense James Schlesinger: Lofgren, *Programmed to Fail,* 136.

The F-16 was produced at lower cost: Coram, *Boyd,* 302.

The Air Force bought both: Eileen Bjorkman, "The Outrageous Adolescence of the F-16," *Air & Space Magazine,* March 2014.

Northrop and Fairchild Republic went head to head: Hal Sundt, *Warplane: How the Military Reformers Birthed the A-10 Warthog* (Lyons Press, 2024), 73-74.

The Gatling-style gun: "A-10C Thunderbolt II," US Air Force, last modified December 2020, https://www.af.mil/About-Us/Fact-Sheets/Display/Article/104490/a-10c-thunderbolt-ii/.

Five were shot down: Alfred Price, "To War in a Warthog," *Air & Space Forces Magazine,* August 1, 1993.

Packard approached reform: Poole, *Adapting to Flexible Response,* 389.

"Successful development, production, and deployment": Department of Defense, *Acquisition of Major Defense Systems,* DOD Directive 5000.1 (Washington, D.C.: Department of Defense, July 13, 1971), 1.

By the mid-1990s: Greenwalt and Patt, *Competing in Time,* 25.

Greenwalt and Patt show a stunning correlation: Greenwalt and Patt, *Competing in Time,* 25.

Packard, who advocated for cutting acquisition regulations: Lofgren, *Programmed to Fail,* 124.

"Programs shall be structured": Department of Defense, *Acquisition of Major Defense Systems,* 4.

Packard's 5000 series: Department of Defense, *Acquisition of Major Defense Systems,* 2, 3.

***A Quest for Excellence*:** David Packard, et al., *A Quest for Excellence: Final Report to the President* (Washington, D.C.: President's Blue Ribbon Commission on Defense Management, June 1986): xiii.

So, a new process: Bill Greenwalt and Dan Patt, *Required to Fail: Beyond Documents: Accelerating Joint Advantage through Direct Resourcing and Experimentation* (Washington, D.C.: Hudson Institute, February 2025), 26.

Eight US servicemen: "Operation Eagle Claw," U.S. Army Airborne & Special Operations Museum, accessed October 1, 2025, https://www.asomf.org/operation-eagle-claw/.

There were incidents of friendly fire: Ronald H. Cole, *Operation Urgent Fury: The Planning and Execution of Joint Operations in Grenada, 12 October – 2 November 1983* (Washington, D.C.: Joint History Office, Office of the Chairman of the Joint Chiefs of Staff, 1997), 6.

another paper by Greenwalt and Patt: Greenwalt and Patt, *Required to Fail,* 17.

"hidden curriculum of requirements": Greenwalt and Patt, *Required to Fail,* 16.

"With no dedicated technical assessment capability": Greenwalt and Patt, *Required to Fail,* 16.

CHAPTER 6: THE LAST SUPPER AND THE GREAT SCHISM

"a greater defeat": Michael Peck, "Why China's Orbital Bombardment System Is Not America's Sputnik Moment," *Forbes,* October 27, 2021.

It was a critical milestone: *The CORONA Story* (Chantilly, VA: Center for the Study of National Reconnaissance, September 2013), 3.

Fairchild C-119 and Lockheed C-130: Robert D. Mulcahy, ed., *Corona Star Catchers: Interviews with Air Force Aerial Recovery Flight Crews of the 6593d Test Squadron (Special), 1958–1972* (Chantilly, VA: Center for the Study of National Reconnaissance, June 2012), 105; *The CORONA Story*, 37-38, 48.

Much like fighter pilots: Mulcahy, *Corona Star Catchers*, 196.

"missile gap": *The CORONA Story*, 61.

The program didn't return much: Donald E. Welzenbach, "Observation Balloons and Reconnaissance Satellites," Central Intelligence Agency, September 1999, "Secret" declassified, 23.

Both programs were vying: "U-2S/TU-2S," Air Force, updated September 2015, https://www.af.mil/About-Us/Fact-Sheets/Display/Article/104560/u-2stu-2s/.

Powers survived: "Capt. Francis Gary Powers," National Air and Space Museum, accessed October 1, 2025, https://airandspace.si.edu/support/wall-of-honor/capt-francis-gary-powers.

Over 12 years: Curtis Peebles, *The Corona Project: America's First Spy Satellites* (U.S. Naval Institute Press, 1997), 259.

The photos proved: Peebles, *The Corona Project,* 114-115.

The success of CORONA: Peebles, *The Corona Project,* x.

"The United States of America": *The CORONA Story*, 121.

Naturally, the CIA: *The CORONA Story*, 31.

Lockheed was the prime contractor: "First Successful Corona Remote Sensing Satellite Built by Lockheed Martin Marks 50 Year Anniversary," Lockheed Martin, accessed October 1, 2025, https://news.lockheedmartin.com/2010-08-25-First-Successful-Corona-Remote-Sensing-Satellite-Built-by-Lockheed-Martin-Marks-50-Year-Anniversary.

but Eastman Kodak developed: *The CORONA Story*, 56.

and General Electric made: *The CORONA Story*, 24.

General Mills: Welzenbach, "Observation Balloons and Reconnaissance Satellites," 21.

Most of the budget: Gregory C. Allen and Doug Berenson, "Why Is the U.S. Defense Industrial Base So Isolated from the U.S. Economy?" *CSIS Commentary,* August 20, 2024.

Chrysler made cars: "Chrysler SM-78/PGM-19A Jupiter Intermediate Range Ballistic Missile," National Museum of the United States Air Force, accessed October 1, 2025, https://www.nationalmuseum.af.mil/Visit/Museum-Exhibits/Fact-Sheets/Display/Article/3625335/chrysler-sm-78pgm-19a-jupiter-intermediate-range-ballistic-missile/.

Goodyear had an aerospace subsidiary: Stephen W. Lasswell, "History of SAR at Lockheed Martin (previously Goodyear Aerospace)," *Proceedings of the SPIE* 5788 (May 2005): 1-12.

But today, that 6 percent: Allen and Berenson, "Why Is the U.S. Defense Industrial Base So Isolated?"

"knew the fundamentals": Harry C. Thomson and Lida Mayo, *The Ordnance Department: Procurement and Supply* (U.S. Army Center of Military History, 1991), 113.

Although these cities: William J. Perry, *My Journey at the Nuclear Brink*, (Stanford University Press, 2015), 6-8.

Thanks to the GI Bill: Perry, *My Journey at the Nuclear Brink*, 8-9.

At EDL, SIGINT was done: Perry, *My Journey at the Nuclear Brink*, 19.

As CEO for thirteen years: Perry, *My Journey at the Nuclear Brink*, 27.

"We were undertaking a business": Perry, *My Journey at the Nuclear Brink*, 22.

So ESL was entirely capitalized: Perry, *My Journey at the Nuclear Brink*, 23.

"Unlike HP": Steve Blank, "Story Behind "The Secret History" Part III: The Most Important Company You Never Heard Of," *Steve Blank,* April 6, 2009, https://steveblank.com/2009/04/06/story-behind-%E2%80%9Cthe-secret-history%E2%80%9D-part-iii-the-most-important-company-you-never-heard-of/.

It would be up to Perry: William Perry, interview by Alfred Goldberg and Rebecca Welch, Historical Office of the Office of the Secretary of Defense, October 18, 2004, 3, https://history.defense.gov/Portals/70/Documents/oral_history/OH_Trans_PerryWilliam10-18-04.pdf.

"tank for tank, missile for missile": Perry, interview by Goldberg and Welch, 8.

"to be able to see all high-value targets": Rebecca Grant, "The Second Offset," *Air & Space Forces Magazine,* June 24, 2016.

The goal of this concept: Jaspreet Gill, "Return of CJADC2: DoD officially moves ahead with 'combined' JADC2 in a rebrand focusing on partners," *Breaking Defense,* May 16, 2023.

So, to implement the Second Offset: Perry, *My Journey at the Nuclear Brink*, 36-37.

The technology underpinning: Peter Westwick, *Stealth: The Secret Contest to Invent Invisible Aircraft* (Oxford University Press, 2020), 48; Perry, *My Journey at the Nuclear Brink*, 27, 36.

The Air Force wasn't interested: Westwick, *Stealth,* 27.

He made the Air Force: Perry, *My Journey at the Nuclear Brink*, 36-37.

"must be used sparingly": Perry, *My Journey at the Nuclear Brink*, 37.

Perry intervened: Perry, *My Journey at the Nuclear Brink*, 40-41.

He required both services: Thomas C. Hone, Gregory A. Angel, and Roger C. Easton, *The Politics of Naval Innovation* (occasional paper, U.S. Naval War College,1994), 39-40.

We got the Tomahawk: Perry, *My Journey at the Nuclear Brink*, 39.

"Without Dr. Perry's direct intervention": Hone, Angel, and Easton, *The Politics of Naval Innovation*, 40.

To secure freedom of action: Perry, *My Journey at the Nuclear Brink*, 36-37.

"Rather than giving my time": Perry, *My Journey at the Nuclear Brink*, 81.

These numbers improved during the war: John T. Correll, "Daylight Precision Bombing," *Air & Space Forces Magazine,* October 1, 2008.

The Gulf War delivered the report card: Correll, "Daylight Precision Bombing".

"no longer did airmen have to plan": Grant, "The Second Offset".

The stealthy attack aircraft: Krepinevich, *The Origins of Victory*, 393.

Precision strike remained a near monopoly: Barry D. Watts, *The Evolution of Precision Strike* (Washington, D.C.: Center for Strategic and Budgetary Assessments, 2013), 2.

Around 25 executives: Jonathan Chang and Meghna Chakrabarti, "'The last supper': How a 1993 Pentagon dinner reshaped the defense industry," *WBUR,* March 1, 2023.

For example, five companies: Defense Acquisition Universiry, *Chapter One Overview of DOD Manufacturing Management* (Fort Belvoir, VA: Defense Acquisition University), 2. https://www.dau.edu/sites/default/files/Migrated/ToolAttachments/Defense-Manufacturing-Management-Guide-for-PMs.pdf.

"We expect defense companies": Chang and Chakrabarti, "The last supper."

"integrate, disintegrate, or disappear": Mike Benitez and Jake Chapman, hosts, *The Merge,* episode 22, "Military Tech Titan: Norm Augustine," January 7, 2024.

"payoffs for layoffs": Bernie Sanders, "Payoffs for Layoffs Have to Stop," *Los Angeles Times,* July 11, 1996.

Today, these five contractors: Alexandra G. Neenan, *Defense Primer: Department of Defense Contractors,* CRS Report No. IF10600,

(Washington, D.C.: Congressional Research Service, June 6, 2024), https://www.congress.gov/crs-product/IF10600.

"During 1985–1988": Watts, *The US Defense Industrial Base,* 26.

Adding to the "reforms": Watts, *The US Defense Industrial Base,* 24.

Goodyear sold its aerospace subsidiary: Jonathan P. Hicks, "Loral to Acquire Goodyear Division," *The New York Times,* January 13, 1987.

Ford did the same: Paul C. Judge, "Ford Selling Aerospace Unit as Military Spending Slows," *The New York Times,* January 13, 1990.

Loral experienced success: Thomas Heinrich, "Cold War Armory: Military Contracting in Silicon Valley," *Enterprise & Society* 3, No. 2 (June 2002): 265.

One year later, Texas Instruments sold: Allen R. Myerson, "Raytheon Wins Arms Unit in Texas, Though at High Price," *The New York Times,* January 7, 1997.

For all the caricatures: MAC Group, *Impact on Defense Industrial Capability of Changes in Procurement and Tax Policy 1984–1987* (Cambridge, MA: The MAC Group, 1988), D-9.

Activity-based costing (ABC): Watts, *The US Defense Industrial Base,* 58.

Company strategy focused: Watts, *The US Defense Industrial Base,* 25.

There was no bold technologist or founder: Robin Sidel, "Warburg Pincus to Acquire TransDigm for $1.1 Billion," *The Wall Street Journal,* June 9, 2003.

It acquired companies: Peter Westberg, "TransDigm: The Story of the Controversial Aerospace Giant," *Quartr,* August 13, 2024.

Among his many gifts: J. Ronald Fox, *Defense Acquisition Reform 1960-2009: An Elusive Goal* (U.S. Army Center of Military History, 2011), 165-166.

By this time, Perry was: "Les Aspin resigns as Defense Secretary, Dec. 15, 1993," *Politico,* December 15, 2010,

"probably beyond fixing": Perry, interview by Goldberg and Welch, 27.

The statute requires: Federal Acquisition Streamlining Act of 1994, Public Law No. 103-355, § 8104, 108 Stat. 3243 (1994) (codified as amended at 10 U.S.C. § 3453 (formerly at 10 U.S.C. § 2377)).

"military, economic, and policy": William J. Perry, "A New Way of Doing Business" (official memorandum, Washington, D.C.: Department of Defense, June 24, 1994), 1.

"My passion for this goal": Fox, *Defense Acquisition Reform,* 152.

CHAPTER 7: MONOPSONY: THE ORIGINAL SIN

What does the Lockheed Electra: "SR-71 Blackbird," Strategic Air Command, accessed October 1, 2025, http://www.strategic-air-command.com/aircraft/reconnaissance/sr71_blackbird.htm.

"It may be impossible": Clarence L. Johnson, *Kelly: More Than My Share of It All* (Smithsonian Books, 1989), 160.

"What are they doing?" Rich and Janos, *Skunk Works,* 313.

Kelly designed more than forty airplanes: "Kelly Johnson: Architect of Air," Lockheed Martin, October 1, 2020, https://www.lockheedmartin.com/en-us/news/features/history/johnson.html.

But as Rich pointed out: Rich and Janos, *Skunk Works,* 316.

"Imagine if the Lockheed team": Eric Lofgren, "The Five Big Inventions of the SR-71," *Acquisition Talk,* October 18, 2022.

Additionally, Walmart's focus: Hedrick Smith, "Who Calls the Shots in the Global Economy?" *PBS,* November 16, 2004.

Walmart is now one-third the size: Market data as of July 17, 2025.

While the Air Force eventually operated: David J. Lynch, "How the Skunk Works Fielded Stealth," *Air & Space Forces Magazine,* November 1, 1992.

Working with the monopsony: Jeff Foust, "BAE Systems wins approval for Ball Aerospace acquisition," *Space News,* February 14, 2024.

"the defense industry is financially healthy": Office of the Under Secretary of Defense for Acquisition and Sustainment, *Contract Finance Study Report* (Washington, D.C.: Department of Defense, April 2023), 5.

While cash paid to shareholders: *Contract Finance Study Report,* 18, 34.

(for comparison, Palantir): Palantir Technologies Inc. *Form 10-K 2024,* Denver, CO: Palantir Technologies Inc, 2024, 73.

Lockheed Martin, for example: Lockheed Martin Corporation, *Form 10-K 2024.* Bethesda, MA: Lockheed Martin Corporation, 2024, 44, 66.

The Americans and their Coca-Cola: Dimitris Xygalatas, "What Cargo Cult Rituals Reveal About Human Nature," *Sapiens.org,* October 20, 2022.

"goosing stock prices": Craig Hooper, "Why Navy Secretary Carlos Del Toro Blasted America's Big Shipbuilders," *Forbes,* February 20, 2024.

Similarly, politician Rahm Emmanuel: Laura Kelly, "Rahm Emanuel rips US defense firms, calls for punishments in final Tokyo missive," *The Hill,* December 24, 2024.

The fee may be: "Cost-Plus Contracts in Government Contracting: An In-Depth Guide," *Deltek,* accessed October 1, 2025, https://www.deltek.com/en/government-contracting/guide/government-contract-types/cost-plus-contracts.

The contractor assumes the risk: "Firm-Fixed-Price Contracts," Defense Acquisition University, accessed October 1, 2025, https://www.dau.edu/glossary/firm-fixed-price-contracts.

If these features are so obvious: Carley Welch, "After industry pushback, Army pledges to revise software acquisition – up to a point," *Breaking Defense,* September 6, 2024.

The Pentagon would rather pay: Pete Modigliani and Matt MacGregor, "Rethinking Contracting Norms for a Modern Defense Industrial Base," *Defense Tech and Acquisition*, March 5, 2024.

SpaceX reduced launch costs: James Pethokoukis, "Moore's Law Meet Musk's Law: The Underappreciated Story of SpaceX and the Stunning Decline in Launch Costs," *Faster, Please!,* March 26, 2024.

SpaceX did it for under $400 million: *Statement of Tim Hughes, Senior Vice President for Global Business & Government Affairs Space Exploration Technologies Corp. (SpaceX): Testimony before the Senate Subcommittee on Space, Science & Technology, Committee on Commerce, Science & Technology*, 115th Cong. (July 2017) (statement of Tim Hughes, SpaceX Senior Vice President), 4.

The primes get direct reimbursements: Eric Lofgren, "Defense primes have an advantage in OTAs due to a quirk in IRAD," *Acquisition Talk,* May 18, 2022.

Long gone are the days: Rich and Janos, *Skunk Works,* 15-16.

He worked hard to ensure: Miller, *Chip War*, 29-30.

That fact helps explain: Miller, *Chip War,* 31-32.

Private R&D: Gregory Arcuri, "Innovation Lightbulb: A Trend in U.S. Research and Development Expenditure," *Center for Strategic & International Studies,* June 16, 2023.

"a key source of innovation": "Independent Research & Development (IR&D)," Defense Acquisition University, accessed October 1, 2025, https://www.dau.edu/acquipedia-article/independent-research-development-ird.

There was no requirement: Lorell, *U.S. Combat Aircraft Industry*, 54.

It was only after the aircraft's: "North American P-51D Mustang," National Museum of the United States Air Force, accessed October 1, 2025, https://www.nationalmuseum.af.mil/Visit/Museum-Exhibits/Fact-Sheets/Display/Article/196263/north-american-p-51d-mustang/.

He alleges that Northrop: Rich and Janos, *Skunk Works,* 306.

William D. Hartung argues: William D. Hartung, *Prophets of War: Lockheed Martin and the Making of the Military-Industrial Complex* (Bold Type Books, 2012), 72.

Operating margins are around 11 percent: *Department of Defense Contract Finance Study Report*, 23.

they are valued at just: Shyam Sankar, "Why Increasing the Value of Defense Primes Is Good for the Country," *War on the Rocks,* May 1, 2024.

Meanwhile, technology companies: Sankar, "Why Increasing the Value of Defense Primes Is Good."

For example, many of the government's: CACI International Inc, *Form 10-K 2024*, Reston, VA: CACI International Inc, 2024, 23.; Booz Allen Hamilton Holding Corporation, *Form 10-K 2024*, McLean, VA: Booz Allen Hamilton Holding Corporation, 2025, 8.; General Dynamics Corporation, *Form 10-K 2024*, Reston, VA: General Dynamics Corporation, 2024, 46.; Leidos Holdings, Inc., *Form 10-K 2025*, Reston, VA: Leidos Holdings, Inc., 2025, 78.

"one wonders if a nation": McNaugher, *New Weapons Old Politics*, 84.

In 1958, the top twenty-five defense contractors: Jacques S. Gansler, *The Defense Industry* (The Massachusetts Institute of Technology Press, 1980), 39.

Although Raytheon is credited: "Raytheon Company: Historical Background," Raytheon Company, January 1999, https://rjl.home.xs4all.nl/Raytheon_histback.html.

"the government business is too volatile": Daniel E. Slotnik, "Thomas L. Phillips, C.E.O. Who Diversified Raytheon, Has Died," *The New York Times,* January 28, 2019.

Raytheon sold Data Systems: Jay P. Pederson, ed., *International Directory of Company Histories,* vol. 38 (St. James Press, 2001), 374-375.

"the acquisition proved to be": Harvey M. Sapolsky, Eugene Gholz, and Caitlin Talmadge, *US Defense Politics: The Origins of Security Policy,* Fourth Edition (Routledge, 2021), 159.

Goodbye to the publishing house: Pederson., *International Directory of Company Histories,* 375-376.

Under the leadership: George M. Skurla and Wiliam H. Gregory, *Inside the Iron Works: How Grumman's Glory Days Faded* (U.S. Naval Institute Press, 2004), 146, 151.

The bus business lost: Skurla and Gregory, *Inside the Iron Works,* 154.

"I saw the money come out": Skurla and Gregory, *Inside the Iron Works,* 163-164.

"Still remains the conundrum": Skurla and Gregory, *Inside the Iron Works,* 154.

In 1994, Grumman fell victim: Calvin Sims, "Northrop Bests Martin Marietta to Buy Grumman," *The New York Times,* April 5, 1994.

"telecom satellites developed": Heinrich, "Cold War Armory," 266.

While it receives just 42 percent: "Top 100 Defense Companies: Top 100 for 2025," *Defense News,* accessed October 1, 2025, https://people.defensenews.com/top-100/.

The 346 dead: "Key events in the troubled history of the Boeing 737 Max," *The Associated Press,* July 8, 2024.

the two astronauts: Eric Berger, "Starliner's flight to the space station was far wilder than most of us thought," *Ars Technica,* April 1, 2025.

and the door that flew off: Minyvonne Burke and Jay Blackman, "FAA to investigate Boeing after door plug falls off Alaska Airlines plane midair," *NBC News,* January 11, 2024.

Gansler contemplated a law: Gansler, *The Defense Industry,* 268.

On average, US primes: "Top 100 Defense Companies: Top 100 for 2024."

As a result, both contractors: Christopher E. Kubasik, "A Letter to the Leaders of DOGE," L3Harris, January 15, 2025, https://www.l3harris.com/newsroom/editorial/2025/01/letter-leaders-doge.

Contractors also need to comply: "The Cost Accounting Standards (CAS) Guide for Government Contractors," BDO, September 7. 2022, https://www.bdo.com/insights/industries/government-contracting/the-cost-accounting-standards-cas-guide-for-government-contractors#:~:text=CAS%2C%20GAAP%20and%20FAR,million%2C %20unless%20an%20exemption%20applies.

In addition to special accounting systems: Department of Defense, *Report to Congress on FY 2024 Activities Defense Contract Audit Agency* (Washington, D.C.: Department of Defense, March 31, 2025), 3.

Companies must also provide: Defense Logistics Agency, *Defense Logistics Acquisition Directive—Required Certified Cost or Pricing Data* 15.403-4 (Washington, D.C.: Department of Defense, September 2024), https://www.acquisition.gov/dlad/15.403-4-requiring-certified-cost-or-pricing-data-10-u.s.c.-2306a-and-41-u.s.c.-chapter-35.

Chris Kubasik estimates: Kubasik, "A Letter to the Leaders of DOGE."

This is a legal designation: 10 U.S. Code § 3014 (2022).

"there is no EU company": *The future of European competitiveness: Part A | A competitiveness strategy for Europe* (Luxembourg: Publications Office of the European Union, 2025), 6.

The S&P 500 last added a defense company: When excluding Mergers and Acquisitions and spin-offs, Textron's addition to the S&P 500 in 1978 was the most recent defense company added before Palantir.

While there are legitimate reasons: Mikayla Easley, "Pentagon updates decades-old classification policy for space programs," *Defense Scoop,* January 18, 2024.

"Each project had a specific quota": Rich and Janos, *Skunk Works,* 296.

"Facility accreditation should be": Matt MacGregor and Pete Modigliani, "The DIB Delivers with Key Insights," *Defense Tech and Acquisition,* January 23, 2025.

Love them or hate them: Forecast International, "Top 100 Defense Contractors 2023," *Defense and Security Monitor,* March 1, 2024.

CHAPTER 8: BUILDING FOR SCALE

It prioritized creating reports: Douglas M. O'Reagan, *Taking Nazi Technology: Allied Exploitation of German Science After the Second World War* (Johns Hopkins University Press, 2019), 31-35.

Finally, a report was written: O'Reagan, *Taking Nazi Technology,* 163-165.

"The lasting legacy of FIAT": O'Reagan, *Taking Nazi Technology,* 53.

Operation Paperclip prioritized human capital: O'Reagan, *Taking Nazi Technology,* 39.

"Wehrner von Braun and his able group": "Who Really Develops Missiles?" *Aviation Week,* September 23, 1957, 21, https://archive.aviationweek.com/issue/19570923.

Von Braun's work: "Wernher von Braun," Encyclopedia Brittanica, https://www.britannica.com/biography/Wernher-von-Braun.

Founded in 2005 by Peter Thiel: Mario Gabriele, "No Rivals: The Prophet (Part I)," *The Generalist,* June 12, 2025.

While other VC firms: Trae Stephens, "The future of defense funding with Founder's Fund's Trae Stephens | StrictlyLA VC," interview by Connie Loizos, *TechCrunch,* March 1, 2024.

Anduril was founded: Jeremy Stern, "American Vulcan," *Tablet,* https://www.tabletmag.com/feature/american-vulcan-palmer-luckey-anduril.

As of this writing, Anduril is valued: Julie Bort, "Anduril raises $2.5B at $30.5B valuation led by Founders Fund," *TechCrunch,* June 5, 2025.

The company makes autonomous weapons: "Anduril Building Arsenal-1 Hyperscale Manufacturing Facility in Ohio," Anduril Industries, January 16, 2025, https://www.anduril.com/article/anduril-building-arsenal-1-hyperscale-manufacturing-facility-in-ohio/.

Trae grew up: Steven Levy, "Trae Stephens Has Built AI Weapons and Worked for Donald Trump. As He Sees It, Jesus Would Approve," *Wired,* September 25, 2024.

His mother was a substitute teacher: Adam Fishman, host, *Startup Dad,* episode 17, "Two married company founders on starting companies and family," October 5, 2023.

The best the dean could do: Jeff Phaneuf and Josh Pickering, hosts, *Defense Tech Underground,* episode 6, "Trae Stephens—In Pursuit of Good Quests," August 20,2024.

While he did eventually pick: Natasha Mascarenhas, "The Rise of Founders Fund's Faithful Warrior," *The Information,* July 12, 2024.

Palantir operated unprofitably: Lizette Chapman, "Palantir Jumps Most Since 2020 on First Annual Profit, AI Demand," *Bloomberg,* February 5, 2024.

SpaceX, founded in 2002: Kiel Porter, Loren Grush, and Edward Ludlow, "Musk's Undisclosed Starlink Costs Undercut Profitability Claims," *Bloomberg,* April 10, 2024.

yet today it's the most valuable: Tabby Kinder, Stephen Morris, and Ivan Levingston, "SpaceX heads to $400bn valuation in share sale," *Financial Times,* July 8, 2025.

Of Founders Fund's thousands of investments: Santi Ruiz, "How to Rebuild the Arsenal of Democracy," *Statecraft,* November 6, 2024.

Uber's success sparked: Trae Stephens, "Venture Capital's Space for Sheep," *Pirate Wires,* May 2, 2024.

"During World War II": Converse, *Rearming for the Cold War,* 13.

The program was established in 1982: Gabrielle Athanasia, "RAI Explainer: The Small Business Innovation Research Program," *CSIS Perspectives on Innovation Blog,* July 8, 2022.

"Keep your equity and IP. Change the world": "America's Seed Fund: Powered by the Small Business Administration," Small Business Administration, accessed July 21, 2025, https://www.sbir.gov/.

Today, the Department of War: "Office of Small Business Programs," Department of Defense, accessed October 1, 2025, https://business.defense.gov/Programs/.

From 2016 to 2022, one percent: Ben Van Roo, "Emerging tech is transforming war in real-time, yet the biggest DOD incubator is stuck in the past," *Beyond Visual Range—AI, Defense, and Policy,* May 4, 2022.

"The most powerful tool": Stephen Miran, *Brittle Versus Robust Reindustrialization* (New York, NY: Manhattan Institute, February 22, 2024).

The top one-hundred: "SVDG NatSec 100: 2025 Edition," Silicon Valley Defense Group, accessed October 1, 2025, https://www.natsec100.org/.

"The types of businesses that suck": Trae Stephens in discussion with Madeline Hart, January 27, 2025.

Despite all of the private money: Heather Somerville, "Investors Are Betting on Defense Startups. The Pentagon Isn't," *The Wall Street Journal,* January 25, 2024.

"I believe there's some combination": Trae Stephens in discussion with Madeline Hart, January 27, 2025.

In the past seven and a half years: Trae Stephens in discussion with Madeline Hart, January 27, 2025.

Trae admits that Founders Fund: Trae Stephens, "The future of defense funding," interview.by Connie Loizos

Only the top 25 percent: Alexander Edlich, et al., *Braced for Shifting Weather: McKinsey Global Private Markets Report 2025* (McKinsey & Company, May 2025), 88.

In 2024, Google spent: Miles Kruppa and Lauren Thomas, "Google Paid $2.7 Billion to Bring Back an AI Genius Who Quit in Frustration," *The Wall Street Journal,* September 25, 2024.

Meta went on an aggressive hiring spree: Mark Gurman and Riley Griffin, "Meta Poached Apple's Pang with Pay Package Over $200 Million," *Bloomberg,* July 9, 2025.

"If the entrepreneur seeks": Bruce Gibney, "What happened to the future?" Founders Fund, accessed October 1, 2025, https://foundersfund.com/2017/01/manifesto/.

"define the legitimate interest": 10 U.S. Code, §3771 (2021).

Yet too often, the government: Shyam Sankar, Caitlin Dohrman, and Madeline Zimmerman, "The Military's Insistence on Owning Commercial Intellectual Property is Limiting Innovation," *War on the Rocks,* January 16, 2024.

Lockheed was thus unable: Thomas Heinrich, "Military Contracting in Silicon Valley," *Enterprise & Society* 3, no. 2 (June 2002): 266.

The government was so possessive: Leandra Bernstein, "The Complicated History of US Commercial SAR: Market Competition and National Security," *Kratos Space,* February 22, 2023.

Venture money has since: Aria Alamalhodaei, "Umbra is a Silicon Valley outsider — they prefer it that way," *Tech Crunch,* July 19, 2023.

Even still, the bulk of EO companies' business: Theresa Hitchens, "US SAR satellite imagery firms say draft ITAR changes still too restrictive," *Breaking Defense,* October 28, 2024; Theresa Hitchens, "SAR-satellite startup Capella Space creates 'federal' unit for US government sales," *Breaking Defense*, January 31, 2025; Ignacio Gonzalez, "Planet Labs More Than Doubles Backlog as Defense Spending Grows," *Bloomberg,* March 20, 2025.

In 2024, 86 percent: Alexander C. Karp and Nicholas W. Zamiska, *The Technological Republic: Hard Power, Soft Belief, and the Future of the West* (Crown Currency, 2025) 77.

"Noyce had never liked the business": Tom Wolfe, "The Tinkerings of Robert Noyce: How the Sun Rose on Silicon Valley," *Esquire Magazine,* December 1983.

There is no personal bankruptcy: Ryan McMorrow, Wenjie Ding, and Nian Lu, "Chinese venture capitalists force failed founders on to debtor blacklist," *Financial Times,* January 5, 2025.

In 2019, WeWork prepared: Annie Palmer, "WeWork Pulls IPO Filing," *CNBC,* September 30, 2019.

Just three years later: Dominic-Madori Davis, "How a16z's investment into Adam Neumann further solidifies the 'concrete ceiling'," *TechCrunch,* August 16, 2022.

For example, the KC-46: John A. Tirpak, "KC-46 Losses Now Top $5.4 Billion as Boeing Takes a New $406 Million Charge," *Air & Space Forces Magazine,* January 26, 2022.

"We have a couple": Lucas Owens, 'It just doesn't work': Boeing CEO takes aim at fixed-price contracting, " *Missouri Business Alert,* June 5, 2023.

CHAPTER 9: WHEN UNDERDOGS GO ON OFFENSE

"his coffin should be": "World Battlefronts: BATTLE OF FRANCE: Supreme Commander," *TIME,* June 19, 1944.

"Let us thank God": Jerry E. Strahan, *Andrew Jackson Higgins and the Boats That Won World War II* (Louisiana State University Press, 1994) 3.

"Alligator Ark[s]": Strahan, *Higgins and the Boats,* 166.

Higgins' biographer, Jerry Strahan, reports: Strahan, *Higgins and the Boats,* 1.

He hoped his bona fides: Strahan, *Higgins and the Boats,* 28.

"We *know* that we have designed": Strahan, *Higgins and the Boats,* 29.

That didn't stop the BCR: Strahan, *Higgins and the Boats,* 31.

"satisfactory and successful": Strahan, *Higgins and the Boats,* 32.

Compared to his rivals' boats: Strahan, *Higgins and the Boats,* 35.

"the Higgins boat is considered": Strahan, *Higgins and the Boats,* 37.

The failed design: Strahan, *Higgins and the Boats,* 38.

The Navy didn't want to test it: Robert Coram, *Brute: The Life of Victor Krulak, U.S. Marine* (Tantor and Blackstone, 2021), 87.

Meanwhile, the chief of naval operations: Strahan, *Higgins and the Boats,* 46-47.

It continued to award contracts: Strahan, *Higgins and the Boats,* 47.

"Through the unfathomable process": Strahan, *Higgins and the Boats,* 47.

During tests, it performed spectacularly: Strahan, *Higgins and the Boats,* 62.

"fancy dancing": Strahan, *Higgins and the Boats,* 76.

"we were properly registered": Strahan, *Higgins and the Boats,* 78.

"bias and prejudice": Strahan, *Higgins and the Boats,* 79.

"Navy has consistently refused": Strahan, *Higgins and the Boats,* 77.
Cowed, the admiral rescinded: Strahan, *Higgins and the Boats,* 79.
"I pointed out to them": Strahan, *Higgins and the Boats,* 77.
Instead of holding an open competition: Strahan, *Higgins and the Boats,* 102.
"Higgins's tank lighter came through fine": Strahan, *Higgins and the Boats,* 106.
The 1,100 tank lighters were built: Strahan, *Higgins and the Boats,* 107.
"The Bureau of Ships has grown like a mushroom": Strahan, *Higgins and the Boats,* 85-86.
In 1994, 50 years after: Federal Acquisition Streamlining Act of 1994, Public Law No. 103-355, § 8104, 108 Stat. 3243 (1994) (codified as amended at 10 US Code § 2377).
In 2016, Palantir sued the Army: *Palantir USG, Inc. v. United States,* Docket No. 1:16-cv-00784 (Fed. Cl. 2016) ("Palantir Complaint").
During the wars in Iraq and Afghanistan: Jen Judson, "30 Years: MRAP—Rapid Acquisition Success," *Defense News,* October 25, 2016.
The problem was compounded: Palantir Complaint at 20-23.
The Beltway's best were on it: Steven Brill, "Trump, Palantir, and the Battle to Clean Up a Huge Army Procurement Swamp," *Fortune,* March 17, 2017.
The product was borderline unusable: Palantir Complaint at 26.
"a piece of shit": Brill, "Trump, Palantir, and the Battle to Clean Up a Huge Army Procurement Swamp."
"Intelligence analysts in theater": Palantir Complaint at 6.
"a theater-wide, web-based advanced analytical platform": Palantir Complaint at 44-46.
Yet, in a microcosm: Palantir Complaint at 45-46.
"offline for months": Palantir Complaint at 46.
When connections were spotty: Palantir Complaint at 29-31.
More than three dozen: Brill, "Trump, Palantir, and the Battle to Clean Up a Huge Army Procurement Swamp."
"Marines are alive today": Brill, "Trump, Palantir, and the Battle to Clean Up a Huge Army Procurement Swamp."

The 82nd Airborne had requested: Palantir Complaint at 48.
"All the bullet points the Army can list": Palantir Complaint at 6.
In response, the Army sent: Palantir Complaint at 50.
Ultimately, the Army's chief of staff: Palantir Complaint at 50.
With controversy over DCGS: Palantir Complaint at 9-10.
ATEC's report found: Palantir Complaint at 10.
In a display right out of Orwell's *1984*: Palantir Complaint at 52-53.
"suggestion was a minor one": *Palantir USG, Inc. v. United States,* 129 Fed. Cl. 218, 255 (2016).
"ensure that any and all copies": Palantir Complaint at 53.
"Colonel Stock's May 2012 request": Palantir Complaint at 54.
"works pretty damn good": Palantir Complaint at 57.
Another bombshell: Palantir Complaint at 10-11.
"outside of the normal acquisition process": Palantir Complaint at 51.
They had done so: Palantir Complaint at 32.
The "new" phase of the program: Palantir Complaint at 34-35.
During market research: Palantir Complaint at 36.
Carter was the first secretary of defense: Marcus Weisgerber and Patrick Tucker, "New Pentagon Chief Carter to Court Silicon Valley," *Defense One,* April 16, 2015.
"we're reaching out": Ash Carter, "Networking Defense in the 21st Century (Remarks at CNAS)," Department of Defense, June 20, 2016.
When Palantir saw that the Army: Brill, "Trump, Palantir, and the Battle to Clean Up a Huge Army Procurement Swamp."
For example, Boeing and Lockheed: Aaron Mehta and Lara Seligman, "Boeing, Lockheed Decline Lawsuit over B-21 Bomber," *Defense News,* February 26, 2016.
while Northrop Grumman protested: Mark Pomerleau, "After nearly 5 years of litigation, Navy awards next system in advanced airborne electronic attack," *Defense Scoop,* September 12, 2024.
GAO denied the protest: Edda Emmanuelli Perez, *GAO Bid Protest Annual Report to Congress for Fiscal Year 2024* (Washington, D.C.: Government Accountability Office, November 14, 2024), 5.
"we don't have a business": Doug Philippone in discussion with Madeline Hart, March 12, 2025.

"the Army acted arbitrarily": *Palantir USG, Inc. v. United States,* 129 Fed. Cl. 218, 290 (2016).

"As Palantir argues": *Palantir USG Inc. v. United States,* No. 17-784 C (U.S. Court of Federal Claims, November 9, 2016), 103. Redacted Opinion, US Court of Federal Claims, 103.

But the Army's FASA violation: Jen Judson, "Palantir — who successfully sued the Army — has won a major Army contract," *Defense News,* March 29, 2019.

"In years of writing": Brill, "Trump, Palantir, and the Battle to Clean Up a Huge Army Procurement Swamp."

In March 2019, Palantir won: Judson, "Palantir — who successfully sued the Army — has won a major Army contract."

CHAPTER 10: BREAK THE MONOPSONY

"we afforded redundant Air Forces": Stephen Rosen, "Service Redundancy: Waste or Hidden Capability?," *Joint Force Quarterly* 1 (Summer 1993), 38.

"centralizing decision making": Harvey M. Sapolsky, *The Polaris System Development: Bureaucratic and Programmatic Success in Government* (Harvard University Press, 1972), 204.

With Polaris, we gained: Poole, *Adapting to Flexible Response,* 6.

He received a frigid welcome: Sheehan, *A Fiery Peace in a Cold War*, 4-5.

"Kaiser Wilhelm": Sheehan, *A Fiery Peace in a Cold War,* 7.

Bennie's father: Sheehan, *A Fiery Peace in a Cold War,* 5.

He would say the Pledge of Allegience: Sheehan, *A Fiery Peace in a Cold War,* 7.

And when he went to college: Sheehan, *A Fiery Peace in a Cold War,* 13-14.

Upon graduation, he joined the Army Air Corps: Sheehan, *A Fiery Peace in a Cold War,* 26-27.

He was itching to fight: Sheehan, *A Fiery Peace in a Cold War,* 32.

He proved his bravery: Sheehan, *A Fiery Peace in a Cold War,* 40.

In twenty months: Sheehan, *A Fiery Peace in a Cold War,* 44.

After the war, Schriever took on: Sheehan, *A Fiery Peace in a Cold War,* 129.

Standing six feet three inches: Sheehan, *A Fiery Peace in a Cold War,* 12.

"without a doubt the handsomest": Sheehan, *A Fiery Peace in a Cold War,* 295.

"missile gap": "50th Anniversary of the Missile Gap Controversy," John F. Kennedy Presidential Library and Museum, accessed October 1, 2025, https://www.jfklibrary.org/events-and-awards/kennedy-library-forums/past-forums/transcripts/50th-anniversary-of-the-missile-gap-controversy.

While the United States pursued: Converse, *Rearming for the Cold War,* 211.

"I don't think anybody in the world knows": Robert L. Perry, *The Ballistic Missile Decisions* (Santa Monica, CA: RAND, October 1967), 6.

Bush advocated for consolidating: Rosen, "Service Redundancy," 38.

Almost ten years later: Sheehan, *A Fiery Peace in a Cold War,* 199.

This miniaturization was essential: Sheehan, *A Fiery Peace in a Cold War,* 193-194.

Von Neumann enthusiastically wrote: Sheehan, *A Fiery Peace in a Cold War,* 215.

Even with this special status: Sheehan, *A Fiery Peace in a Cold War,* 268.

"interference from those nitpicking sons of bitches": Sheehan, *A Fiery Peace in a Cold War,* 228.

If it had been discovered: Sheehan, *A Fiery Peace in a Cold War,* 272-73.

"a research and development program": Converse, *Rearming for the Cold War,* 496.

The IRBMs had a distance requirement: Sheehan, *A Fiery Peace in a Cold War,* 347.

while ICBMs had a far greater requirement: Converse, *Rearming for the Cold War,* 394.

Bennie got his missile programs: Sheehan, *A Fiery Peace in a Cold War,* 299, 317.

Overseeing them: Sheehan, *A Fiery Peace in a Cold War,* 324-25.

Beginning in 1954: Sapolsky, *The Polaris System Development,* 13.

Schriever's Thor: Sheehan, *A Fiery Peace in a Cold War,* 322.

"a pack of amateurs": Sheehan, *A Fiery Peace in a Cold War,* 347.

In another, the range safety officer: Sheehan, *A Fiery Peace in a Cold War,* 343-44.

The third flew nearly 1,400 nautical miles: Sheehan, *A Fiery Peace in a Cold War,* 347.

By stealing a march: Sheehan, *A Fiery Peace in a Cold War,* 347.

Schriever took the Army's challenge: Sheehan, *A Fiery Peace in a Cold War,* 299, 348.

"cancelled as expeditiously as possible": Sheehan, *A Fiery Peace in a Cold War,* 358.

Many Navy officers: Sapolsky, *The Polaris System Development,* 5.

Also, the Army thought: Sapolsky, *The Polaris System Development,* 22.

"the farthest east the Navy could hope": Sapolsky, *The Polaris System Development,* 24.

The initial results were promising: Sapolsky, *The Polaris System Development,* 27.

The Navy compromised on key things: Sapolsky, *The Polaris System Development,* 27.

The weight-to-yield ratio: Sapolsky, *The Polaris System Development,* 30.

"Our religion is to build Polaris": Poole, *Adapting to Flexible Response,* 252.

Reeling from this betrayal: Sapolsky, *The Polaris System Development,* 32.

"nearly forced to eliminate": Sheehan, *A Fiery Peace in a Cold War,* 366.

He had at least two contractors for each: Converse, *Rearming for the Cold War,* 499.

Raborn pursued a similar approach: Sapolsky, *The Polaris System Development,* 92.

"eleven different methods": Sapolsky, *The Polaris System Development,* 141.

Deliberate duplication: Converse, *Rearming for the Cold War,* 499.

Both ICBMs were awarded contracts: Greenwalt and Patt, *Competing in Time,* 18.

The liquid-fueled Atlas and Titan: Sheehan, *A Fiery Peace in a Cold War,* 409.

He once faked an intelligence report: Sheehan, *A Fiery Peace in a Cold War,* 246.

"Blow! Blow! Blow!": Sheehan, *A Fiery Peace in a Cold War,* 348-49.

Initially, the Air Force hadn't planned: Sapolsky, *The Polaris System Development,* 39.

Plus, Hall had long wanted: Sheehan, *A Fiery Peace in a Cold War,* 409.

The innovative decision: Sheehan, *A Fiery Peace in a Cold War,* 410-411.

Hall wanted to generate: Sheehan, *A Fiery Peace in a Cold War,* 413-14.

Hall's briefing on Minuteman: Sheehan, *A Fiery Peace in a Cold War,* 415.

Minuteman development proceeded: Poole, *Adapting to Flexible Response,* 6.

Polaris started development in 1956: Converse, *Rearming for the Cold War,* 540.

Minuteman started development in 1957: Poole, *Adapting to Flexible Response,* 258; Greenwalt and Patt, *Competing in Time,* 18.

It saw action in the Cuban Missile Crisis: Sheehan, *A Fiery Peace in a Cold War,* 450.

The father of the ICBM: Sheehan, *A Fiery Peace in a Cold War,* 470-71.

"The history of the missile": "ARMED FORCES: The Bird & the Watcher," *TIME,* April 1, 1957.

(GPS modernization): Laura Heckmann, "Timeline for Troubled GPS Programs Continues to Grow," *National Defense,* November 12, 2024.

(*Virginia*-class submarine production): Ronald O'Rourke, *Navy Virginia-Class Submarine Program and AUKUS Submarine (Pillar 1) Project: Background and Issues for Congress,* Report No. RL32418, Washington, D.C.: Congressional Research Service, February 11, 2025).

The two were exceptional: Sapolsky, *The Polaris System Development,* 40.

"Looking back it is quite possible": Sapolsky, *The Polaris System Development,* 204.

In losing Jupiter: "Evolution of the US Army Aviation & Missile Command," US Army Aviation and Missile Life Cycle Management Command, accessed October 1, 2025, https://history.redstone.army.mil/ihist-evo.html.

He retired and became a priest: Sheehan, *A Fiery Peace in a Cold War,* 468.

Or, it would be industry: Jake Chapman, "Moving Toward Defense as a Service," *War on the Rocks*, November 29, 2024; Justin Johnson, "Combatant Commands as Customers?" *War on the Rocks,* May 8, 2025.

(recall that David Packard): Fredrickson, *The Laird-Packard Way*, 85.

CHAPTER 11: THE FACTORY IS THE WEAPON

In the early 2000s: Dan Wang, *Breakneck: China's Quest to Engineer the Future* (W.W. Norton & Company, 2025), 73.

The agency had to spend $69 million: Wang, *Breakneck*, 73.

Grove—born András István Gróf: Andrew S. Grove, *Swimming Across: A Memoir* (Warner Books, 2001), 1.

When the Nazis occupied Hungary: Grove, *Swimming Across*, 42-45.

His father had been conscripted: Grove, *Swimming Across*, 19-20.

Grove, then a second-year chemistry student: Grove, *Swimming Across*, 225.

So, after much agonizing: Grove, *Swimming Across*, 232-233.

He adopted a new, Americanized name: Grove, *Swimming Across*, 273.

"If they had got killed over it": Joshua Cooper Ramo, "Andrew Grove: A Survivor's Tale," *TIME Magazine*, December 29, 1997.

By contrast, Andy Grove brought: Andrew S. Grove, *Only the Paranoid Survive: How to Exploit the Crisis Points That Challenge Every Company* (Crown Business, 1996), 84.

"strategic inflection points": Grove, *Only the Paranoid Survive*, 32-35.

Nearly 90 percent of the world's: Ramo, "Andrew Grove."

Intel's $114 billion market cap: Walter Isaacson, "Andrew Grove: Man of the Year," *TIME Magazine*, December 29, 1997.

"the Digital Revolution has created": Isaacson, "Andrew Grove."

"The old economy was geared": Isaacson, "Andrew Grove."

"of any nation ever": Isaacson, "Andrew Grove."

"if the brutal facts": Andy Grove, "Thinking Strategically," *The Wall Street Journal*, January 22, 2007.

"Could we pull off the Manhattan Project today?" Grove, "Thinking Strategically."

Grove wrote that American elites fetishized: Andrew Grove, "How to Make an American Job," *Bloomberg Businessweek*, July 5, 2010.

"a general undervaluing of manufacturing": Grove, "How to Make an American Job."

"chain of experience": Grove, "How to Make an American Job."

"rebuild our industrial commons": Grove, "How to Make an American Job."

"responsibility to maintain the industrial base": Grove, "How to Make an American Job."

"develop a system of financial incentives": Grove, "How to Make an American Job."

"If we want to remain a leading economy": Grove, "How to Make an American Job."

"I can't believe what I read": James Altucher, "Andy Grove From Intel Is Wrong," *The Wall Street Journal*, July 6, 2010.

"So what if we have outsourced": Altucher, "Andy Grove From Intel Is Wrong."

"Chimerica": Niall Ferguson and Moritz Schularick, "'Chimerica' and the Global Asset Market Boom," *International Finance* 10, no. 3 (2007).

Made in China 2025: PRC State Council, *Notice of the State Council on the Publication of "Made in China 2025"*, trans. Ben Murphy (Washington, D.C.: Center for the Study of Emerging Technology, May 8, 2015), https://cset.georgetown.edu/wp-content/uploads/t0432_made_in_china_2025_EN.pdf.

Closer to home, Intel fell behind: Dylan Patel, Doug O'Laughlin, Myron Xie, Jeff Koch and Sravan Kundojjala, "Intel on the Brink of Death," SemiAnalysis, December 9, 2024, https://semianalysis.com/2024/12/09/intel-on-the-brink-of-death.

It never caught up: Patel, et al., "Intel on the Brink of Death."

In 2023, the total factor productivity: "U.S. Bureau of Labor Statistics, Manufacturing Sector: Total Factor Productivity [MFGPROD]," retrieved from FRED, Federal Reserve Bank of St. Louis, October 9, 2025, https://fred.stlouisfed.org/series/MFGPROD.

And indeed, total factor productivity: "U.S. Bureau of Labor Statistics, Private Nonfarm Business Sector: Total Factor Productivity [MFPNFBS]," retrieved from FRED, Federal Reserve Bank of St. Louis, October 9, 2025, https://fred.stlouisfed.org/series/MFPNFBS.

Private investment in capital goods: Austin Bishop and Blake Seitz, *Re-industrialise: Building Capacity, Security, and Prosperity in a De-globalising World*, (London: Alliance for Responsible Citizenship, February 2025) 7.

South Korea had more than 1,000 industrial robots: "Global Robot Density in Factories Doubled in Seven Years," International Federation of Robotics, November 20, 2024, https://ifr.org/ifr-press-releases/news/global-robot-density-in-factories-doubled-in-seven-years.

China had 470 robots: "Global Robot Density."

The United States had just 295 robots: "Global Robot Density."

As Rob Atkinson: Robert D. Atkinson, "Accelerating Digital Technology Adoption Among U.S. Small and Medium-Sized Manufacturers," Information Technology & Innovation Foundation, April 19, 2024, https://itif.org/publications/2024/04/19/accelerating-digital-technology-adoption-among-smes/.

Adoption of digital technology: Atkinson, "Accelerating Digital Technology."

In 2023, the National Association of Manufacturers: Nicole V. Crain and W. Mark Crain, "The Cost of Federal Regulation to the U.S. Economy, Manufacturing and Small Business," National Association of Manufacturers, October 2023, 5, https://www.nam.org/wp-content/uploads/2023/11/NAM-3731-Crains-Study-R3-V2-FIN.pdf.

This regulatory bill: Crain and Crain, "Cost of Federal Regulation."

"in which bits were unregulated": Tyler Cowen, host, *Conversations with Tyler*, episode 1, "Peter Thiel on Stagnation, Innovation, and What Not To Name Your Company," April 6, 2015, https://conversationswithtyler.com/episodes/peter-thiel/.

The Trump deregulatory actions: "EPA Launches Biggest Deregulatory Action in U.S. History," Environmental Protection Agency, March 12, 2025, https://www.epa.gov/newsreleases/epa-launches-biggest-deregulatory-action-us-history.

"Congratulations. Give that man one chip": Paul A. Eisenstein, "Tesla's Elon Musk Goes Broke," *The Detroit Bureau*, June 2, 2010.

And instead of relying on third parties: Greg Reichow, "Tesla's Secret Second Floor," *WIRED*, October 18, 2017.

"We didn't leverage the way other people built": Doug Newcomb, "Writing the Tesla Code That Helped Spur a Revolution," *Motortrend*, March 3, 2024.

As early as 2017, the company's former head of production: Reichow, "Tesla's Secret Second Floor."

"We often joked": Reichow, "Tesla's Secret Second Floor."

It was able to increase production: "Airbus + Palantir," Palantir Technologies, accessed October 2, 2025, https://www.palantir.com/impact/airbus/.

Similarly, Panasonic uses our software: "AIP + Mixed Reality with Panasonic Energy of North America | AIPCon 3," posted March 13, 2024 by Palantir Technologies, YouTube, https://www.youtube.com/watch?v=nUlnb1N6H9E.

The company is able to take workers: "AIP + Mixed Reality."

The company's head of manufacturing, Kieth Flynn: Keith Flynn and Matt Steckman, discussion with Blake Seitz, May 2, 2025.

"you're mid-eight figures": Keith Flynn and Matt Steckman, discussion with Blake Seitz, May 2, 2025.

"You don't have to be really good": Keith Flynn and Matt Steckman, discussion with Blake Seitz, May 2, 2025.

"hyperscale manufacturing facility": "Anduril Building Arsenal-1 Hyperscale Manufacturing Facility in Ohio," Anduril Industries, January 16, 2025. https://www.anduril.com/article/anduril-building-arsenal-1-hyperscale-manufacturing-facility-in-ohio/.

Production is expected to start in 2026: Keith Flynn and Matt Steckman, discussion with Blake Seitz, May 2, 2025.

The company's operating system: Stephen Losey, "Air Force starts ground testing Anduril collaborative combat aircraft," *Defense News*, May 1, 2025.

The company boasts: "The future of defense manufacturing with Anduril CEO Brian Schimpf," Lux Capital, November 15, 2024, https://www.luxcapital.com/content/the-future-of-defense-manufacturing-with-anduril-ceo-brian-schimpf.

"Rebuilding the Arsenal": "Rebuild the Arsenal," Anduril Industries, 2024, https://www.rebuildthearsenal.com/rebuild-the-arsenal.

Kevin Czinger is the founder: "Divergent Technologies, Inc. Announces Closing of Upsized $230 Million Series D Capital Raise," *PR Newswire*, November 13, 2023,

He remembers the North American X-15: Kevin Czinger, discussion with Madeline Hart and Blake Seitz, March 21, 2025. Unless otherwise specified, all information and quotations in this section are derived from personal author interviews with Kevin Czinger.

The Obama administration dangled: Jim Motavalli, "Coda Makes Plans for Battery Plant in Ohio, Pending Federal Loan Approval," *The New York Times*, May 25, 2010.

In a sign of the times: Motavalli, "Coda."

The Czinger 21C: Jim Motavalli, "Czinger on Czinger: The Incredible $2 Million 21C Hypercar Is a Family Project," *Penta*, May 23, 2023.

CHAPTER 12: ANTI-PLAYBOOK FOR FOUNDERS

Similarly, America wouldn't have launched: Greenwalt and Patt, *Competing in Time,* 19.

Soviet submariners: Dave Oliver, *Against the Tide: Rickover's Leadership Principles and the Rise of the Nuclear Navy* (U.S. Naval Institute Press, 2014), 53.

There were so many deaths: Vladimir V. Stefanovsky, "Their System Still Needs Victims..." *U.S. Naval Institute Proceedings* 118, no. 8 (August 1992).

The Defense Officer Personnel Management Act: Bernard D. Rostker, Harry J. Thie, James L. Lacy, Jennifer H. Kawata, Susanna W. Purnell, *The Defense Officer Personnel Management Act of 1980: A Retrospective Assessment,* (Santa Monica: RAND, 1993).

"the US Navy's enemies": James Fallows, "The Rise of Hyman Rickover," *The New York Review,* April 1, 1982.

Yet Congress intervened: Francis Duncan, *Rickover and the Nuclear Navy: The Discipline of* Technology (U.S. Naval Institute Press, 1989), 14, 233-234.

"one person showed me an email chain": Nabeel S. Qureshi, "Reflections on Palantir," *Nabeelqu*, October 15, 2024.

"padlocked on budgets": Tony Carr, "We Need Different Generals," *The Radar,* January 24, 2025.

The Naval Ordnance Test Center: Ron Westrum, *Sidewinder: Creative Missile Development at China Lake* (U.S. Naval Institute Press, 2013), 250.

"Projects should determine the organization": Westrum, *Sidewinder,* 68.

"overriding the exclusive jurisdiction": Edward N. Luttwak and Eitan Shamir, *The Art of Military Innovation: Lessons from the Israel Defense Forces* (Harvard University Press, 2023), 88.

Following the directive: Beasley, *Knudsen*, 271-272.

E-M would be foundational: Franklin C. Spinney, "Genghis John," *U.S. Naval Institute Proceedings* 123, no. 7 (July 1997).

Upgraded versions are still: "RTX's Raytheon awarded $736 million contract to produce AIM-9X missiles," RTX, October 10, 2024, https://www.rtx.com/news/news-center/2024/10/10/rtxs-raytheon-awarded-736-million-contract-to-produce-aim-9x-missiles.

In 1950, 600 Raytheon engineers: Westrum, *Sidewinder,* 45.

Starting in 1946, McLean: Westrum, *Sidewinder,* 31.

With no money for his mission: Westrum, *Sidewinder,* 41-42.

McLean gave the effort inconspicuous names: Howard A. Wilcox, "Sidewinder," *Invention & Technology* 5, no. 2 (Fall 1989).

"Sidewinder got authorized": Westrum, *Sidewinder,* 113.

"I found he had no interest": Westrum, *Sidewinder,* 136.

"It was a turkey shoot": Preston Lerner, "Sidewinder," *Air & Space Magazine,* November 2010, https://www.smithsonianmag.com/air-space-magazine/sidewinder-57687913/.

In 1957, the Air Force finally bought: Westrum, *Sidewinder,* 161.

However, Falcons flew so poorly: Lerner, "Sidewinder."

The Navy's Sparrow: Westrum, *Sidewinder,* 210.

Developed at one-tenth the cost: Westrum, *Sidewinder,* 209.

Early on, the Soviets created: Westrum, *Sidewinder,* 205-206.

The Sidewinder's hit rate: Rowland White, "Her Majesty's Death Ray: How The AIM-9L Sidewinder Vanquished The Argentine Air Force," *The War Zone,* November 27, 2020.

"McLean hated formal requirements": Westrum, *Sidewinder,* 57.

CHAPTER 13: MOBILIZE

"I (Shyam) was in the audience": Shyam Sankar, "War Footing: The Secretary of War's speech was a rallying cry. Reformers must heed it," *First Breakfast,* November 13, 2025, https://www.firstbreakfast.com/p/war-footing.

But the high-low mix was never implemented: Scott Bledsoe and Mike Benitez, "Re-thinking the High-Low Mix, Part I: Origin Story," *War on the Rocks,* January 25, 2017.

The orders stress that buyers: Exec. Order 14271, 3 C.F.R. 16433-16435 (2025).

"measured and calculated risks": Exec. Order 14265, 3 C.F.R. 15621-15624 (2025).

Other Transaction Authorities: Exec. Order 14265, 3 C.F.R. 15621-15624 (2025).

They call for a systematic review: Exec. Order 14265, 3 C.F.R. 15621-15624 (2025).

They kickstart a shipbuilding revival: Exec. Order 14269, 3 C.F.R. 15635-15641 (2025).

And they streamline: Exec. Order 14318, 3 C.F.R. 35385-35388 (2025).

"comprehensive transformation": Pete Hegseth, "Army Transformation and Acquisition Reform" (official memorandum, Washington, DC: Department of Defense, April 30, 2025).

And it recognizes the primacy of people: Pete Hegseth, "Army Transformation and Acquisition Reform."

"disestablishment of JCIDS": Pete Hegseth and Steve Feinberg, "Reforming the Joint Requirements Process to Accelerate Fielding of Warfighting Capabilities" (official memorandum, Washington, DC: Department of Defense, August 20 2025).

Force Design 2030: Andrew Feickert, *U.S. Marine Corps Force Design Initiative: Background and Issues for Congress,* CRS Report No.

R47614 (Washington, D.C.: Congressional Research Service, 2024).

Fostering Reform and Government Efficiency in Defence (FORGED) Act: Fostering Reform and Government Efficiency in Defense Act (FoRGED), S. 5618, 118th Congress (2024).

National Next-Generation Opportunities for Venture Acceleration and Technological Excellence (INNOVATE) Act: INNOVATE Act, S.853, 119th Congress (2024).

And there are efforts to mobilize: "Army Launches Detachment 201: Executive Innovation Corps to Drive Tech Transformation," U.S. Army, June 13, 2025, https://www.army.mil/article/286317/army_launches_detachment_201_executive_innovation_corps_to_drive_tech_transformation.